D0913245

The Seven Faces
of
Information Literacy

Christine Bruce

Adelaide
Auslib Press
1997

This publication is available from

Auslib Press Pty Ltd
PO Box 622 Blackwood South Australia 5051
Tel (08)8278 4363   Fax (08)8278 4000

National Library of Australia cataloguing-in-publication data

Bruce, Christine Susan.
  The seven faces of information literacy.

  Bibliography.
  Includes index.
  ISBN 1 875145 43 5.

  1. College teachers - Australia - Attitudes. 2.
  Universities and colleges - Australia - Faculty -
  Attitudes. 3. Library orientation for college students -
  Australia - Public opinion. 4. Information retrieval -
  Australia. 5. Libraries and education - Australia - Public
  opinion. I. Title.

025.5240994

'access, to and critical use of information and of information technology is absolutely vital to lifelong learning, and accordingly no graduate - indeed no person - can be judged educated unless he or she is 'information literate...' (Candy, Crebert and O'Leary 1994, p.xii)

Phenomenography is a 'research specialisation aimed at the mapping of the qualitatively different ways in which people experience, conceptualise, perceive and understand various aspects of ... the world around them' (Marton 1988, p.178)

Publisher's note: *The Seven faces of information literacy* is substantially the author's doctoral thesis (less appendices), presented to the University of New England, Australia in 1996. It is believed to be the first Australian doctoral thesis on information literacy and one of few worldwide. This has been a primary motivation in making it more widely available than normally occurs with doctoral theses. Readers are invited to communicate with the author about her research at the address given on the back cover.

Contents

Preface

The Seven faces of information literacy examines the varying experience of information literacy amongst higher educators and proposes a relational model of information literacy as an alternative to the behavioural model that dominates information literacy education and research. After establishing the importance of information literacy in higher education, the metaphor of an *information literacy wheel* is used to examine problems associated with the behavioural model and to propose the adoption of a relational approach. The three spokes of the wheel analysed are descriptions of information literacy, information literacy education and research.

Following discussion of these three aspects are details of an empirical study into information users' conceptions of information literacy. The study was conducted to form an initial hub for the relational information literacy wheel—a detailed picture of the different ways in which information literacy is experienced, or conceived amongst a group of experienced information users, in this case higher educators. The resulting conceptions, represented by 'categories' describing them, provide a picture of the phenomenon of information literacy, that is a picture of information literacy as it appears to people. This picture becomes the centrepiece of the relational information literacy wheel, in the same way that lists of attributes are central to the behavioural model.

This new picture of information literacy was obtained using a phenomenographic research approach. In using this approach the study continued a tradition of merging information needs and uses and educational research. Data gathered from lecturers, librarians, counsellors and staff developers were subjected to an iterative analysis resulting in categories of description representing different conceptions of information literacy. Each category is distinguished by a particular way of focussing on the world which correlates with a particular meaning associated with information literacy. The categories represent peoples' subjective experience of different parts of the phenomenon which are logically related. These relationships are graphically represented in an outcome space.

The picture of information literacy derived from examining variation in users' conceptions provides a deeper understanding of the phenomenon and completes the proposed relational model. The outcomes also pave the way for new approaches to information literacy education and research.

Christine Bruce

Chapter 1

Towards an alternative model for information literacy

In recent years information literacy has emerged as a significant issue in higher and other education. What is meant by information literacy, the changing nature of the world which has generated the need for information literacy, and strategies for fostering information literacy have been the subject of considerable discussion. *The Seven faces of information literacy* contributes to the conversation through proposing an alternative 'relational' model for information literacy to stand alongside the 'behavioural' model which presently dominates information literacy scholarship. It is with the progressive development of the new model that this book is concerned. The model unfolds through the initial chapters with a review of developments in describing information literacy, information literacy education, and information literacy research, including proposals for a relational treatment of these. This is followed by a report of an empirical study, the outcomes of which are central to the relational model, then by a discussion of the contribution made by the research outcomes and the new model to the three major facets of information literacy scholarship.

The empirical research, conducted to establish an initial core for the new model, was a study of higher educators' conceptions of information literacy. The focal question addressed was: What are the varying ways in which higher educators conceive of information literacy? The research approach adopted for the study was phenomenography, a Swedish approach which has had a considerable impact on thinking about teaching and learning in higher education. Phenomenography developed from a desire to understand how students approached learning tasks and how they conceived of learning. From this work emerged the phenomenographic 'project' of describing conceptions and a 'relational approach to teaching and learning' which have informed this study. In addition, descriptions of the varying ways in which some aspect of the world is conceived have come to be described as its phenomenography (Marton 1981a, p.181). Thus the centrepiece of the relational model proposed may be described as a phenomenography of information literacy.

The purpose of this chapter is to establish the background to this study of the meaning of information literacy. It explores the historical and continuing emergence of information literacy, the limitations in our present understandings of the phenomenon, and leads into the remainder of the work using the following headings:

- Why has the idea of information literacy taken root?
- The rise and spread of the information literacy movement
- Information literacy related challenges to higher education

- Information literacy under scrutiny

- What was the research problem?

- Towards a relational model of information literacy

- Establishing the boundaries of the study

- Synopses of the remaining chapters

Why has the idea of information literacy taken root?

The concept of information literacy has its roots in the emergence of the information society, characterised by rapid growth in available information and accompanying changes in technology used to generate, disseminate, access and manage that information. Since the publication of the American Library Association's *Final Report* (1989), written by a group of librarians and other educators, the concept of information literacy has been widely adopted by the information and education professions. This interest in information literacy is largely a result of its close association with the idea of lifelong learning.

> Ultimately information literate people are those who have learned how to learn. They know how to learn because they know how information is organised, how to find information, and how to use information in such a way that others can learn from them. (American Library Association Presidential Committee on Information Literacy 1989, p.1)

The importance of information literacy to lifelong learning has captured the imagination of higher educators all over the world in a way that the earlier concepts of 'user education' and 'information skills' did not. In Australia, Candy, Crebert and O'Leary (1994), in their report *Developing lifelong learning through undergraduate education*, highlight the importance of information literacy both as part of the profile of a lifelong learner and as an important element of the teaching-learning process. The emphasis placed on information literacy is revealed in their declaration that:

> ...access to and critical use of information is absolutely vital to lifelong learning, and accordingly no graduate—indeed no person—can be judged educated unless he or she is information literate. (Candy, Crebert and O'Leary, 1994 p.xii)

In South Africa Behrens (1992, 1994) and Gevers (1995) also endorse this relationship between information literacy and lifelong learning, and this endorsement has led to considerable activity in South African universities related to information literacy education as it has previously, particularly in the United States and Australia.

This association with lifelong learning explains the growth in interest in information literacy. Other explanations must be sought, however, for why the idea initially germinated and took root. The foundation for such explanation is the importance of the 'world of information' to information professionals. For many, changes in the world of information have been a sufficient justification for the introduction of the concept of information literacy. It is, in part, an understanding of this world, which is considered necessary to ongoing learning.

At least two models of the information universe, as it is in the late twentieth century, have been developed for teaching purposes, and published. The first is a model which represents an information professional's mental map of the information environment (Rubens 1991, pp.278-9) This two part mental map is comprised of the prebibliographic terrain, which includes institutional answer providing sources, and the bibliographic terrain, which includes bibliographic answer providing sources. The second is a model derived from exploring the life-world of information users (Huston 1990, p.694). The three information universes in this model are the universe of everyday information, comprising natural communication networks; the universe of scholarly knowledge, including 'natural and designed' communication networks, and information storage and retrieval systems, comprising designed and rational communication networks. Huston (1990, p.693) also introduces the idea of the 'information web', as another way of describing the information universe and differentiates between the webs of networked researchers, librarians and novices. Fundamentally, she argues, it is the need to communicate which underlies the existence of the information universe. The webs are seen as 'communication systems' which 'individuals must navigate in order to obtain data that they can forge into information' (Huston 1990, p.693).

The need for the use of the term *information literacy* has also been attributed to librarians determined to promote the cause of library or information based education. Nonetheless the genesis of the concept has come from the need to describe something very real. That 'something', has been the information literate individual, the ideal 'information consumer' in a rapidly and continually changing world of information. These changes in the world of information are characterised by increases in the volume of information, changes in information technology and changing communication patterns. Towards the end of the twentieth century these changes are accelerating and likely to be ongoing. People, to function effectively in their personal and professional lives, need to understand and interact effectively with their ever changing information environment. Recognition of this need, often described in terms of 'empowerment' of the individual, contributed further to the emergence of the concept of information literacy.

Also influencing the emergence of the concept were barriers to information access. The information explosion itself constitutes a barrier to information access, as do the costs of information searching, the limited availability of information sources, ignorance that new tools for information retrieval exist and poor skills for using the tools that are available (Dennis 1990, pp.39-40). These barriers, which potentially prevent people from exploiting their information environments, underline the need for a concept such as information literacy.

Consequently, information literacy is recognised as important in private life (Curran 1990, 1993; Owen 1995) and in the workplace (Behrens 1992; Doyle 1992; Takle Quinn 1991). It is now considered necessary to educate students, both undergraduates and research students, to cope with the changing information environment, and to provide professional development opportunities for those who must foster information competence. In broad terms students and staff in higher education institutions must be helped to be information literate. Until now, as libraries are regarded as a 'significant public access point to this universe of information', it has been predominantly librarians who have claimed responsibility for playing 'a key role in preparing people for the demands of today's information society' (Breivik 1991a, p.33). This scenario is changing, however, as lecturers and staff developers are developing greater interests in the possible contribution of information literacy to education.

The rise and spread of the information literacy movement

The information literacy movement has grown out of a concern with the potential role of libraries and librarians in education, in both school and tertiary settings. This concern first emerged in the late 1960s, in relation to school settings, alongside early developments in computer based information technology. Although the first mention of the term 'information literacy' is usually attributed to Zurkowski (1974), much of the rhetoric of information literacy began to appear in the mid 1960s. Roe's (1965 a,b; 1969 a,b) discussion of these matters, for example, resembles today's discourse on information literacy. He links 'the intimidating growth of knowledge and the age of rapid technological change' with the need to 'learn to learn' (Roe 1969a, p.196) and points to the need for:

- children to be taught to be self reliant, able to obtain information for themselves, weigh evidence, make responsible decisions
- libraries to provide the resources required for students to work on in the process of learning to learn
- a closing of the gulf between those teachers who have little understanding of libraries and librarians and those librarians who have little understanding of education, its objectives, problems and methods
- courses for teacher librarians to integrate the study of librarianship with the study of education
- courses for teachers to be oriented towards 'the active use of libraries in teaching and learning and ...(focus) on practical experience in the use of library materials as a critical feature of teaching method
- the need to address the poor image of libraries and librarians (adapted from Roe 1969a, pp.196-8)

Roe (1965b) outlines the problems which keep libraries and librarians from ensuring a critical role in education and identifies possible remedies, including:

- lobbying of administrators and government by pressure groups and influential individuals (p.192)
- revised strategies for teacher training (p.194)
- revised strategies for librarian training (p.196)
- the determined perseverance of exceptional individuals (p.199)

Although we recognise, today, that libraries are only one component of an individual's information networks, all of these, thirty years later, continue to be critical strategies for achieving the adoption of information literacy programs. Furthermore, it seems that the intrinsic value of information literacy is no longer as easily recognised. Whereas Roe pointed to the emergence of the information society as impelling serious attention to 'fashionable talk about children 'learning to learn'' (1969b, p.184), librarians and others now appeal to the learning to learn discourse to ensure that their call for information literacy education is heard.

Paul Zurkowski (1974) first used the term *information literacy* in a report to the US National Commission on Libraries and Information Science titled *The Information service environment, relationships and priorities.* In this report Zurkowski advocates the establishment of a national program aimed at achieving information literacy within a ten year time frame. He describes information literacy in terms of an individual's capacity to use information tools and primary sources to address problems. The idea was, a few years later, defined as being about individual and organisational awareness of 'the knowledge explosion and how machine-aided handling systems can help identify, access, and obtain data and documents needed for problem solving and decision making' (Horton 1983, p.16). It has also been described as a core competence needing 'cooperative information skill curriculum development between educational sectors and in collaboration with stakeholders' (Burnheim 1992, p.195).

Rapid and widespread acceptance of the concept of information literacy since the release of the American Library Association's *Final report* (1989) has led to renewed emphasis on information literacy in all education sectors. Information literacy is making a significant impact on educational curriculum as the relationship between information literacy and autodidactics that is 'the independent pursuit of learning without formal institutional structures' (Candy 1991, p.411) is recognised. Today the meaning of information literacy has broadened considerably and the term represents a convergence of interests in the need to educate those who must live and work in our information society.

Since the 1970s the importance of information literacy has been represented by librarians committed to serving the information society and bridging the gap between the information rich and the information poor. In the late 1980s and 1990s, interest in information literacy mushroomed on all continents: America (ALA 1989; Doyle 1992, 1996; Farmer and Mech 1992), Europe (Hartsuijker 1986; Pettersson 1994), Australia (Booker 1993, 1995, 1996; Kirk 1986), Asia (Breivik 1992), and Africa (Behrens 1990,1992, 1994).

The international move towards information literacy is seen in the publication of United Nations' guidelines for the training of teachers in the integration of libraries and information skills into curriculum (Hall 1986). This document, which focuses on schools, identifies three areas for implementation of programs: 1)information skills and teachers' professional development, 2)information skills and the school library and 3)learning how to learn and the school library. It includes case studies illustrating the implementation of such strategies in Zimbabwe, England, and the US.

In Britain, during the 1980s the British Library Research and Development Department gave priority to 'research examining the nature of information skills and illuminating the problems of teaching and learning those skills' (Kuhlthau 1990, p.23). The focus of attention here was also on schools; a range of reports on information skills and curriculum arose out of this work (for example, Hounsell and Martin 1983; Marland 1981). Perhaps the most enduring outcome was Marland's (1981) taxonomy of information skills, which continues to underpin information skills and information literacy programs.

Also in Europe considerable developments were taking place in the university sector where the importance of information skills instruction, particularly in relation to libraries was being increasingly recognised. Fjällbrant (1988, pp.229-30) contributed to the transition of user education programs from being targeted at orientation to education. Her implementation, at the Chalmers University of Technology in Gothenburg, Sweden, of subjects designed to introduce postgraduate students and researchers to electronic and other information networks continues to be regarded as a model. With the emphasis being on education and the evaluation of information, Fjällbrant and her colleagues were targeting information literacy goals as they are understood today although the term itself was not being used. In the school sector, however, in the Netherlands, information literacy was an articulated goal in the mid 1980s. Computer and information literacy were the focus of a range of curriculum innovations (Hartsuijker 1986).

In the southern hemisphere, Australian librarians and educators have been protagonists for information skills and later information literacy education. In the late 1970s and 1980s the trend towards information skills education in schools compares with trends in Britain, with some state departments of education releasing guidelines to assist teachers working with information skills (see, for example, Education Department of Tasmania 1984; New South Wales Department of Education 1988). Kirk (1986) traces the steps in the school sector towards an emphasis on information literacy. She notes evolving concerns for literacy, computer literacy, technological literacy and the early establishment of the relationship between information skills and learning skills.

During the early 1990s, the release of a range of Government reports focusing on the need for information skills paved the way for intensive interest in information literacy in all education sectors (Hazell 1993), including the Jones, Ross, Carmichael and Mayer reports. This interest in information literacy has found a focal point in two conferences, held in Adelaide in December 1992 and 1995 by the University of South Australia Library (Booker 1993, 1996). The first conference held in late 1992 brought together teachers, librarians, academics and industry representatives to discuss future directions. The second, held in 1995, brought together a similar group to discuss recommendations for the articulation of information literacy curriculum across sectors.

In the university sector aspects of information access and management were taught throughout the 1980s and into the early 1990s under the guise of reader, or user education. A discernible shift towards information literacy has since occurred. This shift in direction has been augmented by interest from lecturers, a level of interest which has resulted in CAUT (Committee for the Advancement of University Teaching) grants being awarded to projects concerned with information literacy (see, for example, Appleton 1993; Birkett 1993; McKinnon 1993). More recently, the previously mentioned *Developing lifelong learners through undergraduate education* (Candy, Crebert and O'Leary 1994) identified information literacy as a key characteristic of lifelong learners and an essential element of undergraduate curriculum.

Early developments of the information literacy movement in the United States are documented by Breivik (1991b, p.226). The publication of *Nation at risk* in 1983, targeting educational reforms whilst ignoring issues associated with the information society and the role of library and information professionals, triggered advocacy for information literacy. Breivik asserts that the first US educational reform report to acknowledge the role of libraries in education was published in 1985, but that the view of the library profession's involvement was limited.

Rader (1990a, p.19) points to the importance of the bibliographic instruction movement in the evolution towards information literacy. Two major landmarks in the development of bibliographic instruction are therefore important to the emerging understanding of information literacy. The first bibliographic instruction 'think tank', held in 1981, discussed the role and strategies of librarians and libraries in learning; the second 'think tank', held in 1989, determined that information literacy was a broader concept than bibliographic instruction. By the early 1990s the emphasis of library instruction in schools and higher education had begun to shift from a bibliographic instruction to an information literacy focus (Kuhlthau 1990).

Up until the mid 1980s the most significant events in the development of information literacy in the US were in the school sector. In 1987 the focus shifted to include tertiary institutions, with the convening of a national symposium for leaders in higher education, including librarians to explore the role of libraries in the search for academic excellence. An important outcome of this symposium was the establishment of the ALA (American Library Association) Presidential Committee on Information Literacy in the same year. This was followed in 1988 by the publication of *Information power: guidelines for school library programs*, and the *Final report* of the ALA Presidential Committee in 1989. Also in 1989 the National Forum on Information Literacy was convened to act as an umbrella organisation for the promotion of information literacy (Breivik 1993).

In the tertiary sector the integration of information literacy into the curriculum began to receive the serious attention of lecturers (Farmer and Mech 1992). Prior to this the information literacy movement had largely been adopted by those involved in bibliographic instruction. Not surprisingly changes in bibliographic instruction programs to encompass the many and varied aspects of information access and management meant that the term 'bibliographic instruction' no longer adequately conveyed the nature of the designated programs.

Other geographic regions, with the exception of South Africa (Behrens 1990; Marais 1992; September 1993), have been comparatively silent in the ongoing information literacy conversation. This silence does not suggest lack of interest as Breivik (1992), for example, mentions interest generated by Hannelore Rader in China. We may expect other nations to begin to contribute to the conversation through the literature and other forums in coming years.

Information literacy related challenges to higher education

The concept of information literacy has considerable significance for the higher education community. Along with other educational sectors, this community must ensure that its members are empowered to utilise the changing information environment both within the academic context and in the wider community. Further, the changes in the world of information, which are present in the microcosm of the scholarly community, need to be accounted for in both research and teaching-learning contexts. The aim is to ensure relevant and timely research outcomes and graduates who are able to contend with the world of information independently.

The notion that information literacy is important to learning in higher education has been stressed many times during the early to mid 1990s:

- Information literacy is a key characteristic of lifelong learners (Candy, Crebert and O'Leary 1994)

- Information literacy is an essential focus of undergraduate curriculum (Candy, Crebert and O'Leary 1994)

- Information literacy is a core competence which needs to be developed with increasing sophistication in the journey from school to work (Burnheim 1992, p.195)

- Information literacy is important to the improvement of the teaching learning process (Simmons 1992, p.15)

- Information literacy is emerging as one of the most critical literacies for an educated person in the 21st century (Farmer 1992, p.103)

- The threshold issue for colleges and universities in the Middle States region is the need for a campus-wide commitment to information literacy as a strategy that will improve the immediate learning experiences of each student in every discipline and one that will enhance the student's lifelong learning (Commission on Higher Education 1995, p.1).

Information literacy is important to higher education curricula both in terms of the *what* and the *how* of learning. These terms, used by the advocates of a relational approach to teaching and learning, refer to the *content* and the *process* of learning. In relation to information literacy education the *what* refers to the content of learning about information literacy, that is metalearning about information literacy. Students need to understand what information literacy is, as well as learn to engage in the processes of effective information use. This latter aspect, the *how* of learning, refers to the implementation of teaching-learning strategies which enhance information literacy whilst simultaneously developing substantive knowledge. Approaches presently used for information literacy education will be discussed in chapter four.

Alongside the importance of information literacy sit a series of challenges to higher educators. The first of these stems from difficulties noted by Glass Schuman (1990, p.4), who assigns the idea of the information society, a society in which individuals have access to, and are empowered by, the volumes of information being generated, to the realms of fantasy. Her pointing to the difficulty which people have in dealing with the information society, together with the overwhelming experience of library anxiety (Mellon 1986) and information anxiety (Wurman 1989), bring into focus the major information literacy related challenge to higher education:

- *To graduate students who are information literate*

This challenge, of graduating information literate students, brings with it two further challenges:

- *To provide access to the increasing number and manner of information resources and systems to staff and students*

- *To provide opportunities for students and staff to learn to use information effectively*

Challenges of providing access bring with them problems of deciding what services should be provided to discrete groups in the academic community. These services are sometimes provided by a Division of Information Services, or equivalent, comprising such units as computing services, the university library, and audiovisual services. Although a wide range of information sources and systems usually available, funding constraints often require that limitations be placed on the availability of some systems and services.

In university libraries for example, services such as interlibrary loans and access to a full range of commercial online databases, are often only available to university staff and research students. Undergraduate students are usually limited to the resources available within their own library or library system; although as commercial live databases are charging more competitive rates these are also being made available on a limited basis to undergraduates. Similarly telecommunications networks such as AARNet and the Internet may not always be accessible to undergraduate students. This scenario is usually acceptable where traditional academic curricula are taught, without emphasis on information literacy education. When information literacy education becomes a priority at all levels of higher education, then the widening of access to all students is critical. This makes the challenge issued to libraries relevant to other information service providers in the university: '...a library that does not transcend its own limitations falls into the same entrapment of classroom and text book learning' (McCrank 1992, p.493).

Challenges of providing opportunities for learning to use information effectively are directed at curriculum developers, lecturers and librarians involved in curriculum design, implementation and evaluation. Students need to learn 'to survive in information rich environments' (Eisenberg and Small 1993, p.263). Designing these programs poses further challenges for educators.

- *How should information literacy programs be designed, implemented, evaluated? Do students' information literacy needs differ at different levels, and if so how?*

- *What is the role of libraries and computer centres in the design, teaching and resourcing of information literacy education, and furthering the experience of information literacy?*

The challenges at undergraduate and postgraduate level may differ. Postgraduate students experience an initiation into the world of information as part of their induction into research culture. This initiation can be seen as a learning experience during which their experience of information literacy is likely to change. Undergraduates and other coursework students are not likely to become familiar with the world of information related to their discipline/area of professional interest unless their courses are structured to provide them with the relevant opportunities. The challenge in postgraduate education is therefore to foster the experience, in a research context, which necessarily forces students into encountering the challenges of the information environment. For undergraduates, the challenge is to provide them with contexts which will require them to encounter the information environment. In both undergraduate and postgraduate education there is an ongoing challenge to ensure that experiences gained in the academic environment are transferable to professional and other contexts.

Both information services divisions and educators generally, however, are responding to these challenges whilst our understanding of information literacy, particularly the different ways in which it is experienced, is still limited. Our limited insights into the experiences of information users make it difficult to communicate the nature of information literacy and make it difficult to design and evaluate information literacy programs (Arp 1990). An overview of the limitations in our understanding of information literacy is presented in the following section.

Information literacy under scrutiny

Despite the widespread acceptance and use of the idea of information literacy in a range of educational forums, the idea of information literacy has been scrutinised, and challenged, several times since the mid 1980s. The meanings we presently have access to, which will be the focus of attention in following chapters, come from scholarly descriptions of information literacy, information literacy education programs and some research studies. Nevertheless our understanding of information literacy is problematic. The term *information literacy* is:

> ...not well defined by theoreticians and practitioners in the field, and so a great deal of confusion will occur unless we continue to articulate the parameters of this question.' (Arp 1990, p.49)

Amongst practitioners and scholars of information literacy and information literacy education there is lack of precision in use of the term. This is evident in the uncertainty about the distinction between information literacy, bibliographic instruction and library skills programs. This uncertainty points to a lack of clarity about the nature of information literacy, and the difference between this phenomenon and its predecessors, such as library literacy. Evidence for this uncertainty is found in periodic use amongst practitioners, and in scholarly writing, of *information literacy* alongside other terms, such as 'information skills', 'library skills' and 'bibliographic instruction'. Examples are found in a range of document types, from journal articles (Fatzer, van Pulis and Birchfield 1988) to curriculum guides (Cody, Grassian and Jacobson 1992). The following phrases are extracted from these documents:

...information literacy/library skills

...library/information literacy instruction (Fatzer, van Pulis and Birchfield 1988, p.77)

...library/information literacy skills instruction (Gratch 1992)

In the introduction to a new bibliographic instruction course syllabus:

...information literacy or user education or bibliographic instruction

and in the objectives, '...bibliographic instruction/information literacy' occurs (Cody, Grassian and Jacobson 1993). These other terms, in most critical writing, are not considered the same as *information literacy*.

Lack of precision in the use of varying terms, such as those above, is compounded by varying use of *information literacy* itself. A range of definitions and descriptions of information literacy found in contemporary literature on the subject, and discussion about the differences between information literacy, library skills, computer literacy and bibliographic instruction programs continues. These issues are discussed in detail in chapters two and three.

Some writers in this field acknowledge this terminological confusion, including Lawrence McCrank (1992) who details some of the different uses of the phrase, while others point to our present relatively fragmentary understanding of the concept. Others recognise that the skills and competencies which may be said to comprise information literacy are undefined (Kwasni 1990, p.127), and that the 'concept and definition of information literacy continue to emerge' (Ford 1991, p.314). McCrank (1991, p.42) emphasises that those who are committed to furthering the cause of information literacy are 'doomed to partial success unless the concept undergoes further definition, refinement and delimitation of its objectives'. Our lack of understanding is partly due to the recent and continued emergence of both the phenomenon itself and scholarly understanding of it. It is not surprising, given this background, that some scholars have reached the conclusion that 'information literacy is indeed a phrase in quest of a meaning' (Foster 1993, p.344). Another author comes to the lame conclusion that information literacy is another way of expressing one of the outcomes of a sound general education. All that is different is the nomenclature—and perhaps the toys' (Cavalier 1993, p.20).

The terminological confusion described above is accompanied by scepticism on the part of some scholars regarding the validity of the concept of information literacy (Coons, Schlabach and Barnes 1989, p.4), and criticism of existing descriptions (Foster 1993). Vareljs (1991, p.1) asks: What is information literacy? Is it simply the latest buzz word...? White (1992, p.78) similarly does not favour the phrase, and Foster (1993, p.346) regards its use as primarily 'an exercise in public relations'. Lack of conviction about the term information literacy is not a denial of the phenomenon which it labels, it is possibly symptomatic of the lack of a sufficiently deep understanding of it.

Problems of meaning are accompanied by discrepancies in the paradigms associated with information literacy. Although researchers are leaning towards qualitative approaches (Doyle 1992), and constructivist approaches to teaching and learning are being preferred by educators (Todd 1995, Kirk 1995), the primary picture of information literacy prior to the development of the relational model, was painted in terms of attributes of individuals. In addition, these understandings were predominantly the views of information literacy scholars and researchers rather than the views of information users. Fundamentally, the only picture of information literacy which was available was framed in the declaration that information is objective and literacy is a characteristic of individuals. New ways of thinking about information (Dervin 1994) must be allowed to transform our understanding of information literacy as well as our teaching practices. Similarly, contemporary scholars of literacy are arguing for a move away from the idea of literacy as the unified possession of an individual or as a set of transportable skills, and toward the idea of literacy practices-that...shape...the everyday lives of individuals and communities' (Freebody 1994).

Clearly a coherent framework for information literacy is required which reflects changes in thinking about information and literacy and which may better serve the needs of practitioners interested in reflective, problem based and resource based approaches to teaching and learning. Although the relational model of information literacy may not be completely consonant with some of these approaches, given its emphasis on changing ways of conceiving of phenomena, it is not in conflict with them.

The research presented here, is the second substantial work concerned with the meaning of information literacy. The first was completed by Doyle (1992), at about the same time that the ground work for this study commenced. Doyle used the Delphi technique to achieve a consensus definition of information literacy amongst a large pool of information literacy scholars. So why was the second study, my own, conducted? The two studies, although sharing very similar intentions—to enhance our understanding of information literacy—are very different in character. Doyle's study served particular political ends. She sought to work within a paradigm acceptable to curriculum authorities in the United States and to provide outcome measures for assessing learning. My study also has a political purpose. It is intended to bring our understanding of information literacy into a new educational paradigm which has slowly been gaining acceptance in the higher education community. The major differences between Doyle's approach to information literacy and the approach captured in the relational model are found in Table 1.1.

As this study progressed, further evidence was found in the literature to support the idea that it was reasonable to seek variation in people's experience of information literacy. For example, Plomp and Carleer attribute problems in relation to developing information and computer literacy programs in schools in the Netherlands' to varying interpretations:

> Information and computer literacy as a label for a new domain may mean different things to different people. This can be partly a consequence of not being well informed about the goals and content of (information and computer literacy), but also because what is being conceived as (information and computer literacy) is still developing. (Plomp and Carleer 1987, p.58)

Table 1.1 Contrasting characteristics of alternative pictures of information literacy

Doyle's (1992) picture of information literacy	The relational picture of information literacy
derived from scholars' views	derived from users' experiences
derived from seeking consensus	derived from seeking variation
derived using the Delphi Technique	derived using phenomenography
recommends constructivist approaches to teaching and learning	recommends relational approaches to teaching and learning
sees information literacy as measurable	does not see information literacy as measurable
sees information literacy as definable	sees information literacy as describable–
sees information literacy as quantifiable, asks how much has been learned?	does not see information literacy as quantifiable, asks what has been learned?
portrays information literacy in terms of attributes of persons	portrays information literacy in terms of conceptions ie subject-object relations
focuses on personal qualities of the individual apart from the environment	focuses on personal qualities in relation to the environment

Curran and Cavalier both supply further evidence to suggest that their thinking about information literacy differs from that of those with whom they interact:

> Information literacy does not mean knowing how to read. It does not mean knowing how the information place. Many people however do not understand this. In their confusion they announce at meetings that their libraries are heavily into information literacy because of some computer-assisted tour that they have created. (Curran 1993, p. 258)

> When I asked a Pro-Vice Chancellor of a university in Sydney, did she know the term information literacy she disappointed me by saying 'Yes, I do'. While she was not actually able to define the term, she thought it probably meant effective use of libraries. (Cavalier 1993, p. 19)

What was the research problem?

The aim of this study was originally to enhance our understanding of information literacy through describing conceptions of information literacy amongst a group of information users, that is higher educators. In order to approach this task it was clear that new ways of thinking about describing information literacy, information literacy education, and information literacy research were required. To capture the dominant paradigm, and the alternative one being proposed, two information literacy wheels were created. As the study progressed, the wheels came to represent alternative models for thinking about information literacy. Thus the initial aim of the study broadened to constructing an alternative relational model for information literacy, to which the empirical study contributed one part. The focal problem addressed in the empirical study is described further in this section, and the alternative models are presented in the next.

The empirical part of the study, wherein data was gathered from a group of participants for analysis, sought higher educators' conceptions of information literacy Marton describes the set of conceptions uncovered as representing the 'collective intellect' of a population:

> The collective intellect can be seen as a structured pool of ideas, conceptions underlying the possible interpretation of reality, and it is enhanced steadily as new possibilities are added to those previously available. (1981, p.181)

Conceptions of information literacy may be defined as qualitatively different relations between individuals and some aspect of their information environment which could not be predetermined. Varying conceptions are also often described as different ways of seeing, experiencing or understanding a phenomenon. The set of conceptions taken together, represent the phenomenon being studied. Higher educators were chosen as participants because their varying experience of information literacy may be expected to shape that of higher education graduates.

The study had the following purposes stemming from its primary aim:

- to identify varying conceptions of information literacy amongst one group in the higher education community that interacts extensively with information

- to develop descriptions of information literacy which reflect the experience of information literacy amongst the study's participants

- to develop deeper and/or new understandings of information literacy as a result of the variation identified

- to ascertain the implications of the variation identified for stakeholders involved in teaching and learning information literacy in universities

Engaging in such a study required three changes in approach to information literacy. These were changes in relation to ways of describing information literacy, ways of teaching information literacy and ways of researching information literacy. These three changes, discussed below, provided an internally consistent framework within which to conduct the empirical study into varying experiences of information literacy.

Towards a relational model of information literacy

Scholarly understanding of information literacy is informed by writings focusing on descriptions of information literacy, information literacy education and a limited number of research studies. These understandings have been cast in a framework which regards information literacy in terms of attributes of individuals, which sees learning to be information literate as acquiring the relevant attributes, and which focuses on researching the views of experts. To date these views have been mainly informed by behaviourist and information processing paradigms. They are depicted as an information literacy wheel in Figure 1.1a.

Uncovering varying conceptions of information literacy required a different framework within which to approach information literacy in all three areas: descriptions of information literacy, information literacy education and research. The empirical study, therefore, was framed within three changes in our ways of thinking about information literacy, each of which was eventually translated to form a key element in the relational model of information literacy. These are also graphically depicted in an alternative information literacy wheel in Figure 1.1b.

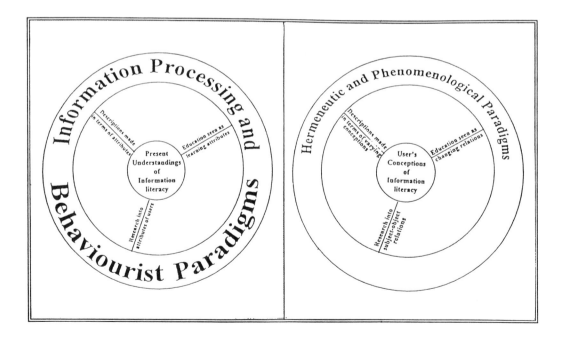

Figure 1.1a Dominant paradigms informing understandings of information literacy

Figure 1.1B Alternative paradigms informing understandings of information literacy

Each of the proposed changes is described below:

- *Towards a relational view of information literacy.* This involved a change from describing information literacy in terms of attributes (skills, knowledge and attitudes) to describing it in terms of varying conceptions or experiences which are defined in terms of relations between people and aspects of the world.

- *Towards a relational view of information literacy education.* This involved a change from viewing learning information literacy as the acquisition of attributes to viewing it in terms of changing conceptions or ways of experiencing aspects of the world.

- *Towards researching relations between users of information and aspects of the world.* This involves a change from researching both the understandings of experts and information users to researching conceptions, or the varying relations between people and aspects of the world.

These shifts, which will be examined in detail in subsequent chapters are grounded in an experiential, or phenomenological, world view. Although the shifts have been initiated to frame the study of higher educators' conceptions, when the alternative information literacy wheel is considered as a potential information literacy model, its central core is clearly empty. The central core of the wheel representing the dominant paradigm is readily available, in the form of lists of attributes of information literate people. The outcomes of the study, described in later chapters, allowed the completion of the wheel and its transformation into an alternative model for information literacy.

The completion of this study is significant for the following reasons. It has:

- yielded descriptions of information literacy, in the form of conceptions, which are based on information users' experiences

- enhanced our understanding of how information literacy appears to people

- paved the way for trialing an approach to information literacy education based on seeing learning as changing conceptions

- paved the way for continued application of the phenomenographic approach in information literacy research

- provided a basis for awareness raising about differences in conception amongst tertiary educators

- provided a basis for enhancing communication amongst educators who may conceive information literacy differently.

The primary contribution of the study, however, is in the adoption of a conceptual framework which views information literacy relationally, that is in terms of varying conceptions. The study makes a contribution to the theory of information literacy, both in adopting such a framework and in devising descriptions of information literacy which are consistent with that framework.

This contribution has immediate implications, listed above, for information literacy education in higher education institutions. It also has wider implications for information literacy education generally, for the professional development of librarians and other educators, and for future research efforts.

Establishing the boundaries of the empirical study

Firstly, the empirical research conducted was intended to explore one of the problems associated with information literacy. The primary question is one associated with meaning.

What are the different ways in which information literacy is experienced by people? The outcomes contribute to the relational model of information literacy. What curriculum developers and researchers may do with this model, although of interest to the study, is of secondary importance.

Secondly, the study inquires into how information literacy is experienced, not into what it is. The question being posed is 'What are the different ways in which information literacy is conceived, that is, seen, experienced, or understood? not 'What is information literacy?' However, if we accept that a phenomenon 'may be seen as a complex of the different ways in which it can be experienced' (Marton 1992, p.4), discovering the varying ways in which information literacy is conceived provides insights into the latter problem.

Thirdly, the range of conceptions discovered belong to the context from which they are derived, that is the academic culture of higher education institutions. Descriptions of these conceptions portray the varying experience of members of the group who belong to that culture. The conceptions do not belong to individuals or the discrete groups which make up the culture. The study does not address the question of whether the experiences of the various subgroups differ.

Fourthly, conceptions of information literacy identified in this context are a subset of those belonging to the larger context in which information literacy is experienced by a wide range of people in wide range of situations. Although the conceptions identified here are likely to apply to contexts other than the higher education arena, the phenomenon will need to be explored in those contexts to discover further variation in the experience of information literacy.

Finally, the conceptions were discovered as a result of interviews which took place in 1994. Although it is unlikely that the categories describing them will be rendered obsolete, it is likely that ways of conceiving of information literacy will change over time. In the context of continuing rapid change in the world of information it is difficult to predict how information literacy may be conceived in the future. It is not within the boundaries of this study to do so.

Organisation

The Seven faces of information literacy develops a relational model of information literacy and reports the empirical study which contributes to that model. It reflècts an emerging picture of information literacy. In each chapter pictures of information literacy are presented, against the backdrop of the relevant literature belonging to the moments in time with which the chapter is concerned. Thus, the second, third and fourth chapters examine developments pertaining to information literacy advocacy and scholarship that were available in early 1994, the time when I was beginning to form the relational model. At that time most available literature was dated 1993 or earlier.

On completion of the data analysis, the outcomes of the study were discussed in relation to the earlier literature review and documents that had since become available. New directions for information literacy are therefore proposed, together with the complete relational model, in the seventh chapter, within the context of developments in information literacy scholarship available up to early 1996.

The remaining chapters are organised as follows:

Chapter Two: Historical and contemporary descriptions of information literacy

Chapter two deals with the first spoke in the information literacy wheel: descriptions and definitions of information literacy. It opens with a review of concepts influencing the idea of information literacy, such as information technology, literacy, library literacy, computer literacy and information skills. It then reviews the varying ways in which the concept of information literacy is understood from the early 1970s to the close of 1993. The chapter concludes with a summary of paradigms influencing contemporary approaches to information literacy and proposes the use of an experiential paradigm which allows information literacy to be described from a second order perspective. This becomes the first element of the relational model of information literacy.

Chapter Three: Information literacy education

Chapter three deals with the second spoke in the information literacy wheel: information literacy education. It describes predecessors to information literacy education, including library instruction and bibliographic instruction, then examines contemporary approaches to information literacy education to the close of 1993. The chapter concludes with a summary of educational theory underpinning contemporary approaches to information literacy education and proposes, as an alternative, the relational view of teaching and learning, involving changing ways of seeing the world. This becomes the second element of the relational model of information literacy.

Chapter Four: Information literacy research

This chapter focuses on the third spoke in the information literacy wheel. It reviews the background to research into information literacy focusing particularly on the area of information needs and uses. It then examines existing research into information literacy and highlights research directions recommended in the literature, again to the close of 1993. The last part of the chapter argues for a change in research approach from exploring the characteristics of people, to describing their conceptions or ways of experiencing aspects of the world. This becomes the third element of the information literacy model framing the subsequent inquiry into higher educators' conceptions of information literacy.

Chapter Five: Thematising conceptions of information literacy

Chapter five examines the research approach called phenomenography and the specific techniques designed to uncover tertiary educators' varying conceptions of information literacy. Included in the chapter are descriptions of the participants in the study, the data gathering instruments and the pilot study through which these were trialed. The analysis techniques used for identifying conceptions from the data gathered, the form of the research findings, and the basis on which these findings are defended, are also described.

Chapter Six: Descriptions of conceptions of information literacy

This chapter contain the outcomes of the empirical study, the beginnings of a core for the new relational model. It opens with a description of the collective experience of information literacy amongst higher educators in the form of an outcome space. The section outlines the variation in the conceptions uncovered and describes the logical relations between them. A detailed analysis of each conception, including its structural and referential components, in the form of categories of description, follow.

Chapter Seven: New directions for information literacy

This final chapter summarises the research outcomes. It reviews the significance of the study and the contribution made to the theory of information literacy, information literacy education and the future research agenda. It establishes new directions for information literacy scholarship based on the completion of the relational model for the phenomenon. Attention is focused on implications for higher education stakeholders with responsibility for teaching and learning, staff developers and researchers.

Chapter 2

Descriptions of information literacy

This chapter examines descriptions of information literacy that were available in the literature before the empirical study was commenced. These descriptions form the first spoke in the *information literacy wheel* introduced in the previous chapter. They represent prevailing trends in writing about information literacy, and are likely to influence the views of those responsible for information literacy education. Most importantly, they demonstrate the considerable variation in how information literacy is being treated in the literature. Then, towards the close of the chapter, I argue for the first of the three shifts in thinking about information literacy which frame my empirical study into higher educators' varying conceptions of the phenomenon. This is the change from describing information literacy in terms of personal attributes, to describing it in terms of experiences or conceptions.

To understand the range of contemporary descriptions of information literacy present in the literature, it is first necessary to know something of other concepts that have influenced, and are continuing to influence them. These, and the varying descriptions of information literacy are examined under the following headings:

- Conceptual influences on information literacy

- Varying descriptions of information literacy

- Towards an alternate approach to describing information literacy: from attributes to conceptions

Conceptual influences on information literacy

The idea of information literacy has been influenced by five other concepts associated with elements of the emerging information society: information technology literacy, computer literacy, library literacy, information skills, and learning to learn. These concepts, depicted in Figure 2.1, all coexist with the idea of information literacy and are themselves subject to ongoing discussion about their meaning. Each one is also systematically differentiated from, or incorporated into, contemporary descriptions of information literacy. This has led to information literacy sometimes being used as a subsitite term for one of the other concepts. Information skills, library skills and information technology skills, for examples, are at times interpreted as information literacy,

That the various terms should be clearly differentiated from information literacy, however, is '...not mere semantic fussiness. Well intentioned people are often confused on this issue' (Curran 1993, p.262). It is as much to distinguish between these ideas and information literacy, as to demonstrate their relationship with that phenomenon, that these ideas are now elaborated. The impact of the conceptual influences on our understanding of the phenomenon will be seen in the net section of this chapter which reviews varying approaches to describing information literacy.

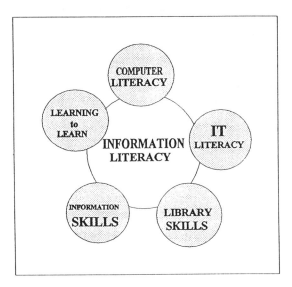

Figure 2.1   Concepts influencing and coexisting with information literacy

Information technology literacy (ITL)

Associated with the information age are the many technologies being developed and used for producing, managing, storing, disseminating and accessing information. Some of the more familiar of these include personal computers and their associated software, mainframe computers, telecommunications, CDRom, online databases and interactive videodiscs. Making an impact on higher education since the early 1990s have been facilities such as the Internet, gophers, Archie, Veronica, World Wide Web (WWW) and Wide Area Information Systems (WAIS). All these are used in many facets of society including the higher education sector where their intended function is to support teaching and learning, research and scholarly communication. The concept of information technology literacy, which has emerged in parallel with other concepts such as information skills and information literacy, focuses primarily on a person's ability to use these new and continually changing technologies.

In the *Encyclopedia of library and information science*, information technology literacy is described as knowledge

> In the broadest sense, ITL is the knowledge which allows an individual to function and effectively in whatever circumstances one finds him/herself in a technologically oriented society. (Penrod and Douglas 1986, p.76)

When that description is elaborated, eight competencies are identified which together, Penrod and Douglas argue, comprise a definition of information technology literacy. These are the ability to:

- operate and communicate with technological devices
- understand how subsystems fit together to form systems or networks
- erstand documentation and how to utilise applications software
- understand the basic jargon or terminology of information technology
- solve problems through the use of technology
- identify and use alternate sources of information
- discuss the history and future of information technology
- have some insight into the ethical and human impact issues of information technology (Penrod and Douglas 1986)

Thematised, or brought into focus in this description are the technologies, typically electronic technologies although this is not made explicit, which help people to use information. Many elements of information literacy, as it is described in the literature, such as valuing information, being able to identify information problems, evaluating information and understanding what happens as knowledge is transformed in various stages of its life cycle, are not recognised as important elements of information technology literacy.

Of particular interest, however, is the inclusion of the sixth ability: 'identify and use alternate sources of information'. Its presence in the definition of information technology literacy points to an area of overlap between this concept and the ideas of information skills and information literacy. The ability to identify and use information sources is usually, as will be seen later, identified as an important part of the information skills taxonomies that underpin information literacy curricula. For some scholars, however, the idea of information literacy is so closely aligned to information technology literacy that the terms are treated as synonymous, that is information literacy is simply used as a new label for information technology literacy.

Computer literacy

'Computer literacy is an understanding of what computer hardware and software can do' (Kuhlthau 1990, p.16). In this sense it is a component of information technology literacy. There is, however, a range of definitions of computer literacy and some disagreement about what it includes, for example whether or not computer literacy includes a knowledge of programming (Levin 1983). The concept is often associated with the use of personal computers, but may be interpreted as having a broader meaning. Over the years there has been a shift in orientation from describing computer literacy in terms of operating computers to a focus on their application and use (Kuhlthau 1990, p.16). Following is a selection of goals that capture the broader dimensions of computer literacy:

- being able to program computers
- knowing how to use software packages
- understanding about the structure and operation of the computer

- knowing about the history of computers
- understanding the economic, social and psychological impact of computers
- developing literacy in a personal computer environment; and
- being able to turn naturally to the computer for problem solving. (Trauth 1986, p.252)

The relationship between computer literacy and information literacy is also complex. In some descriptions of information literacy, computer literacy plays a prominent role, usually involving a claim that information literacy goes beyond computer literacy (Horton 1983). Many advocates of information literacy point out that not all information is available through computers and that 'computer stored information is only as good as the sources from which it is taken' (Breivik and Gee 1989, p.12). Computer literacy is, however, usually recognised as 'a subset of information literacy' (Breivik 1993, p.13).

Library literacy

The concept of library literacy, or library skills, can be defined as the ability to use libraries. There are two main approaches to interpreting the concept of library literacy. The first of these is a narrow interpretation which focuses on a person's ability to retrieve information from library resources. Behrens (1990, p.355), for example , claims that 'library skills concentrate on the mechanics of obtaining information...The skills required are essentially lower level location skills, not higher level intellectual skills'. In this view library skills are seen as the ability to use the range of tools for accessing information available through libraries. These may include the library online catalogue, other electronic databases, microfiche, videodiscs, Internet sources and so on; indeed in most university and other libraries a broad range of information technologies can be encountered. The focus, however, is on the effective use of the tool, and the location of the information required, rather than on problem solving, evaluation and other elements of the process of using information. The second approach adds to familiarity with location skills, the notion of interpretation skills within the library context. Interpretation skills involve using information once it has been found. They encompass critical thinking, particularly the ability to evaluate and synthesise information. In this second approach to the idea of library literacy, location and interpretation skills are inseparable (Kuhlthau 1990, p.15). Unfortunately, the recognition of process skills beyond locating information as being an essential part of library literacy is not 'commonly acknowledged' (Kuhlthau 1990, p.15).

When library skills are recognised as incorporating the broader skills of information use, which are engaging in formulating information problems, finding, managing, evaluating and synthesising information, then the concept comes close to the ideas of information skills and information literacy. The context in which the skills are used, and the particular nature of the tools through which information is found, are the differentiating factor, making library literacy a subset of the other two. In describing a broader view of library literacy Kuhlthau suggests that the library be seen as an information system within which students can learn the essential components of other information systems (Kuhlthau 1990, p.15). Essentially, the library is considered a microcosm of the world of information; once learned about, students are able to apply their understanding of information systems to those beyond the library.

This broader view of information literacy may explain why it is that some librarians refer to library skills as information literacy. For them, the library is one context within which information literacy can be learned, and then applied in future to other contexts. This claim can only be defended, however, when an appropriate process approach is taken to teaching and learning library use.

Information skills

The idea of information skills dates from around the mid 1980s. It was around that time that most of the relevant taxonomies were developed. This makes the term *information literacy* somewhat older than the term *information skill*. Nevertheless, the idea of information skill has competed strongly with that of information literacy, and continues to do so. In general, the term *information skill* may be said to focus on the intellectual processes of information use. Although the idea has mainly been promoted by those with an interest in teaching library use, the processes involved are decontextualised and thus made relevant to learning in contexts outside the library. Where these skills are taught in relation to the use of library resources, it is stressed that they are not intended to be specific to libraries, nor to any one library or its collections. The skills are described as 'information based, not library based' (Kirk 1986, p.84). This approach recognises that the skills are applicable to the library context, but that they can also be used in other information settings.

Not only do the processes reflect an abstraction away from library use, they also reflect an abstraction away from information technology. The ability to use information technology, while required in some applications of information skills, fades into the background in the taxonomies describing them. Both libraries and information technology are seen only as sources of information relevant to one aspect of the overall process. The close association of information skills with library skills is seen, however, in the early references to *library and information skills*. Perhaps the most famous information skills taxonomy, the 'Big six skills', was designed as:

> ...a library and information skills curriculum designed around (1) the information problem-solving process and (2) Bloom's taxonomy of cognitive objectives. The emphasis is on developing a logical, critical thinking approach to information problem-solving and not on those skills associated with merely locating and accessing information sources. (Eisenberg and Berkowitz 1988, p.99)

The six skills proposed by Eisenberg and Berkowitz are:

- **Task definition**: determining the nature of the information problem and defining the purpose for the information search
- **Information seeking strategies**: determining the type of sources and strategies for acquiring the sources required to meet a previously defined information task
- **Location of & access to information**: finding sources and retrieving specific information from sources
- **Use of information**: applying information to defined information needs

- **Synthesis**: integrating, structuring and repackaging information to meet defined task
- **Evaluation**: judging the information problem solving process and whether the information need was met. (Eisenberg and Berkowitz 1988, p.101)

A few years later, Eisenberg and Small (1993, p.269-270) similarly describe information skills as comprising 'information acquisition methods, information seeking process and information problem solving skills'. More specific aspects involve topic analysis, information seeking, storing, evaluation and presentation. All of these components are included in most information skills taxonomies. Another such taxonomy, which appeared before the Big six skills, is that developed by Marland. Marland's taxonomy is based on questions which need to be addressed when working with an information problem:

- What do I need to do? (formulation and analysis of need)
- Where could I go? (identification and appraisal of likely sources)
- How do I get to the information? (tracing and locating individual sources)
- Which sources shall I use? (examining, selecting and rejecting individual sources)
- How shall I use the resources? (interrogating resources)
- What should I make a record of? (recording and storing information
- Have I got the information I need? (interpretation, analysis, synthesis and evaluation
- How should I present it? (presentation, communication and shape)
- What have I achieved? (evaluation). (Marland 1981, cited in Behrens 1990, p.356)

Many information skills taxonomies (for example, Marland 1981; Irving 1986; and Kirk 1986) have influenced heavily descriptions of information literacy. For example , the ALA (1989) description of information literacy draws from them extensively. It will be seen later in this chapter, that in some interpretations no distinction is made between information skills and information literacy. As is the case with other concepts which I have described, information skill is often simply relabelled information literacy. Alternatively, information skills may be considered as one aspect of information literacy.

Learning to learn and lifelong learning

The ideas of learning to learn, self direction in learning and lifelong learning are not unconnected. All of them have captured the attention of information literacy scholars and practitioners. Learning to learn involves developing those skills which lay a foundation for self direction and lifelong learning (Candy 1991, pp.317-342).

The idea of learning how to learn has become important across the educational sectors. It has been applied in primary schools, secondary schools, colleges and workplace learning programs. Gibbs (1983) defines learning to learn as '...a developmental process in which people's conceptions of learning evolve'. In creating this definition he is careful to discriminate between learning to learn and learning to study or acquiring study skills. Candy (1991, p.320) refers to Gibbs' interpretation as focusing on the 'higher order aspects of learning to learn'.

Mumford (1986), focusing on the need for managers to continue to learn, describes learning to learn as being about understanding one's own learning processes. This is similar to the idea of learning to learn as being about acquiring self knowledge and being able to address questions like *'How do I learn best*? and *'Where do I learn best?'* (Naisbitt and Aburdene 1985, p.134). According to Naisbitt and Aburdene learning to learn prepares people to continue to learn in our society that is continually changing, necessitating the regular updating of skills and knowledge. Learning to learn is therefore a prerequisite for lifelong learning. In some approaches to learning to learn, learning though information gathering plays an important role. It may be this focus which makes the concept of learning to learn attractive to those writing about information literacy. A number of anecdotes illustrating learning to learn, which capture this focus, include descriptions of an adult learning to learn from new acquaintances at a conference, a child learning to learn from library resources, and a journalist learning to learn by 'gathering information piece by piece, source by source, formulating and testing hypotheses' (Naisbitt and Aburdene 1985, p.134). For many, these illustrations would serve as descriptions of learning to be information literate.

Summary of concepts influencing the idea of information literacy

The five concepts influencing information literacy reviewed above, are apparently simultaneously discrete and interrelated. Computer literacy, for example has been recognised as a subset of information technology literacy. Information skills overlap somewhat with information technology literacy and library literacy. Information skills and computer literacy are not outside the boundaries of learning to learn. Some interrelations between these concepts and information literacy have also been touched on. The relationships between these concepts and information literacy will be explored further in the net section which examines the varying ways in which information literacy is described.

Varying descriptions of information literacy

The concept of information literacy has been interpreted in varying ways since the early 1970s when it was first considered. Two decades later, in response to the need to gain consensus among scholars, the following definition was developed using the Delphi Technique:

> Information literacy is the ability to access, evaluate and use information from a variety of sources. (Doyle 1992, p.5)

A more recent definition is even more concise:

> Information literacy is the ability to use information... (Curran 1993, p.258)

As a rule, however, information literacy scholars prefer to describe information literacy rather than to define it. The American Library Association's statement, reproduced below, comes closest to what may be considered an authoritative description, in the sense that it is regularly referred to by scholars and practitioners:

> To be information literate, a person must be able to recognise when information is needed and have the ability to locate, evaluate and use effectively the information needed... Ultimately information literate people are those who have learned how to learn. They know how to learn because they know how information is organised, how to find information, and how to use information in such a way that others can learn from them. (ALA Presidential Committee on Information Literacy 1989, p.1)

Critical features of this description are the focuses on information skills and lifelong learning, which are grounded in knowledge of the world of information, the capacity to navigate that world and communication skills. The description has nevertheless been criticised for its strong library orientation (Lenox and Walker 1992, p.4), and is by no means the only available description of information literacy. The tendency to describe information literacy is accounted for as follows:

> Information literacy is difficult to define but easier to describe because it is an abstraction, an ideal, and an interlocking set of skills and knowledge that is characterised by an ability or behaviour rather than a specific subject domain. (Lawrence McCrank 1992, p.485

The tendency towards description is evident in Bjorner's summary of the characteristics of information literacy, which she claims to be widely accepted in the evolving understandings of the phenomenon:

- To be information literate is an acquirable characteristic of an individual
- Information literacy is action-oriented; it is demonstrated in problem-solving and decision making which enable others to learn from an information-literate individual
- Information literacy operates in a broader arena than just a single discipline; an information literate individual can always find information needed for a new task or decision, and skills are useful in occupational as well as personal activities
- There are skills involved in the demonstration of information literacy and the skills once learned can be used throughout a lifetime
- The skills involved include finding and using information
- An information literate person is able to deal effectively with new technologies to handle information (Bjorner 1991, p. 151)

Given the diversity of concepts that form the background to information literacy, and the ongoing changes in the world of information, it is not surprising that information literacy has been, and continues to be, understood in a range of ways. I have chosen to analyse the variation in how scholars are describing information literacy because these differences are of special interest to the empirical study which will be described later. They are of interest not only because they represent the thinking of scholars about the phenomenon, but also because people's conceptions, or experience of information literacy, may reflect elements of these understandings, at least in part. It is not unusual for researchers investigating conceptions to discover that people's conceptions resemble contemporary, and historical, scholarly thinking about the phenomenon being studied.

In what follows I examine the different ways in which information literacy is described in the literature arising out of scholarly reflection on the subject, as opposed to descriptions of education programs or research studies. I have focused mainly on contemporary literature, from 1990 onwards, simply because most of the discussion has been taking place since then. Material from earlier attempts at describing information literacy is included to provide a historical perspective. The historical development of the concept of information literacy is important because, as I have already pointed out, contemporary conceptions, or understandings of a phenomenon, are often found to reflect its history.

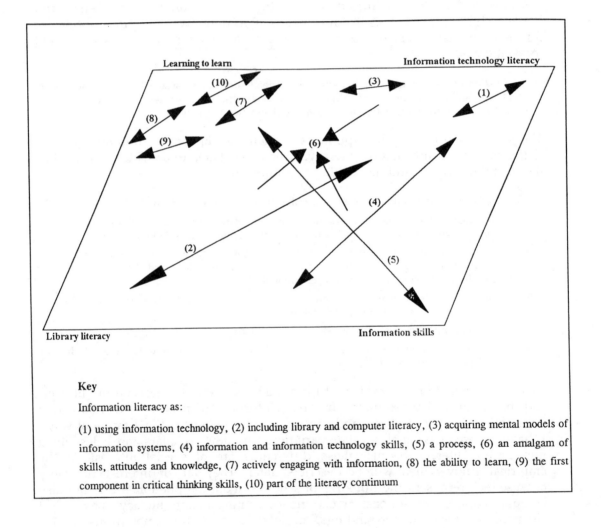

Figure 2.2   Arrowgraph showing proximity of interpretations of information literacy to related concepts

Although the following descriptions of information literacy are qualitatively different, they are not intended to be mutually exclusive. Authors writing about information literacy may focus on more than one of the different interpretations at different times. These different interpretations are shown below in an 'arrowgraph', after which each is described in detail. An arrowgraph is a tool commonly used by thesaurus developers to graphically portray the relationships between terms. Here it is used to portray something of how the various interpretations of information literacy are related to each other and to its companion concepts described earlier.

Information literacy as using information technology

This way of describing information literacy closely resembles the idea of information technology literacy discussed earlier. It is very much a systems-based approach, with its advocates focusing on the technology-based information systems of various kinds together with the knowledge and skills required to use them. Horton (1983) describes information literacy as involving awareness of the knowledge explosion and how technology can help with information related tasks in problem solving and decision making. Specific systems and services he lists include online databases, electronic mail, abstracting and indexing services, telecommunications services, government information sources and library networks (Horton 1983, p.16). The focus is very much on information technology, knowledge of what is available, and the motivation to use it. In this approach computer literacy is a 'prerequisite to information literacy' (p.16). Skills and competencies required for using information, the processes that are focal points in some other descriptions, recede into the background.

The focus on the ability to use information technology as a key element in information literacy is also highlighted by Johnston (1986) and Demo (1986). Demo (1986) describes information literacy as an intellectual skill that enables the mastery of new communications and information technologies such as microcomputers, cable television, electronic publishing, fibre optics, satellite communication, videotext, online databases, CDRom and robotics. Similarly Johnston (1985) focuses on the need to master technological tools, for example microcomputers, electronic mail, bulletin boards and commercial database searching, as well as the skills necessary for survival in an electronic environment. These include finding, manipulating and scanning electronic text, wordprocessing, keyboarding and using idea organisers (Johnston 1986).

As can be seen from the arrowgraph (Figure 2.2) information technology literacy is one of the major areas of convergence for the various interpretations of information literacy. A resurgence of interest in this approach has also occurred since the Internet and its associated technology has become more widespread.

Information literacy as including library and computer literacy

Although there has been a push for generic, that is non-library specific, definitions of information literacy, the term continues to be used interchangeably with 'library-based research' (McCrank 1992, p.487). In general, this involves some emphasis on the computer driven information sources available in libraries. Consequently information literacy is sometimes described as a combination of library literacy and computer literacy. Kuhlthau (1990, p.14), for example , defines information literacy this way. The approach to library literacy being drawn upon here is that which includes higher order skills of information interpretation and use as well as the locational skills. Similarly, Ford focuses on the role of computers in information provision and management and the skills required for effective use of academic libraries (Ford 1991, p.313

A variation of this approach is that which describes information literacy as an extension of library and computer skills. Authors so describing information literacy are working at extending the boundaries of information literacy, recognising that information might come from places other than libraries and be accessed from sources other than computers. In this interpretation library and computer literacy are seen as necessary but insufficient for information literacy (Behrens 1990, p.355; Breivik 1993).

Despite the label for this view of information literacy, its advocates are not necessarily system oriented as opposed to information user oriented. Kuhlthau, in particular, favours a strong process approach to information literacy arising out of her interest in how users engage in using the library for research (see for example Kuhlthau 1993).

Information literacy as acquiring mental models of information systems

Huston (1990) puts forward an interpretation of information literacy that differs significantly from the other descriptions presented here. For Huston, the idea of information literacy revolves around seeing the world as a configuration of information systems. The information user, to be information literate, must understand that information systems are the products of the need to communicate, and must also develop appropriate mental models of those systems:

> ...a fundamental definition of information literacy must acknowledge the value of knowing how to navigate systems that affect our everyday existence - like complex social, political, economic and work environments. (Huston 1990, p.692)

This view rejects the idea that information literacy comprises processes or behaviours. It suggests instead that particular mental models of information systems are required to ensure information access:

> ...individuals desiring information will have to extend their own expertise; this requires that they acquire the considerable conceptual knowledge necessary for thinking like expert searchers. (Huston 1990, p.695)

For Huston, it is acquiring those mental models which constitutes information literacy.

Information literacy as a combination of information and technology skills

The view of information literacy as a skill dominates the historical and contemporary literature on the subject. The earliest descriptions of information literacy as skills-based were relatively underdeveloped. They pointed, for example , to the skills and techniques required for 'using the wide range of information tools as well as primary sources' (Zurkowski 1974). Minor variations on this theme include Burchinal's description of information literacy as a 'set of skills' that are applicable to employment as well as private activities (Burchinal 1976, p.11) and descriptions of information literacy as the mastery of search and evaluation processes (Kobasigawa 1983, cited in Henri and Dillon 1992).

In the mid 1980s information literacy was also described in relation to library skills with the caveat that information literacy involves understanding and evaluating information and is not dependent on libraries as a source (Breivik 1985, p.723). Breivik provides an extended description of information literacy *skills*, characterising information literate students as those who can:

- understand processes for acquiring information, including systems for information identification and delivery
- evaluate the effectiveness of various information channels, including libraries, for different kinds of needs
- master basic skills in acquiring and storing their own information
- consider public policy issues relating to information, for example copyright, privacy and privatisation of government information. (Breivik 1987, p.46)

In the late 1980s there continued to be a strong emphasis, in this approach, on library use for the development of information literacy. Thus information literate individuals were described as having acquired a 'lifelong habit of library use' (ALA 1989, p.4).

In the early 1990s this way of describing information literacy continued to reflect the skills based approach of the 1970s and 1980s. Rader's (1990a,b) description of information literacy is virtually identical with that provided by Breivik in 1987. There is a heavier emphasis, however, on 'survival in the age of information and technology' (Rader 1990a, p.20), and the context of the 'global electronic environment' (Rader 1990a, p.21). Information literacy is here considered to incorporate computer literacy (Behrens 1990, p.355; Rader 1990a, p.20). Kwasnik (1990) presents a variation to this type of description, claiming that the necessary information and technology skills are at present undefined. They do, however, include 'attention to and selection of data, the individual processing of data in the human mind, and skills which enable the individual to interact with the environment'. Some skills she sees as required include:

- the acquisition, through experience, of a large body of knowledge, within which to integrate new knowledge
- an ability to organise existing knowledge conceptually, to remember it, to recognise it, to reorganise it
- conceptual flexibility
- an ability to not only analyse a problem into its components but to also view it in a larger context; an ability to switch from one viewpoint to another
- to use the above to define one's information requirements effectively, ...to translate an inchoate information need into the language of a system (computer, library, index) so the system can be used to advantage' (Kwasnik 1990)

Information literacy as a process

This approach is one in which information literacy and the processes labelled 'information skills', earlier in this chapter, are seen as the same. It is characterised by the claim that information literacy is the ability to apply information skills to a range of situations. The processes of information literacy outlined by adherents to this view (Bjorner 1991; Henri and Dillon 1992, p.106) may be directly equated with earlier descriptions of information skills.

The information literacy process approach may be represented through Bjorner's description of information literacy as the capability to:

- recognise an information need
- be motivated to satisfy that need
- develop a strategy to find the needed information
- carry through the strategy
- organise, evaluate and utilise the information in a satisfactory fashion (Bjorner 1991,p.151)

The six skills, or processes outlined by Kirk and Todd can be seen to draw heavily on Marland's taxonomy reproduced earlier:

- defining the tasks for which information is needed: what do I really want to find out and what do I need to do?
- locating appropriate sources of information to meet needs: where can I find the information I need
- selecting and recording relevant information from sources: what information do I really need to have
- understanding and appreciating information from a range of sources, and being able to combine and organise it effectively for best application: how can I best use this information
- presenting the information learned in an appropriate way: how can I most effectively present this information
- evaluating the outcomes in terms of meeting needs and increases in knowledge: did I achieve my purpose and what have I learned from this? (Kirk and Todd 1993, p.129)

The idea of information literacy as a process is very strong in the literature. It is a core understanding which is accepted by many scholars. Thus information literacy is described as extending 'the process of learning information skills to all ages and at all times' (Rader 1990a), the ability to apply a model of information gathering behaviour to new situations with the skills to go about it (MacAdam 1990), and the 'ability to select and apply information skills and strategies' (Henri and Dillon 1992, p.106). Eisenberg and Small (1993) describe information skills, which are the processes of locating, accessing, using analysing and presenting information, as research skills.

Information technology and library literacy do not feature in this approach. Skills in these areas are incidental to, rather than central to the process. Describing information literacy as a process has greatest affinity to describing it as the ability to learn.

Information literacy as an amalgam of skills, attitudes and knowledge

Differing from the view of information literacy as a process, or as a skill, is the view of information literacy as involving a combination of skills, attitudes and knowledge. Based on the framework provided in Bloom's taxonomy, this approach to information literacy focuses on the need for skills, attitudes and knowledge (Nahl-Jakobovits and Jakobovits 1993). It brings together emphases on information and technology-based skills encompassed in the approaches just described, with emphases on values and various kinds of knowledge about the information society, its systems, tools and sources. Thus Lenox and Walker (1992, p.4) add to information and critical thinking skills the capacity to 'challenge the validity of information,...seek corroboration before adopting information,...understand the political social and economic agendas of information creation and dissemination'. Kuhlthau (1990, p.17) describes information literacy in terms of knowledge, skills and attitudes such as 'persistence, attention to detail and scepticism'. Gratch summarises this approach in describing information literacy as comprising four components:

- an attitude that appreciates the value and power of information
- an awareness of the diversity of information forms and formats
- an understanding that information is not necessarily knowledge until it has been analysed questioned and integrated....
- a process to access and assess information critically and effectively. (Gratch, cited in McHenry, Stewart and Wu 1992, pp.55-56)

Information literate individuals are described as able to 'organise their own information searches, evaluate information, build their own online databases and know how to manage electronic files' (Rader 1990a, p.20). Information technology literacy is also a marked feature of this approach, with individuals being required to contend with developments in the information environment and associated technological change (Ford 1991, p.314).

Information literacy as actively engaging with information

One of the earliest approaches to information literacy came as a response to the flood of fragmentary, and often decontextualised information presented to people through the mass media. In this sense it is similar to the idea of media literacy (Aufderheide and Firestone 1993). Hamelink (1976) argues that the presentation of fragments of information to the public by the mass media 'keeps people from shaping their own world' (p.120). 'A new information literacy is necessary for liberation from the oppressive effects of the institutionalised public media' (p.120). In his interpretation, information literacy is seen as an alternative way of using information in which the individual shifts from being a passive recipient of predigested information, to achieving personal power in the information context (p.122). In this approach there is no focus on information technology or skills for accessing information. The focus is rather on the individual taking an active role in engaging with the information environment.

Hamelink's approach is influenced by the thought of Paulo Freire and is similar to that adopted by Huston (1988) in developing programs for educating information users. It is also opposed to the economic rationalist influence which pervades descriptions of information literacy as perceived by Curran (1993). In the latter, the welfare of the nation, rather then the individual is stressed. This type of description has since received very limited attention in contemporary writing about the concept.

Information literacy as the ability to learn

Unlike the description of information literacy as engaging actively with information, this approach is skills-based like some of those previously described. However the focus goes beyond the skills to the personal outcomes for those who have mastered them. Thus information literacy is described as a 'characteristic of self-directed independent learners who are prepared for lifelong learning' (Breivik 1987, p.46).

This description is reflected in part by scholars of self-directed learning who describe information location and use as a characteristic of individuals with this trait (see, for example , Candy 1991). The reasoning underlying this approach is that information literate individuals, those who have the requisite skills, attitudes and knowledge, have acquired key attributes required for learning.

For some, information literacy is seen as more than just one among many characteristics of learners; it is equated with the capacity to learn. Emphasis is placed on equipping individuals for lifelong learning with the appearance that no more than information literacy is required. The description of information literate people as 'those who have learned how to learn' (ALA 1989, p.4) reflects the thinking of such scholars. Behrens, for example , describes the information literate person in vivid, if not gender neutral, terms

> The ability of the information literate person to handle information effectively will positively affect his quality of life. He has learned how to learn, is thus able to operate dynamically in his own education and therefore has control over the way in which he communicates, works and lives. (Behrens 1990, p.357)

This idea is reflected in the titles of monographs appearing in the early 1990s such as *Information literacy: learning how to learn* (Vareljs 1991) and *Information literacy: developing students as independent learners* (Farmer and Mech 1992). For authors taking this focus, information literacy becomes a tool for personal empowerment (ALA 1989; Behrens 1990; Lenox and Walker 1992).

Information literacy as the first component in the continuum of critical thinking skills

Kuhlthau (1990), Lenox and Walker (1992), among others, point to the role of critical thinking in information literacy. Critical thinking skills that need to be mastered, according to Kuhlthau (1990) are those listed by Beyer:

- determining the factual accuracy of a statement
- distinguishing relevant from irrelevant information, claims or reasons
- detecting bias
- identifying unstated assumptions
- identifying ambiguous or equivocal claims or arguments
- recognising logical inconsistencies or fallacies in a line of reasoning

- distinguishing between warranted or unwarranted claims
- determining the strength of an argument. (Beyer 1985, cited in Kuhlthau 1990

Breivik (1991a, p.226), however, takes a different stance, describing information literacy as the first port of call in the application of critical thinking skills, arguing that it is an essential first step to be able to identify and retrieve an 'adequate, accurate and up to date body of information'. Breivik's argument is that appropriate solutions to problems are not likely to be found if the problem solver's information base is inadequate.

Information literacy as part of the literacy continuum

Whereas most approaches treat information literacy as a qualitatively different kind of literacy, such as visual literacy, social literacy or science literacy, this approach describes the phenomenon as part of the literacy continuum (Arp 1990; Behrens 1990, p.355; Breivik 1991b, p.29; Breivik and Gee 1989, pp.22-23). In this sense information literacy is seen simply as an extension of traditional literacy requirements for the information age; in which case, as Arp (1990) argues, the term is redundant. Alternatively, information literacy is regarded as an overarching literacy, incorporating all other types of literacy. Breivik (1991c pp.10-11), for example, claims that with the attainment of information literacy 'all other literacies will have been achieved'.

Towards an alternate approach to describing information literacy: from attributes to conceptions

In previous sections of this chapter I have described a range of interpretations of information literacy found in scholarly description. These descriptions form the first spoke of the information literacy wheel representing the present dominant approach to information literacy (See Figure 2.3a). I now turn to examining the main features and limitations of these descriptions and argue for describing information literacy as experiences, or 'conceptions' (See Figure 2.3b).

Although not explicitly stated by the authors concerned, the varying descriptions that I have examined are most strongly influenced by behaviourist and information processing paradigms. Except for the critical approach evident in seeing information literacy as engaging actively with information, and the constructivist approaches that may underlie the 'mental model' and 'learning to learn' perspectives, contemporary critics either lean towards behaviourist and information processing approaches or draw on the work of others who use them. It is the very adoption of these approaches, to a greater or lesser degree, that has led to the descriptions that dominate our picture of information literacy. These are descriptions which emphasise attributes of individuals, that is knowledge, skills and attitudes, or processes of information use which individuals need to master. The tendency to describe information literacy this way, may be partly due to the relative familiarity of the skills-based curriculum models that can be derived from the descriptions. These curriculum models will be analysed in the following chapter.

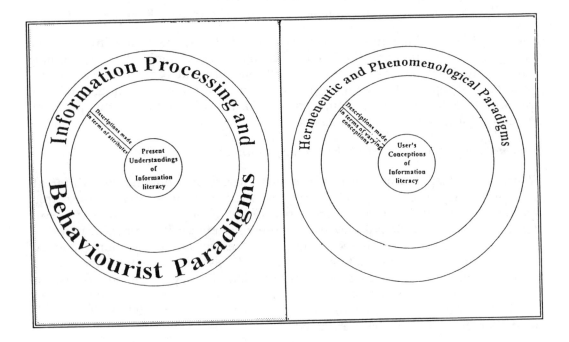

Figure 2.3a Describing information literacy
as attributes of people

Figure 2.3b Describing information literacy
in terms of people's perceptions

As the various authors do not usually make explicit their theoretical positions, it is not possible, or fair, to label any of them as having adopted a single position. It is possible, however, to identify the major views that have influenced thinking about information literacy to varying extents:

- **Dualism** Strictly interpreted as 'the hypothesis that mind and body are separate entities' (Sutherland 1994, p. 127), dualism can be reinterpreted in the context of information literacy scholarship as an approach to the world which involves seeing the information user as separate from his or her environment. This has led to descriptions of information literacy which are framed as attributes of individuals without accounting for how they interact with elements of the information environment. The information user is described as having particular capabilities, whilst the relation between the individual and his or her world is ignored. For example , in some instances information literacy is described as being able to use modern information technology. How the person approaches, or interacts with that technology is not a concern

- **Behaviourism** This has been defined as 'a psychological theory based on the analysis of observable behaviour' (Rowntree 1981, p. 22) that has led to descriptions of information literacy which are informed by Bloom's taxonomy, and therefore framed as various forms of knowledge, skills and attitudes. The information user, to be described as information literate must exhibit behaviours that demonstrate these abilities. A wide range of the descriptions of information literacy analysed in the previous section fall into this category; they are identifiable through their emphasis on skills

- **Information processing** Usually associated with 'the organisation, manipulation duplication and distribution of information using computers' (Verma 1993, p.83), information processing theory has influenced a range of disciplines leading to the formulation of linear processes to assist in various forms of problem solving. This approach has led to descriptions of information literacy which are framed as sets of information skills and processes which individuals should adopt. As a rule, these are in the forms of linear descriptions of the process, which if followed will result in the desired outcome, that is information used effectively. The description of information literacy as a process, a very influential one, leans towards this position, although many educators adopting it would use it within a constructivist framework.

- **Constructivism** Defined as 'the doctrine held, among others by Piaget, that complex mental structures are neither innate nor passively derived from experience, but are actively constructed by the mind' (Sutherland 1994, p.91), constructivism has focussed on critical thinking, decision making and problem solving as well as a broader interest in learning, which feature in some descriptions of information literacy. This view has had a greater explicit influence on teaching and learning programs preceding information literacy, as will be seen in the following chapter, than it has had on information literacy and information literacy education itself. At present its influence on thinking about information literacy continues to grow, but has not displaced the skills based approaches which dominate

- **Economic rationalism** This has led to the view that information is a commodity that must be efficiently accessed and managed for the profit of the individual, the economy and society. Information literacy is, in this view, seen as the ability to maximise economic advantage. This view permeates much of the justification for the need for information literacy, and is in sharp contrast with the interest in personal and social empowerment which also underpins arguments for information literacy

The resulting descriptions, couched mainly in terms of skills, attitudes and knowledge, are the result of an attempt to fit our thinking about information literacy into the frameworks that have until recently dominated the disciplines of information science and education. These descriptions have been used, to date, to promote the concept of information literacy and to underpin information literacy education programs. They have been developing since the early 1980s and have been becoming progressively more sophisticated. Unfortunately, descriptions are the result of the use of particular theories to describe a phenomenon about which very little is actually known. This may, in part, explain the general dissatisfaction with the concept noted in the first chapter.

What are the problems associated with the prevailing descriptions of information literacy?

The American Library Association's (1989) *Final Report* on information literacy captures the essence of contemporary descriptions. Some limitations of these descriptions are, therefore, highlighted in Foster's criticisms of that report's portrayal:

- they do not allow us to recognise those who are information literate
- the elements of knowledge and skills involved, such as 'knowing how knowledge is organised' and being able to use information, are overgeneralised 'to the point of uselessness'
- the abilities to locate, evaluate and use information are not viewed contextually
- they do not successfully differentiate between the use of libraries and other information environments, that is the descriptions fundamentally mean that 'information literate people are those who know how to use libraries'. (Foster 1993, p.344)

Other limitations of the various descriptions of information literacy are that they:

- are largely based on intuitive recognition and anecdotal reporting rather than any systematic investigation (Kirk and Todd 1993, p.129)

- do not distinguish between information literacy in the academic environment, in the workplace and in everyday life

- represent an attempt to decontextualise the descriptions to make them universally applicable, without having first examined the nature of information literacy in specific contexts

- do not capture the varying ways in which information literacy may be experienced

- explore skills, resulting in a focus on the characteristics required for completing a task rather than focusing on the experience of the task itself (Sandberg 1991, p.2)

- do not take into account the individual's idiosyncratic ways of operating

- describe characteristics of individuals rather than the relations between people and their information environment

The *information skills or process* view of information literacy shares the above flaws and is subject to more specific limitations. It is:

- linear in nature, and therefore does not suggest anything of the recursive and reflexive nature of information use; for example it may still be necessary to retrieve information when information is being 'packaged' for communication

- difficult to differentiate from general problem solving and research processes

- unable to portray the need for some elements, such as evaluation to occur at all stages of the process

In summary, these descriptions of information literacy have gained acceptance without having been subjected to any rigorous testing. As a rule, they have not been derived from observation of the processes of information users; nor have they been examined to determine the extent to which they are applicable or to determine the types of problems to which they might be applicable.

Continuing within the current framework would mean that, to understand information literacy better, we would seek to further explore the skills, knowledge and attitudes which may be required. These attempts would be aimed at consolidating objective definitions of information literacy, accompanied by lists of attributes in the form of skills to be learned, units of knowledge and statements of value to be internalised; all intended to allow the measurement of information competence (see, for example , Doyle (1992)). Although the process approach to information literacy seems unlikely to generate such difficulties, one amplification (Bjorner 1991) generated a list of thirty-four competency statements.

Such an approach would also be fundamentally at odds with the very idea of information literacy, which suggests that knowledge and skills are quickly dated, and that information literacy involves being able to learn and relearn in the face of constant change.

What are the benefits of adopting a relational approach to describing information literacy?

To further our understanding of information literacy requires an approach to describing it which will allow us to focus on the phenomenon itself, as it is experienced by people interacting with the world of information. Philosophers belonging to the phenomenological schools have coined a phrase which captures this kind of intention: *to the things themselves* (Husserl, cited in Ihde 1986). Their goal is to better understand phenomena through studying afresh the ways in which aspects of the world appear to people, without encumbering their insights with previous understandings of the phenomenon being studied. If we accept the idea that information literacy is phenomenal, in other words that it is something which is experienced by individuals, then it becomes possible to seek to understand the nature of information literacy without recourse to the understandings which have been linked to the concept to date.

Describing information literacy in terms of the varying ways in which it is experienced by people, that is their conceptions, is the alternative which I propose. This alternative recognises the argument that as information literacy belongs to the family of literacies, the starting point for understanding it should be through the viewpoint of the literate:

> ...defining literacy objectively is difficult since we are unable to study it except from the viewpoint of 'literate' participants in a 'literate society'. (Kwasnik 1990, pp.127-8)

Studying information literacy from the viewpoint of people who could be considered to be highly effective information users in particular contexts, is the first step towards a relational view of information literacy. Within the relational approach any phenomenon is seen as 'the logically structured complex of the different ways of experiencing an object' (Marton 1993). Information literacy, therefore, may be described as a complex of the different ways in which it appears to people/is seen, experienced or understood. These different experiences of information literacy, are the qualitatively different relations between people and some aspect of the world, known as conceptions.

Conceptions which will be discussed in detail in the fifth chapter, are not found in the mind of an individual, nor are they a characteristic or capability. They are defined as relations between subjects and objects. The simplest example s of this are described by Ihde (1986). Ihde explains that when any multistable phenomenon, such as a picture of a cube, is experienced as something different, this is because the person, or subject, is 'reaching out to' or focusing on the object in particular ways. The conception of, or way of experiencing the cube is not a characteristic of the person or the cube; it is a characteristic of the relation between them.

This approach to information literacy is significantly different from the one usually adopted. It is:

- **experiential**, based on the lived experience of people interacting with the world around them
- **relational**, it focuses neither on the person, nor on the object of interest, but on the relation between them
- **second order**, it represents the views of information users, through their discourses rather than the views of experts

The major implication of this view is that from this perspective, information literacy is neither dichotomous (Arp 1990, p.47), nor part of a continuum (Breivik 1991a), but about qualitatively different ways of interacting with the world. Further, a description of information literacy would be framed in terms of the various ways in which people conceive of it, rather than in terms of personal characteristics. There are several reasons for adopting a relational approach to describing information literacy.

Firstly, it has been argued that 'essential aspects of human competence', of which information literacy is one, are not reducible to a list of attributes (Sandberg 1994, p.20). For Sandberg, clearer insights into what constitutes competence are gained when the idea of competence is interpreted in terms of ways of conceiving of what it means to be competent in a particular situation. This does not mean that attributes need be dismissed, but rather that attributes are 'an integral part of .... conceptions' (Sandberg 1994, p.34).

Secondly, experiences, or conceptions, are more fundamental than attributes. They govern both the way in which a task is accomplished, and the attributes used in accomplishing it (Sandberg 1994, p.3). This means that examining conceptions of information literacy may change our understanding of the attributes involved, and that describing attributes is a task which can only be secondary to identifying the conceptions which constitute information literacy.

Thirdly, this approach allows us to describe information literacy as it is experienced, within particular contexts, before attempting to generalise about its characteristics. In my empirical study, universities have been selected as the initial context within which to explore conceptions of information literacy.

Fourthly, conceptions are holistic descriptions of ways of experiencing, or thinking about phenomena. They focus on a person's interaction with elements of their information universe, thus making the structure of the phenomenon underlying the concept explicit.

The research approach which will allow conceptions of information literacy to be identified is phenomenography. This approach will be described in detail in the fifth chapter. In the following chapter I review information literacy education, the second spoke in the information literacy wheel.

Chapter 3

Information literacy education

Having examined the various approaches to describing information literacy, I now turn to examining the second spoke in the *information literacy wheel*, information literacy education, in the context of higher education institutions. In this chapter I also review programs which have been part of the move towards information literacy education. Insights into information literacy education demonstrate how educators are fostering the process of becoming information literate, sometimes providing further insights into how information literacy is understood. The educators referred to here are mainly librarians in higher education institutions. As the wider community of tertiary educators develops an interest in the information literacy agenda we may expect changes in approach to information literacy education. Such changes are likely to be the result of the greater variety in experience of information literacy which will influence teaching and the likelihood of closer integration with academic curriculum. It is also possible that the views of information literacy education analysed in this chapter will have influenced higher educators' conceptions of information literacy which will be explored in later chapters.

Towards the close of this chapter I argue for the second of the three shifts in thinking about information literacy which frame my empirical study into higher educators' varying conceptions of the phenomenon. This is the shift from seeing learning to be information literate as the acquisition of attributes, to seeing it as coming to conceive of information literacy in different ways. As a result of this change we would design curricula around changing conceptions rather than around desirable attributes.

Information literacy education is examined under the following headings:

- Precursors to information literacy education

- Contemporary approaches to information literacy education

- Curriculum models for information literacy education

- Towards an alternate approach to information literacy education: from skills, knowledge and attributes to changing conceptions

Precursors to information literacy education

Although descriptions of information literacy date back to the 1970s, information literacy education is a more recent development. Teaching-learning programs targeted at fostering information literacy have mainly been developed by librarians, although this is a picture which is gradually changing. Before the emphasis on information literacy, university libraries called their teaching programs *library instruction,bibliographic instruction* or *user education*. The nature of these programs and their relation to information literacy education is subject to ongoing debate. Practitioners, that is librarians teaching these programs, do not always distinguish between them and so the various terms are often used interchangeably with information literacy education and with each other.

The descriptions provided here of *library instruction, bibliographic instruction* and *user education* represent an attempt to demonstrate why the different terms came to be used and some of the distinctions that are made between them at a theoretical level. It will be seen that, although on one hand the changes in terminology, particularly from library to bibliographic instruction were politically engendered, they also represent different ways of thinking about teaching and learning library and information skills. Use of the term *information literacy* to describe a library's teaching program is usually also both a political move, to attract interest in the program, and an acknowledgment of differences in the content and processes used.

Library instruction

Library instruction is the earliest ancestor of information literacy education. The aim of library instruction was, and still is, to ensure that students have the necessary skills to use their libraries. The key content areas of a library instruction program are outlined by Breivik (1982, p.85) as: 'attitudinal concerns, the logistics of using the library, the logistics of using resource tools, the organisation of information, resources and search strategies'. The focus of attention is the library and the resources it contains, usually leading to emphasis on library tours, instruction in the use of the inhouse library catalogue and tools which are commonly used. Another feature of this kind of instruction is awareness raising of the resources contained within the host library collection. In Breivik's content areas listed above, the latter elements such as the organisation of information, resources and search strategies, are also dealt with within the library context.

Library instruction programs may comprise one to one instruction or group instruction within, or in addition to, academic curriculum. In the latter case, student participation is usually voluntary. Irrespective of the level of formality, these programs are usually subject to the influence of educational research and theories (Aluri 1981), and evaluation (Beeler 1975; Breivik 1982).

Differences in library instruction reflect the differences in interpretation of library literacy noted in the previous chapter. Thus, library instruction is sometimes described as being confined to library orientation and location skills (Behrens 1990). This is not, however, always the case, and library instruction, like bibliographic instruction, may include an emphasis on broader information processes. Even during the late nineteenth century some librarians did not favour a narrow approach to library instruction. Perhaps this explains in part why the library instruction of those times is now referred to as bibliographic instruction.

In the late nineteenth and early twentieth centuries, although libraries were not yet transformed and linked by computer technology, their instruction programs were by no means confined to the structures and contents of the host library. Genevieve Walton of the Eastern Michigan University is an example of a librarian who did not confine her teaching programs to locational skills. In the late 1800s she initiated a lecture series which dealt with such diverse topics as 'Ancient writing material and manuscripts, printing and the printing press, libraries, catalogues and classification, reference books and how to use them, and selection and buying of books for private and small school libraries' (cited in Beck 1989, p.442). Walton is described as being:

> .... in the mainstream of the late nineteenth century movement to develop libraries as laboratories for independent reading, offering an alternative to textbooks. She was not just encouraging this among college students but was trying to train teachers who would make library use a part of the education of school children. (Beck 1989, p.443)

All the elements of library instruction are also part of bibliographic instruction and user education which are examined below. Some of the elements, however, such as library tours may cease to be recognised as a core part of the program.

Bibliographic instruction

Bibliographic instruction is the name usually given (particularly in the United States) to teaching programs in academic libraries which acquaint students with the bibliographic structure of their disciplines and enable them to use the necessary bibliographic tools. The term came into use, in the mid 1970s, to differentiate programs focusing on the processes and knowledge required for library based research from the more parochial library orientation programs, both of which had previously been known under the more general label of library instruction.

Bibliographic instruction involves teaching students all facets of using information which has entered the formal domain, that is information which is accessible through libraries. Grey, unpublished literature is also often dealt with. Guidelines for bibliographic instruction programs are provided in *the Model statement of objectives for bibliographic instruction* (Roberts and Blandy 1989, p.181) which has been revised regularly. The Model statement is examined later in this chapter because it is recognised as an example of information literacy curriculum (Kuhlthau 1990, p.17). Important developments in bibliographic instruction include:

- the identification of conceptual frameworks for bibliographic instruction (Baker 1986; Kobelski and Reichel 1981)

- movement towards course integrated instruction programs (Kirk 1984; Kohl and Wilson 1986)

- emphasis on the development of critical thinking skills (Bodi 1988; Engeldinger 1988; Plum 1984)

- the adoption of learning theories for program development, such as Kolb's learning cycle (Svinicki and Schwartz 1988), Bloom's taxonomy

(Jakobovits and Jakobovits 1990), and Knowles' theories of adult learning (Sheridan 1986)

- the development of experimental (American Library Association 1983) and qualitative program evaluation strategies (Frick 1990)

The term *bibliographic instruction* is now considered somewhat misleading as programs bearing this name today consider a wider range of processes and tools than the name implies. Since the mid 1980s there has been growing emphasis, for example, on teaching remote online searching of commercial databases, the use of bibliographic reference management software, the evaluation of the content of documents, and navigation of Internet sources.

In November 1993 the Bibliographic Instruction Section of the Association of College and Research Libraries considered a change of name which would more accurately represent contemporary practice. Although it was unlikely that the term information literacy would replace it, there has been support for the idea that bibliographic instruction programs were predecessors of information literacy programs:

> BI is part of an evolution towards information literacy, just as library orientation and library instruction was a step towards the evolution of BI. (Rader 1990a, p.20)

Lenox and Walker (1992, p.14) also describe bibliographic instruction programs as 'early efforts in the evolution towards information literacy'. They claim that the 'concepts and principles of bibliographic instruction, in years past were a sufficient information literacy program' (Lenox and Walker 1992, p.5). The stated differences between bibliographic instruction and information literacy education echo those emphasised between library skills and information skills. Bibliographic instruction is today considered to be an important strand of information literacy programs; the fundamental difference being that in teaching information literacy 'the information can be anywhere in any format or shape' (Rader 1990a, p.20).

User/Reader education

The terms *user education* or *reader education* are commonly used in public and academic libraries outside the United States, particularly in Europe (Fjällbrant 1976), Britain (Fleming 1990) and Australia (Frylink 1992). These terms have been in use since the early 1960s and has embraced the changes denoted by the labels *library instruction, bibliographic instruction* and now *information literacy*. User education may also include any one or all of the curriculum models suggested by these labels. They may encompass library specific orientation programs, instruction in the use of bibliographic tools and other sources, the processes of information searching from problem identification to evaluation, synthesis and communication. The format of such programs is also variable, ranging from voluntary one to one or group instruction, to accredited academic units.

A useful distinction which has been made in relation to online user education programs, and one which is relevant to user education programs generally, is that between promotion, orientation, training and education (Fjällbrant 1988, pp.229-30). Promotion captures the public relations elements of programs. On a broad scale this may include awareness raising of the existence of the library and resources accessible through it, or awareness raising about the existence and value of other information systems. Orientation ensures that the 'user' is comfortable with the range of types and systems and services provided. Training ensures the ability to use a specific system. Education captures the need for knowledge of broader principles, concepts and strategies which are necessary for understanding, evaluating and using a wide range of systems both within and beyond library structures.

User education programs may be designed on the basis of constructivist approaches similar to those characterising model bibliographic instruction. Interest in fostering reflective practice and critical thinking for example (Walton and Nettleton 1992), mirrors similar work being undertaken in the United States (Gibson 1989; Reichel 1990).

Contemporary approaches to information literacy education

The change in terminology to *information literacy education* within many library teaching programs reflects both real curriculum changes and a political dimension. The political dimension is asserted by Arp who points out that the term *bibliographic instruction* was familiar to librarians but meaningless to those outside that environment. On the other hand the term *information literacy* communicates well with those outside libraries without having yet been properly defined and understood for instruction purposes (Arp 1990). The need to communicate something of the nature of the programs and gain acceptance for them has led to a wide range of library programs being described in terms of information literacy. This practice, together with the varying approaches to describing information literacy, has led to:

> ...disagreement as to whether information literacy demands a mode of teaching different from that developed over the past ten years by library/media specialists and bibliographic instruction librarians. (Bjorner 1991, p.151)

Information literacy and bibliographic instruction are often not well differentiated, a problem which is recognised by critics of information literacy (White 1992, p.78). The lack of distinction is evident in a number of contributions to recent monographs (see for example, Farmer and Mech 1992; Huston 1991) addressing information literacy. In these monographs authors describe classical bibliographic instruction or library instruction without distinguishing between these and information literacy in terms of either content or processes (see, for example, Gaunt and Nash 1992; Porter 1992; Tierney 1992; Wiggins 1992). For example, the following description of an information literacy program at Brigham Young University fits the description of library instruction programs devised by Breivik (1982):

....basic skills instruction was developed in self instructional packages. These included a taped tour and programmed instruction texts for card catalogs, the library's online catalog, and periodical indexes....English composition instructors and librarians would team teach research strategies... (Wiggins 1992, p.79)

Many attempts to distinguish clearly between information literacy education and its forerunners do not succeed. Breivik's (1992, p.10) suggestion, that the essential difference revolves around library instruction being regarded as an 'add on' to curricula, disregards the tradition of ensuring that both library and bibliographic instruction are integrated into students' learning experiences through effective curriculum design.

Wright and Larson (1990, p.104) propose that the feature which separates information literacy from bibliographic instruction and library instruction is the establishment of 'a conceptual framework that supports information gathering activity.' Their proposal, and Lukenbill's (1989) suggestion that information literacy is a process approach to bibliographic instruction, disregard the already well established practice of using a process approach in that context. Research strategy, for example, was identified as a crucial conceptual framework for bibliographic instruction in the early 1980s (Kobelski and Reichel 1981). The suggestion that in information literacy education the information need not come from libraries further ignores the emphasis of the other programs on information sources outside the confines of libraries, such as patents offices, commercial online database hosts and newspaper databases. Differentiating between information literacy education and bibliographic instruction becomes even more difficult when the bibliographic instruction *Model statement of objectives* is described as an information literacy curriculum (Kuhlthau 1990, p.17).

Of some assistance in understanding the fundamental difference between an information literacy and bibliographic instruction program is the idea that information literacy education is based on fostering the skills, knowledge and attitudes which are required for learning from information sources of all kinds; whereas bibliographic instruction focuses on the skills, knowledge and attitudes required for learning from formal, library based, information systems. To make this distinction clear, an information literacy program would aim to ensure that a student could apply his or her information competence to a context in which interviews, for example, were required, whereas bibliographic instruction would stop short at ensuring that students could distinguish whether any documentary sources could supply the information.

In the higher education environment, the skills, knowledge and attitudes learned in both information literacy education and bibliographic instruction are similar; the same processes of recognising an information problem, identifying sources through to evaluating, managing and using the information would be required. However, the context in which these processes are applied would be broader in an information literacy education setting. Therefore, bibliographic instruction, or similar library based programs, can claim to further the interests of information literacy in relation to formal information systems; they may or may not emphasise the transferability of the skills to a wider range of information environments. Information literacy programs would emphasise a range of contexts for the application of skills, such as libraries, commercial information systems, workplace settings and various forms of public and private systems, for example government agencies. In this sense bibliographic instruction is best regarded as a subset of information literacy education.

Curriculum models for information literacy education

Despite the differences in approach to describing information literacy and the apparent difficulties in delimiting information literacy programs, contributors to the discussion accept, at least implicitly, that information literacy is something that can be learned. Given this assumption information literacy is seen in two distinctive ways in relation to education programs:

- as a conceptual framework applicable to all education curricula

- as a program in its own right

In the former approach information literacy is considered to be a vehicle through which learning occurs. It is thus described variously as 'a conceptual framework for the development of educational models and new curricular concepts in addressing information skill development' (Lenox and Walker 1992, p.5), a paradigm supporting the design of curriculum, including those of bibliographic instruction programs (Lowry 1990, p.23), or as summarising the 'underlying principles of quality undergraduate education for a new century' (Bunnell Jones 1992, p.32). In the second approach information literacy is regarded as content to be learned, thus programs are designed with their own supporting curriculum. The emphasis in such programs is on teaching people how to find, evaluate, use and manage resources.

Many of the difficulties associated with designing information literacy education come from the range of descriptions previously analysed. In addition, information literacy educators aim to develop skills in using information from a wide range of sources, considering it essential to incorporate all kinds of information systems and resources into learning experiences:

> Therein lies the dilemma of defining the concept so as to confine the program or else to open up both the definition to the point of meaningless generality and expanding a program to impossible goals. Where is the proper boundary for conceptualisation and hence targeting? (McCrank 1992, p.487)

Curricula which have been devised can be seen as representing an attempt to come to terms with this dilemma. The contribution of curriculum designers to our understanding of information literacy is significant because they have made the most systematic and sustained attempts at describing information literacy. These descriptions are embedded in the curriculum goals, objectives and taxonomies which they have designed and show how the problem of setting boundaries has been dealt with in practical situations.

A number of philosophies of curriculum development influence information literacy curricula leading to the possibility of discipline based, student based, social utilitarian or social reconstruction models (Bjorner 1991, p.152). Student based models are considered to be the most appropriate (Bjorner 1991, p.151) although most of the published curricula are heavily influenced by information theory. Also influential in the development of information literacy programs are the behaviourist learning theories of Skinner and Gagne (Lukenbill 1989, p.171).

The following models, or sets of goals which serve as foundations for information literacy curriculum represent the range being used in higher education. Some of them are regarded as models of excellence. These include the Mann library model, the Jakobovits' taxonomy, the *Model statement of objectives*, Bjorner's information literacy curriculum and the resource based learning model. The first four of these models feature the skills, knowledge and attitudes which students need to acquire. In this way they are consistent with the descriptions of information literacy examined in the previous chapter. Nevertheless, they spell out the knowledge, skills and attitudes involved in more detail. The level of detail provided in the following descriptions is not as extensive as in the primary sources but is sufficient to portray the style of the curriculum involved. The resource based learning model which is advocated in schools, but could be used more in higher education, sits well with the 'information literacy as a conceptual framework' approach to curriculum described earlier. Each model discussed here has been explicitly described in the literature as an example of information literacy curriculum.

The Mann library model

The Mann library model encompasses five goals each of which is subdivided to specify a set of knowledge, skills and attitudes. Specific sources of information are not mentioned. Instead students are required to be able to deal with information formats, such as online databases, and negotiate the structures, such as indexing files etc. The Mann library curriculum was published as an exemplary model in the American Library Association's (1989) report, where it was slightly modified for application to K-12 curricula. The five goals are reproduced below:

Goal A: Understand the role and power of information in a democratic society. (Including such concepts as scholarly communication and the power of information)

Goal B: Understand the variety of the content and format of information. (Including the ability to evaluate information and information sources)

Goal C: Understand standard systems for the organisation of information. (Including understanding sources of information, available through electronic and other media, and their structure)

Goal D: Develop the capacity to retrieve information from a variety of systems and formats. (Developing and implementing strategies for the use of print and electronic sources including library systems)

Goal E: Develop the ability to organise and manipulate information for various access and retrieval purposes. (Including bibliographic file management, word processing, electronic spreadsheets) (Olsen 1992, pp.98 -9)

The Mann library model has also been largely adopted by Cleveland State University, and two further goals included which focus on information process:

- Students can articulate and focus their information needs
- Students are able to evaluate their information search processes (Rader 1991, p. 28)

These two goals, however, are arguably subsumed by Goal D of the Mann library model. Developing the capacity to retrieve information from a variety of formats must involve articulating the information need and evaluating the search process afterwards. There are also some apparent gaps in both models. For example, there is no focus on the conceptual aspects of synthesising and communicating new knowledge gained from the information use processes.

The taxonomic approach

An approach to library and information skills curriculum based on Bloom's taxonomy of affective, cognitive and sensorimotor objectives has been developed by Jakobovits and Nahl-Jakobovits (1987 and 1990). These models have been adapted and expanded to develop information literacy curriculum applicable to the bibliographic instruction context (Nahl-Jakobovits and Jakobovits 1993). Within this approach the emphasis is on:

...integrated behavioural objectives, linking the affective, cognitive and sensorimotor domains within three levels of information literacy instruction: critical thinking or information evaluation skills; using information knowledge or information use skills; and learning to learn or enjoying the benefits of information success (Nahl-Jakobovits and Jakobovits 1993, p.78).

The resultant taxonomy is comprised of nine cells, with each of what are labelled affective, cognitive and sensorimotor objectives being divided into three levels. The first level is the orientation or critical thinking level, the second is the interaction level in which information is retrieved and used, and the third is the internalisation level in which the process is successfully accomplished. The taxonomy includes nine major objectives, three for each of the affective (A), cognitive (C) and sensorimotor (S) domains:

A1: Becoming sensitive to the need to evaluate information
A2: Having the perception of an information need and feeling the excitement of being an independent searcher
A3: Attaining the feeling of personal empowerment
C1: Evaluating the source of information according to appropriate standards
C2: Formulating the question and planning a search strategy
C3: Evaluating the information content and being empowered by it
S1: Coping in an information society and engaging in learning
S2: Recognising the information provided as suitable to the need and experiencing a sense of well being
S3: Facilitating one's life through lifelong information and enjoying its rich benefits. (Nahl-Jakobovits and Jakobovits 1993, p79)

The major discrepancy in this taxonomy is the use of the label 'sensorimotor' for the last set of objectives. They appear to contain further examples of affective and cognitive objectives. This taxonomy is, however, based on the assumption that learning in all three levels (1, 2 and 3 in the above list) is occurring simultaneously (Nahl-Jakobovits and Jakobovits 1993, p.79). The authors also claim that the taxonomy is exhaustive, representing a complete map for all kinds of bibliographic instruction programs, '...the information literate person is skilled in all nine cell areas, although not necessarily to the same extent in each' (p.79). Although described as a taxonomy suitable for the bibliographic instruction context, this taxonomy could be implemented in any learning environment.

Bibliographic instruction Model statement of objectives

The *Model statement of objectives* was created, and continues to be revised by the Association of College and Research Libraries Bibliographic Instruction Task Force. The model statement also emphasises skills and knowledge to be learned. Its behaviourist and information processing orientations are recognised by critics who regard the model statement as a 'significant contribution to the process of task analysis' (Wright and Larson 1990, p.105), the idea being that a comprehensive list of tasks is required to serve as a starting point for an information access curriculum. In task analysis the processes of information processing analysis, task classification, and learning task analysis 'produce a list of tasks and behaviours that collectively represent the beginning of a curriculum' (Wright and Larson 1990, p.105).

Kuhlthau (1990, p.17) identifies the model statement as comprising 'general and terminal objectives of information literacy skills'. These skills, in conjunction with the appropriate attitudes and information search processes, including critical thinking skills, form the basis of information literacy curriculum. The model statement, which has recently been revised to incorporate different levels of curriculum, requires learners to acquire proficiencies that demonstrate they understand:

- how information is identified and defined by experts
- how information sources are structured
- how information sources are intellectually accessed by users
- how information sources are physically organised and accessed

The model statement is not universally accepted as an information literacy curriculum model. Bjorner (1991, p.159) points out that the 'model statement as it now stands seems limited to libraries and library based systems and to only one of the duty areas of the information literacy curriculum working model.' Bjorner's working model is discussed below.

Bjorner's information literacy metacourse

Bjorner's working model of information literacy is described as a metacourse which she suggests may be taught as individual lessons, as concentrated units, or throughout a curriculum spanning several years. The metacourse may span the educational curriculum, from K-12 through to adult and continuing education (Bjorner 1991, p.155). According to Bjorner, individual learning situations in particular courses, subjects or lessons should be seen as contributing to an overall effort spanning many years of education. Details of Bjorner's metacourse are reproduced in chapter four as it represents one of the few outcomes of information literacy research. The eight major competency areas, which are a variation on the information skills theme, are listed below:

A. recognising and accepting an information gap

B. responding positively to the need for an investigation

C. constructing alternative strategies to reduce the information gap

D. evaluating and selecting a strategy

E. acting on a strategy

F. assessing the effectiveness of a strategy

G. using information

H. storing information for future use. (Bjorner 1991, p.157)

Bjorner's metacourse also has apparent deficiencies. Although it emphasises a broad process, the first six of the elements are concerned with information retrieval. Using information, the essential abilities to evaluate, synthesise and communicate are collapsed into a single element labelled information use.

Resource based learning

At the school level there has been a strong emphasis on resource based learning for developing information literacy (Kuhlthau 1991, pp.9 -10). Application of this model to information literacy education in the higher education context has limited presence in the literature (see, for example, McHenry, Stewart and W u 1992; Porter 1992). Its value, however, has been regularly asserted (Breivik 1991a, 1992; Candy 1993; Lenox and Walker 1992). Interest in resource based learning for information literacy education is an intrinsic part of the American Library Association report which calls for:

> ...not a new information studies curriculum but, rather a restructuring of the learning process. Textbooks, workbooks, and lectures must yield to a learning process based on the information resources available for learning and problem solving throughout people's lifetimes.... Such a learning process would actively involve students in the process of:
> - knowing when they have a need for information
> - identifying information needed to address a given problem or issue
> - finding needed information
> - evaluating the information
> - organising the information
> - using the information effectively to address the problem or issue at hand. (American Library Association 1989, p.4)

Authors who have addressed the application of resource based learning to information literacy education have identified a number of its important features. They include:

- adopting resource based learning strategies ensures that 'information literacy is not taught as a separate course but is integrated with learning across the curriculum' (Kuhlthau 1991, p.9)

- resource based learning ensures that information literacy skills are 'learned through application and practice across curriculum areas' (Kuhlthau 1990, p.19)

- knowledge of information processes become an integral part of academic units (Lenox and Walker 1992, p.9)

- in adopting resource based learning strategies lecturers and librarians become learning facilitators rather than conveyors of knowledge (Breivik 1991b, p.226; Lenox and Walker 1992, p.9)

- students 'learn from the information resources of the real world, such as books, journals, television, and online databases' (Breivik 1991b, p.226)

- students engage in active self directed learning in an information rich environment where they learn to communicate an understanding of content, pose questions about the content being learned, reflect on, assess and take responsibility for their own learning (Hancock 1993, p.3)

The emphasis on these features of resource based learning affirms the importance of the interdisciplinary nature of information literacy, its dependence on access to a wide range of resources, and the freedom of the individual to critically select information from them. Also important to a resource based learning program targeting the development of information literacy, particularly in the higher education context, is the idea that students should be required to identify their own information sources. Where students are provided with resources for learning by teachers, they do not learn the skills necessary to navigate the world of information.

The value of resource based learning, and similar curricular strategies such as problem based learning, for information literacy education is readily established. It would not be difficult to adapt existing resource and/or problem based curricula, some of which already include library or bibliographic instruction components, to meet the full range of requirements of information literacy education. That is, students should be learning to identify their own resources from a wide range of formal and informal information sources and systems.

The content of teaching and learning in higher education

In this section I move beyond the general goals of information literacy curricula to probe *what* is taught in information literacy programs reported in the literature, and *how* , that is the teaching strategies used in such programs. This develops a more detailed picture of what is considered to constitute information literacy in the academic context. These details are drawn from a range of articles, appearing, except in one case, since 1990, that report established programs in higher education institutions. As the question of whether bibliographic instruction is a component of information literacy education or one of many teaching areas to which information literacy principles can be applied remains unanswered, only articles explicitly representing information literacy programs were considered.

As my previous examination of varying approaches to information literacy suggests, the idea of teaching the execution of an information based problem solving process is only one of the possible elements of information literacy teaching programs. Thus, programs may focus on a selection, or on a wide range of the following:

Information retrieval

- independent location of literature (Stanford 1992, p.41)

- searching in the electronic environment (Huston 1990, Oberman 1991)

- ability to effectively use bibliographic databases including live commercial databases (Bruce 1994a; Olsen 1992; Porter 1992, p.47)

- the ability to execute processes such as: 1) constructing plans to organise searches for information, 2) using controlled vocabulary and keywords, 3) using logical operators, and 4) understanding and applying concepts of truncation and field qualification in various electronic environments (Olsen 1992, p.99)

- determining the index structure and access points of print and computerised information sources (Olsen 1992, p.99)

- the ability to successfully navigate libraries (Olsen 1992, p.99)

- using card catalogs, online catalogs and periodical indexes (Wiggins 1992, p.79); and

- ability to accurately interpret bibliographic citations from print and computerised information sources and locate the material they represent (Olsen 1992, p.99)

Knowledge of the information universe

- the structure of the information environment (Rubens 1991)

- the conceptual contexts necessary for situating the context of a question, selecting one or more paths, and shifting the search to different pathways (Huston 1990, pp.693-4)

- national and international networks for scholarly communication (Olsen 1992, p.98)

- the purpose and range of reference tools (Gaunt and Nash 1992, p.87)

- knowledge of paper and computerised periodical indexes (Gaunt and Nash 1992, p.86)

- understanding the nature of periodicals (Gaunt and Nash 1992, p.85)

- awareness of library services (Gaunt and Nash 1992, p.85)

- knowledge of specialised information sources relevant to the discipline being studied (Lowry 1990; Tierney 1992; Bruce 1991)

- understanding the power of information and the classification of knowledge (McHenry Stewart and Wu 1992, p.58)

- awareness about the knowledge explosion and the role of technology in helping people identify, access and obtain information (Trauth 1986)

Information management

- knowledge of databases and their structure (Olsen 1992, p.99)

- ability to use specific systems and software packages, eg bibliographic file management packages (Bruce 1991, 1992a; Olsen 1992), word processors (Olsen 1992, p.95), spreadsheets (Olsen 1992, p.95)

- use of the computer for inventing and generating topics and for writing and editing (McHenry Stewart and Wu 1992, p.58)

Thinking skills

- question formulation (Rubens 1991)

- critical thinking, analytical and evaluation skills (Oberman 1991; Walton and Nettleton 1992)

- problem finding and problem solving (Fielder and Huston 1991, p.303)

- reflective practice (Bruce 1992b; Walton and Nettleton 1992)

- ways of focusing on a topic (Gaunt and Nash 1992, p.87)

- development of a research strategy (Gaunt and Nash 1992, p.87, Tierney 1992, p.65)

- the ability to differentiate between types of material typically represented in a library catalog and those that are not (Olsen 1992, p.99)

- assess alternatives for information acquisition, processing and use (Trauth 1986)

Information use context and information presentation

- writing literature reviews (Bruce 1991, 1992a, 1994b; Walton and Nettleton 1992)

- writing abstracts and annotations (Bruce 1990, p.225; Tierney 1992, p.64)

- developing and implementing current awareness strategies (Bruce 1990, 1991)

- writing correct bibliographic citations (Olsen 1992)

Information technology

- operate a personal computer (Olsen 1992)

- use computer based tools appropriate to the information need (Trauth 1986)

- use CDRom (Olsen 1992)

- articulate information needs in terms of technological requirements (Trauth 1986)

- understand and use telecommunications software and systems (Olsen 1992, p.98)

Evaluating information

- distinguishing popular from scholarly treatments of a subject, distinguishing primary from secondary sources, evaluating the quality of information and the usefulness of the content and format of a particular tool based on relevant criteria (Olsen 1992, p.99)

- evaluating the literature search process (Bruce 1991)

- ways of assessing alternative points of view, eg. using tools such as the Alternative Press Index (Gaunt and Nash 1992, p.86)

- analysing the quality of information sources (McHenry, Stewart and Wu 1992, p.58; Tierney 1992, p.64)

In teaching information literacy, both curriculum integrated and extracurricular strategies are used, although the emphasis on curriculum integration indicates that this is the preferred approach. As in most discipline areas a wide range of teaching-learning strategies are used in information literacy programs. Those with a relatively high level of teacher control include specially constructed assignments (Porter 1992), hands on experience, lectures, discussions and written materials (Gaunt and Nash 1992, p.85), taped tours and programmed instruction texts (Wiggins 1992, p.79). Strategies emphasising relatively high levels of student control include a range of adult learning strategies (Sheridan 1986), active and discovery learning strategies (Fielder and Huston 1991, Oberman 1991) and reflective strategies such as the use of diaries (Walton and Nettleton, Bruce 1992), or the 'thinking like a searcher' model (Rubens 1991). These latter strategies intrinsically favour the idea of learning in terms of developing personal heuristics rather than the skills, knowledge and attitudes usually prescribed.

It is clear that the literature of teaching and learning information literacy has been influenced, like the literature of bibliographic instruction before it, by the broader literature of teaching and learning in higher education. However, that part of the literature which focuses on the nature and impact of students' perceptions has not had a discernible impact. The work of Mary Huston presents one of the few examples of attempts to design instruction programs based on the phenomenological perspective that students experience their world, and indeed their learning contexts in significantly different ways. She rejects the idea that information seeking 'like electronic processing is a set of procedures which can be formalised, followed and taught as step by step sequences' (Huston 1990, p.692).

Huston's work, however, does not appear to take the argument for a phenomenological approach to designing teaching-learning strategies to its logical conclusion of specifying learning outcomes in terms of changed ways of experiencing the world. Her goal for teaching and learning is to facilitate the development of

> ...effective teaching, then, should offer a conceptual model that stimulates the development of enabling mental models which can be applied to making database choices and path decisions. (Huston 1990, p.692)

She also describes the student's learning processes and outcomes from a dualistic cognitivist perspective:

> In other words, external information from library sources is received in terms of individuals existing constructions of the topic—as it were, within his or her head. In turn, this new information causes individual's representations of a topic to change. From this perspective, users' cognitive structures can be portrayed as systems that create, motivate and direct searches for relevant information, even as they are influenced by external information. (Fielder and Huston 1991, p.313)

Towards an alternate approach to information literacy education: from learning skills knowledge and attributes to changing conceptions

In this chapter, I have continued to develop the picture of our present understanding of information literacy, through examining information literacy curriculum, programs and teaching-learning strategies. In these approaches, teaching and learning information literacy emphasises acquiring attributes (see Figure 3.1a). I now turn to examining the implications of these views in relation to our understanding of information literacy and argue for adopting a relational view of teaching and learning in information literacy education (see Figure 3.1b).

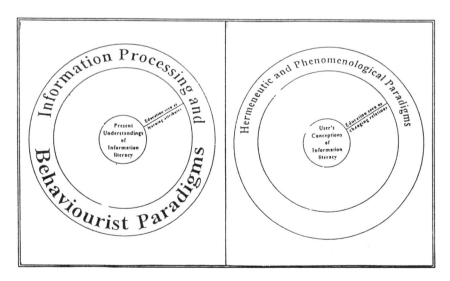

Figure 3.1a Teaching and learning as acquiring attributes of information literacy

Figure 3.1b Teaching and learning as changing conceptions

What are the problems associated with prevailing models of information literacy education?

Although the curricular and teaching strategies demonstrate a move towards student centred models, the dominant paradigms are similar to those which influence descriptions of information literacy examined in the previous chapter. From these perspectives, learning to be information literate is largely about developing skills, knowledge and values, that is acquiring the characteristics of an information literate individual. Bloom's influence, for example, is explicitly recognised by Nahl-Jakobovits and Jakobovits. This means that most curricula are designed around the skills, knowledge and values which an individual needs to acquire. The views of teaching and learning associated with these approaches are, in Biggs' (1990, pp.12-13) terms, predominantly quantitative and institutional. Learning is about 'coverage of a list of facts, skills, concepts and principles that need to be known' and teaching is about communicating the knowledge and skills. Learning also needs to be demonstrated in such a way that it is testable, and competence in skills and knowledge need to be demonstrated in order for academic units to be passed.

Although these views dominate models of information literacy curriculum, the earlier analysis does indicate a shift towards experiential or reflective modes of teaching and learning in bibliographic instruction and some information literacy forums. This appears to be a practitioner based movement, and is yet to influence theoretical writing about information literacy, although the ideas would fit curriculum models which revolve around resource based learning. These approaches are based on substantially different models of teaching and learning; but practitioners involved have not yet been provided with detailed descriptions of information literacy which are compatible with this approach. Advocates of resource based learning may favour interpreting information literacy as learning to learn. However, not distinguishing between these phenomena is as unhelpful to information literacy education as it is to our understanding of information literacy.

In all cases of information literacy curriculum, the question of 'what' needs to be taught, and learned, is not adequately addressed. If *information skills* are the focus, then this raises the problem of whether an information skills curriculum is a sufficient information literacy curriculum. Similarly a focus on information tools and technologies, or on broader processes of resource based and problem based learning seem to skirt around, rather than aim at the target of information literacy. For example, focusing on tools and technologies in relation to information literacy education would not be unlike teaching science students how to use laboratory equipment without any concern for whether or not they understood what it meant to be a scientist. In the case of the more generalised approach, adopting a resource or problem based learning framework without focusing on what it means to be information literate would not be unlike adopting a problem based approach to engineering curriculum without helping students to understand what it means to be an engineer.

Current approaches to information literacy, although focusing more sharply on elements of the world of information than the descriptions examined in chapter two, have also failed to define the concept adequately for educational purposes (Arp 1990). As the above analogies indicate, current approaches are either overly specific, or overly generalised. In all cases they fail to engage the students with the question of what it means to be information literate. This problem is clearest in the ongoing discussion which attempts to unravel the distinction between bibliographic instruction and information literacy programs. Current approaches require a better understanding of the concepts and skills involved, the hierarchical arrangement of concepts and skills, and the development of statements and competencies which are testable (Arp 1990, p.49). They are also likely to lead to ever increasing lists of important knowledge and skills making it difficult for teachers to know what should be the focus of attention in any formal teaching program.

Furthermore, the important knowledge and skills in the world of information are subject to rapid change, paralleling the rate of change in amounts of information and information technology discussed in the first chapter. Content aspects of the curriculum, which are important today, such as the skills required for searching remote online databases may, tomorrow, as a result of technological changes be obsolete. This problem in information literacy education is exactly isomorphic with the educational problems which the concept of information literacy was designed to counteract. The argument here is that the information literate individual should be able to keep up to date in an environment in which relevant professional skills and knowledge are rapidly replaced.

The need to be able to articulate clearly the outcome of information literacy programs is an essential aspect of information literacy curriculum:

> With information literacy we must recognise that we have an expected product the information literate individual—and that we will be expected to produce this product. (Arp 1990, p.49)

One view is that theorists should seek to describe information literacy in such a way that it is measurable (Arp 1990, p.48). During late 1993 the question of how this should be done was raised regularly via the bibliographic instruction listserv (see, for example, Gawrych 1993; Lau 1993; Megill 1993 and Murrey 1993), and poses a dilemma for those responsible for information literacy education. The continuing proliferation of lists of competencies does not appear to have resolved this difficulty. They also lead into a further dilemma, that of testing specific knowledge and skills which have shelf lives as short as the discipline based knowledge which, in part, led to the emergence of the construct of information literacy.

Why adopt a relational approach to information literacy education

In chapter two I argued for adopting a relational approach to describing information literacy. Adopting such an approach would be of little value if we continued to view information literacy education in terms of ensuring that learners acquired the necessary attributes. Consistent with describing information literacy in terms of people's conceptions would be the adoption of a relational view of teaching and learning within the context of information literacy education. Moving towards a relational view of teaching and learning for information literacy education is grounded in the idea that information literacy can be usefully described in terms of conceptions of information literacy, a fundamental change in our understanding of what it means to be information literate, which I have already discussed.

The most fundamental principle underlying a relational view of learning is that:

> ...learning should be seen as a qualitative change in a person's way of seeing, experiencing understanding, conceptualising something in the real world—rather than a change in the amount of knowledge which someone possesses. (Marton and Ramsden 1988, p.271)

Furthermore, such a view implies that 'we do not receive information and then process it internally, but rather we reach out to the world and focus on particular aspects of it' (Prosser 1993, p.21). In relation to information literacy education, this means that how someone conceives of information literacy is of far greater importance to determining what they have learned, than how much knowledge or skill they are able to demonstrate.

A relational view of teaching and learning information literacy would comprise the same features of this approach, outlined by Ramsden (1988, p.26), applied to the information literacy context. I have adapted the first four of Ramsden's features in order to suggest what a relational approach to teaching and learning in information literacy education might involve:

Learning is about changes in conception Applied to information literacy education, this means that learning is about changes in how people conceive of information literacy, or in how they understand, see or experience aspects of their information environment. Of even higher importance to the learner than the knowledge and skills required for using information tools and technology, will be coming to conceive of relevant phenomena in a particular way.

Learning always has a content as well as a process When applied to information literacy education this means that learning to be information literate cannot be achieved in a decontextualised scenario. This means that, like phenomena such as thinking and learning, information literacy does not have a 'life of its own. It is a way of dealing with and reasoning about aspects of subject matter' (Marton and Ramsden 1988, p.274). Information literacy cannot be learned without engaging in discipline specific subject matter.

Improving learning is about relations between the learner and the subject matter, not teaching methods and student characteristics Applied to information literacy education this means that the focus of attention is neither on the student, nor on the teacher, but on the relation between learners and aspects of their information environment. It is these relations which the teacher and learner need to understand and, if appropriate, change.

Improving learning is about understanding the students' perspective This means that it is the role of the teacher, and the learner, to identify how the learner is interacting with elements of his or her information environment. It is the student's conceptions of information literacy and his or her information environment and its elements which need to be explored and revealed. Once this has been achieved it becomes possible for alternative conceptions to be recognised as different, understood and perhaps adopted.

Laurillard's 'prescriptive implications' of viewing learning as a change in conception follow from these four features:

- there must be a continuing dialogue between teacher and student
- the dialogue must reveal both participants' conceptions
- the teacher must analyse the relationships between the student's and the target conceptions to determine the focus for the continuation of the dialogue. (Laurillard 1993)

Other teaching strategies which may assist in changing experiences or conceptions are outlined by Marton and Ramsden (1988).

Adopting a relational view of information literacy education would, therefore, be based on a changed view of what it means to be information literate, and would lead to curricula which emphasise conceptions and experiences rather than attributes of individuals. Adopting such an approach would represent a significant shift from viewing teaching and learning in quantitative (that is, measurable) and institutional terms to viewing them qualitatively (Biggs 1990, p.12). The view of learning which recognises that 'learning not only involves ways of acquiring knowledge, but... of seeing the world in a different way' is recognised by some as a hierarchically sophisticated view which it is desirable for educators to achieve (Biggs 1990, p.12). Similarly, Candy (1991, p. 320) suggests that a focus on conceptions indicates a higher order approach to teaching and learning than thinking in terms of skills and knowledge. This is a view which is gaining widespread acceptance amongst European and Australian tertiary educators (see, for example, Booth 1990; Laurillard 1993; Prosser 1993; Ramsden 1992). The question needs to be asked, however, of why such a qualitative view, and in particular a relational view of information literacy education is desirable?

One of the most persuasive arguments for adopting a relational approach to information literacy education is the repeated observation arising from studies into learning; namely that the acquisition of knowledge and procedures related to a phenomenon is not necessarily accompanied by a change in understanding about that phenomenon. It cannot be assumed that:

> ...if a student obtains new knowledge and acquires new procedures related to a phenomenon, then his or her understanding of that phenomenon will ...change. (Marton and Ramsden 1988, p.272)

In practical terms, based on present thinking about information literacy, this might mean that a student could demonstrate a capacity to perform required tasks, such as formulating an information problem, locating, evaluating and managing information, and yet not recognise the need to adopt these strategies in dealing with information problems in an unfamiliar context.

Secondly, there is ample evidence that students learning about a particular phenomenon do not understand that phenomenon in similar ways. Nor, at the end of a course of study, do they necessarily exhibit the ways of understanding which educators may prefer (Dahlgren 1984a). Essentially, students can have different experiences of the same reality by focusing on different aspects of that reality (Prosser 1993, p.23).

Thirdly, a relational approach to teaching and learning is appropriate if we believe that academic learning is about coming to see the world from the perspective of 'experts'; experts here not being theorists so much as those who have considerable experience of those aspects of the world concerned.

Fourthly, such a view would be consistent with the point already argued, that conceptions of a phenomenon are somehow more fundamental to competence than knowledge and skills.

Finally, such a view may take us some way towards addressing the problem of how to educate people for information literacy without falling into some of the traps evident in the current approach.

In summary, the range of important questions in information literacy education is similar to those which arise in any educational context: Who should teach, in what ways should information literacy be taught, how should students be assessed, how should programs be evaluated, what is the role of libraries in such programs and what is the role of educators, both librarians and other lecturers? Answers to all these questions rest on knowing what should be taught; and at present our programs are largely designed on the basis of the views of information literacy of librarians and scholars rather than the views of information users (Curran 1993, 1990).

If we are to adopt a relational approach to information literacy education, considerable work needs to be done to understand people's varying experience, or conceptions of a range of phenomena: for example the world of information, online databases, indexing structures, telecommunications networks, scholarly communication, the information life cycle, and information searching processes:

> We have to know what views of a particular phenomenon we would like a learner to develop.
> (Marton and Ramsden 1988, p.272)

The starting point chosen in this study is to understand the varying ways of conceiving of information literacy itself. The results of this study will provide an initial map of ways in which information literacy is conceived by higher educators, against which students' perspectives can be compared. They will also provide a set of ways of conceiving of information literacy which may act as 'target conceptions' for teachers and students in formal education settings.

Chapter 4

Information literacy research

Information literacy research forms the third spoke in the *information literacy wheel* introduced in the first chapter. In chapters two and three, ways of understanding information literacy from the point of view of descriptions of the phenomenon occurring in opinion papers and the literature of information literacy education were examined. This chapter examines information literacy research. These studies add further to the picture of information literacy presently available to us. I also argue for the third change in thinking about information literacy which frames my study into varying conceptions of the phenomenon. This is the change from researching people and their attributes in order to understand information literacy, to researching the varying relations between people and aspects of their world. It is also a change from drawing on prior assumptions about the nature of information literacy in research to examining the phenomenon in the light of people's experience. Understandings of information literacy derived from research and the proposed alternative research approach are discussed under the following headings:

- Background to information literacy research
- Research into information literacy
- Research directions recommended in the literature
- Towards an alternate research approach: from identifying attributes to describing people's conceptions
- A preliminary research agenda based on the relational approach

Background to information literacy research

Information literacy research could be seen as belonging to the older, more developed tradition of information needs and uses research. Like the bibliographic instruction research movement which preceded it, however, information literacy research could well draw upon, and contribute to a parallel tradition of educational research. Since little research has yet been conducted into information literacy itself, an overview of developments in the past twenty years is necessary to understand the background to and possible influences on information literacy research.

Trends in information needs and uses research have been analysed and recorded in review articles appearing in the *Annual review of information science and technology*. Dervin and Nilan (1986), capture paradigmatic changes emerging in the mid to late 1980s. Described, for convenience, as the traditional and alternative paradigms, the former has an emphasis on scientific or 'quantitative' approaches, whereas the latter is roughly equivalent to what are commonly identified as inductive, qualitative approaches (Dervin and Nilan 1986, p.16). Today the inductive, qualitative approaches are seen as continuing to be overshadowed by the dominant paradigm which focuses on issues such as measurement and prediction (Stoan 1991; Park 1993).

The two influential paradigms identified by Dervin and Nilan are important to information literacy researchers as they deal with important issues such as the nature of information, views of users and knowledge interests. Essential differences between the two paradigms are summarised in Table 4.1.

Table 4.1   Paradigms in information needs and uses research I
Adapted from Dervin and Nilan (1986)

Traditional paradigm	Alternative paradigm
Information is seen as objective. It is commonly defined as: a) a property of matter, b) any message, document or information resource c) any publicly available symbolic material or d) any data	**Information is constructed by human beings.** It may be defined as: a) that which is capable of transforming image structures or b) any stimulus that alters the cognitive structure of the receiver.
Users are seen as input-output processors of information	**Users are seen as constantly constructing;** free, within system constraints to create from systems and situations whatever they choose
Researchers search for **trans-situational propositions** about the nature and use of **information systems**	Researchers focus on **understanding information use in particular situations** and are concerned with what leads up to and what follows system interaction.
Researchers focus on **externally** observable **dimensions of behaviour and events**	Researchers focus on **how people construct sense** searching for universal dimensions of sense making
Research questions start with the information system, measure use of systems and seek predictors of use	**Research questions start with the user.** The system is examined only as it is seen by the user.
Researchers ask 'what' questions eg what people use what systems, what services do people use?	**Researchers ask 'how' questions** eg how do people define needs in different situation, how do they present these needs to the system, and how do they make use of what the system offers them?
Information needs are defined in terms that designate what in the information system is needed rather than in terms of what users think they need.	**Information needs are defined in terms of the users cognitive structures** eg a) a conceptual incongruity in which the person's cognitive structure is not adequate to the task, b) when the current state of possessed knowledge is less than needed, c) when internal sense runs out.

It can be seen that the 'alternative' paradigm to which information needs and uses researchers are turning is driven by an intrinsic interest in the information user and the user's perspective. This is paralleled in educational research by an interest in the student, or the learner, and his or her perception of learning contexts and phenomena. Other elements of the alternative paradigm, such as focus on cognitive structures and a constructivist approach to information and knowledge also have parallels in modern educational research.

The views of information underpinning the two paradigms are explored by Morris (1994). She contrasts the traditional and constructivist views of information as follows:

> (the traditional view)...sees information as external, objective, as something that exists outside the individual. It is a message transmitted from sender to receiver through a channel... Information in this traditional sense exists in an ordered world that is discoverable, definable, measurable. When we seek information through the traditional paradigm, our goal is to find the external 'information reality' that corresponds to our information need.

> (the constructivist view)...views information not as external or objective, but as ... constructed by the user. Information does not exist in the abstract—it needs to be interpreted... We construct cognitive maps of our environment that are constantly being altered and refined as we experience new information. We are changed by new information.... (Morris 1994, p.21)

Despite the apparent move towards constructivist and user oriented approaches, information needs and uses research continues to be criticised for:

- observing 'users in terms of systems, while only a few studies are finding ways to observe users in terms of users' (Dervin and Nilan 1986, p.9)

- concentrating on the means by which people discover information... rather than upon the ends served by their information seeking behaviour (Stoan 1991, p.247, citing Wilson 1981)

- focusing on systems or intermediaries rather than users (Park 1993)

One unstated, but nevertheless important, characteristic of the 'user driven', qualitative, paradigm described by Dervin and Nilan (1986), is that it remains, like the traditional paradigm, dualist in approach. Individuals are seen as 'self contained' and separate from information systems. The knowledge interest in research has simply shifted from the information system to the user without any apparent accompanying change in how the nature of a phenomenon, as a philosophical construct, is understood. As a result the essential relationship between the information user and his or her world is not being investigated. The alternative paradigm is also strongly influenced by cognitivist and information processing approaches. That is, it focuses on how information is constructed by human beings in the form of cognitive structures such as mental maps.

In educational research, a further shift has occurred since the early 1980s towards focusing on the internal relations, which may vary according to context, between people and aspects of their world (Marton 1981). People and their environments are seen as inextricably linked, such that neither one can be described or understood except in relation to the other. This phenomenological perspective of the world, which underpins research which has made significant advances in our understanding of learning during the 1980s, will be examined later in this chapter.

Since the mid 1980s, there has been a growing interest in the perceptual world of the information user. This has occurred in at least two areas of inquiry: the information related experiences of researchers and the experience of information in undergraduate and postgraduate learning contexts. Despite the entrenched interest in the frequency of researchers' use of information systems and sources (Stoan 1991), studies are emerging which report attempts to understand aspects of the researcher's experience. For example, studies based on intensive interviews have examined scientists' information gathering styles (Palmer 1991), and the strategies applied by researchers when determining the relevance of citations retrieved (Park 1993)

These studies have been both innovative and illuminating. Park's (1993) study, for example, an analysis of how researchers assess the value of citations, provides empirical support for the idea that relevance is not a measurable, but rather a contextually dependent and interpretive, concept. She further concludes that 'relevance can be looked at as a relationship between a user and a citation' (Park 1993, p.329). Unfortunately Park does not pursue the idea of relevance as a relation between user and citation, or the implications of that concept for further research. Instead she focuses on developing a model of her findings which presents the 'factors and thought processes... contributing to selection of a citation' (Park 1993, p.341). Essentially, however, Park adopts a phenomenological stance, describing the essential features of the relation between users and one aspect of their world, without making this explicit.

Qualitative research has also improved our understanding of undergraduate experiences of libraries and information use. Mellon and Kuhlthau used students' journal entries to describe the library research process of new undergraduates (Kuhlthau 1988), and new students' feelings of library anxiety (Mellon 1986). More recently, Andrews (1991) and Sullivan Windle (1993) used the critical incident technique (CIT) to describe undergraduates' perceptions of academic libraries and their staff and the problems which they, the students, experienced. Huston (1990) investigated undergraduate students' and experienced users' mental models of the information universe. The developing interest in this type of research has resulted in the publication of monographs focusing on the role of naturalistic inquiry for information studies (for example, Glazier and Powell 1992; Kuhlthau 1993; Mellon 1990).

The application of qualitative methods in information needs and uses research to the area of postgraduate study and supervision, however, has been limited. Two studies in this area have been identified (Zaporozhetz 1987 and Bruce 1994). The former explored, through interviews, how supervisors advised doctoral candidates for the literature review aspect of their research. The latter study examined research students' conceptions of a literature review. The study of conceptions of the literature review (Bruce 1994b) was the first qualitative study in information needs and uses to adopt explicitly a relational view of a phenomenon, as will be done in this study of the experience of information literacy. My study, therefore is situated in the intersection of two research traditions: the phenomenographic branch of research in higher education with a knowledge interest in people's varying conceptions of phenomena, and qualitative studies in information user research, particularly those focusing on the perceptual worlds of information user

Research into information literacy

For the purposes of this study, research into information literacy is defined as research which explicitly focuses attention on information literacy. There have been many studies into learning and various aspects of information needs and uses, including bibliographic instruction, which shed light on elements of information literacy and the information environment. These studies however, some of which I have discussed in the previous section, do not explicitly seek to illuminate information literacy or its programs; therefore they do not tell us anything about how researchers interpret the idea of information literacy. As I am reopening the question of how information literacy should be interpreted, or understood, I have chosen not to make assumptions about the nature of the phenomenon, a step which would be required if I were to examine research which did not explicitly locate itself within the information literacy domain.

Searches of education and library and information science databases revealed only a small number of journal articles and reports, including dissertations, about information literacy research. Of these studies only three (Bjorner 1991; Doyle 1992; Ochs and others 1991) improve our understanding of how information literacy is interpreted. Other studies, which accept as given contemporary approaches to information literacy, focus on:

- levels of involvement and factors influencing involvement with information and computer literacy in Dutch secondary schools (Plomp & Carleer 1987)

- developing a model of the information intermediary process in facilitating information literacy (Brock 1993)

- the emphasis on information literacy education across selected U.S. teacher education programs (Turner 1992)

- the comparative value of textbooks, computer based drill and practice and computer based tutorials in relation to examination performance in a management information systems course (Hoeke 1988)

- postgraduate students' and supervisors' perceptions of their information needs and personal information competence (Bruce 1990; Hiscock 1993)

Research methods used in these studies included surveys (Bruce 1990; Hiscock 1993; Plomp and Carleer 1987), controlled pre and post testing (Hoeke 1988), content analysis (Turner 1992), and the generation of a model through an extensive literature review and the input of a fifteen member expert panel (Brock

1993). These studies draw on existing descriptions of information literacy in order to pursue their aim. They do not extend our understanding of the phenomenon.

The three studies which deepen our understanding of information literacy in various ways deserve closer attention, both in terms of the strategies used by the researchers and the outcomes achieved. These are:

- the evaluation of Mann Library's information literacy program (Ochs and others 1991)

- the development of a comprehensive definition of information literacy (Doyle 1992)

- the development of an information literacy metacourse (Bjorner 1991)

Each of these studies assumes that information literacy is a valid concept and draws on opinion leaders' and information professionals' understandings, in delimiting or probing the nature of the phenomenon.

Mann Library's program evaluation

Mann Library's information literacy program evaluation had three goals:

- to assess Mann's information literacy program
- to ascertain the information skills which employers would like to see in recent college graduates
- to ascertain the information skills which recent graduates find necessary in their jobs (Ochs and others 1991, p.8)

Both graduates and employers were surveyed to meet these goals. Despite the broadly stated aims of Mann's information literacy curriculum, outlined in chapter three, the researchers responsible for this survey interpreted the character of information literacy very narrowly, focusing entirely on the use of computers for information retrieval and management. Because the understanding of information literacy drawn upon here reflects elements of the information technology based understanding examined in chapter two, information processes, noncomputer related knowledge, skills and attitudes, and noncomputer based information sources were not included in the survey. The survey examined the need to use computers in the workplace, and requirements made of graduates, in six skill areas:

- finding information in computerised databases
- manipulating numeric data with a computer
- creating and managing databases
- writing computer programs
- preparing and producing documents using computers
- using telecommunications networks and software. (Ochs and others 1991, p.12)

Employers, or new graduates who were not involved in using computers were exempt from answering all the questions relating to the defined skills areas. No space was provided in the survey for broader consideration of skills which are not directly computer related. The outcomes of the study were, therefore, confined to statements about computer use. This is reflected in the main conclusions arising from the study:

- Skills in the use of computers are considered in the hiring process.... these skills are valuable to the effective performance of our students' jobs once they have them
- Computers are used in many companies currently and their use is increasing
- Most employers are willing to train good people if they don't have the computer skills needed
- Few employers expect intermediate or advanced skills when they are hiring for very specific positions
- Use of computers does not seem to vary by industry or the size of the organisation a person works for
- Students require less training in mainframe computer programming languages and more training in the use of applications software, including programming with those packages. (Ochs and others 1991, p.17)

This study develops as a result of its assumptions, a picture of information literacy that revolves entirely around the use of computers. The survey design tells us much about the perceived nature of information literacy which is not apparent in the Mann curriculum model: at its core, information literacy is seen to be about the ability to use computers for various applications. Because of the nature of the survey the picture it provides of information literacy needs in the workplace is limited to details of required computer competence. Questions about whether, for example, new employees are required to formulate information problems, develop strategies for identifying information, evaluating, synthesising and communicating information remain unanswered because they were not asked. The survey does, however, develop in considerable detail the computer skills which, in the Mann Library at least, are considered essential to information literacy

A comprehensive definition of information literacy

The second of these studies aimed to create a comprehensive definition of information literacy and to develop outcome measures for this concept (Doyle 1992). Implemented for the U.S. National Forum on Information Literacy, the study was not confined to defining information literacy for a particular educational sector or group of people. In order to develop the definition Doyle used the Delphi technique, comprising three rounds, with a panel of fifty-eight participants. The participants were recognised authorities and opinion leaders from the US, Canada, and Puerto Rico.

Doyle (1992, p.5) claims that the first outcome of the study is a 'comprehensive definition and a list of specific outcomes for the process of information literacy':

- Definition: Information literacy is the ability to access, evaluate and use information from a variety of sources
- Attributes: An information literate individual is one who:
  - recognises the need for information
  - recognises that accurate and complete information is the basis for intelligent decision making
  - formulates questions based on information needs

- identifies potential sources of information
- develops successful search strategies
- accesses sources of information, including computer-based and other technologies
- evaluates information
- organises information for practical application
- integrates new information into an existing body of knowledge
- uses information in critical thinking and problem solving (Doyle 1992, p.2)

Of the outcome measures agreed upon by the expert panel, the outcomes for students amplify the attributes, further illuminating the perceived nature of information literacy. The following list reproduces those outcome measures which do not duplicate items in the attribute statement. Most of the remaining items deal with problem solving and critical thinking.

Students will:

- read with understanding at grade level
- have the ability to access computers and other technologies
- compare and contrast the formats, strengths and weaknesses of various sources such as primary sources, textbooks, databases, indexes, video productions, and human resources
- know how to learn
- be able to judge information based on internal and external criteria
- automatically question assumptions and have the skills to research alternative answers
- have a willingness to look at and understand various points of view
- be able to make informed decisions
- make connections between existing knowledge and new information
- apply problem solving skills regularly...
- use critical thinking skills regularly...
- be able to work individually and in groups
- demonstrate flexibility in ideas and attitudes
- develop and refine oral and written communication skills
- choose appropriate resources to support a proposal, debate, argument. (Doyle 1992, p.14)

The above definitions, attributes and 'outcome measures' represent the consensus view, of opinion leaders and other experts, about the phenomenon of information literacy. Although the availability of a consensus view and the focus which it provides are important, the view represented does not differ substantially from those approaches discussed earlier. Many of the limitations of descriptions of information literacy identified in chapter two apply to this description also. Further, in relation to the need for educational outcome measures discussed in chapter three, many of these statements are not easily assessed.

An information metacourse

The third of these studies into information literacy involved the construction of a working model for information literacy curriculum (Bjorner 1991). Although designed to conform with the curriculum requirements of the US Vocational-Technical Education Consortium of States, Bjorner points out that her metacourse 'which identifies key characteristics of information literate behaviour ... could be the basis for the development of lessons in all disciplines at all levels..' (Bjorner 1991, p.155). Her assumptions about the nature of information literacy differ from those of Ochs and others (1991). Whereas Ochs and others adopted a strong computer skills orientation, Bjorner adopts a process orientation. The outcome of her research was a 'behavioural model which is competency based' (p.156). The model is a 'duty and task listing describing actions taken in specific parts or categories of the total information management process' (p.156). In compiling this list Bjorner has detailed extensively a process approach to information literacy, identifying thirty- four competencies in eight categories:

A.   Recognising and accepting an information gap
  1.   Identify a question to be answered
  2.   Place the question in a context
  3.   Determine the information needed to answer the question

B.   Responding positively to the need for an investigation
  1.   Identify the consequences of not answering the question
  2.   Determine the costs of investigating the question
  3.   Decide on a range of effort to be used to answer the question

C.   Constructing alternative strategies to reduce the information gap
  1.   Identify appropriate information sources
  2.   Determine physical location of sources
  3.   Evaluate skills required to access sources
  4.   Develop action plan(s) for utilising resources

D.   Evaluating and selecting a strategy
  1.   Estimate effectiveness of a strategy in relation to cost, time and effort required for use
  2.   Compare various strategies in terms of estimated effectiveness, cost, time and effort
  3.   Identify the best strategy in terms of estimated effectiveness, cost, time and effort
  4.   Revise a strategy or select another as necessary

E.   Acting on a strategy
  1.   Determine a workplan for implementing the strategy
  2.   Consult the sources required by the strategy
  3.   Note/record the information derived from the sources
  4.   Structure/restructure the information derived from the sources

F.   Assessing the effectiveness of a strategy
  1.   Formulate the answer(s) found by using the strategy
  2.   Compare the answer(s) found with the statement of the question to be answered
  3.   Evaluate the success of the strategy selected in relation to the effectiveness of the answer found, time, cost and effort used
  4.   Determine whether the original question has been answered

G.   Using information
  1.   Identify the audience for the information
  2.   Determine the physical format of presentation
  3.   Select and arrange the intellectual content of the presentation
  4.   Prepare the presentation

H.   Storing information for future use
    1.   Consider storage requirements of discrete information items
    2.   Determine retention value of each item
    3.   Discard items of no continuing value
    4.   Determine physical storage mechanism(s) for items to be retained
    5.   Determine intellectual access points for items to be retained
    6.   Prepare items to be retained according to physical and intellectual access requirements
    7.   File items in personal files. (Bjorner 1991, p.157)

Bjorner's metacourse was designed using the following process. Firstly, she listed the major categories of action taken by individuals working with information retrieval and management. Secondly, for each of the major categories identified she specified tasks which needed to be undertaken (p.156). Thirdly, she asked library and information professionals to provide anecdotal descriptions of recently encountered information problems according to the model designed, which led to some revision of the behaviours listed. Bjorner's portrayal of information literacy was based on and validated by 'expert' views about the nature of information literacy. It is very much a prescriptive model. The information professionals' anecdotes used were analysed for their fit to the model rather than being the basis for the models' development. In addition, the model was based on information professionals', as opposed to information users', ways of dealing with information problems.

As an information literacy process model, this metacourse could be strengthened by additional attention to the processes of evaluating information and recognition of the need for a feedback loop. Its present linear form does not reflect the cyclical nature of information use.

Research directions recommended in the literature

Research into information literacy has been accompanied by suggestions for the future directions of research into this area. The following recommendations draw on research   directions suggested in papers which have contributed to chapters two, three and four. It has   been recommended that attention be given to:

Setting social direction

- formulation of national policy recommendations (Doyle 1992, p.5)

Knowledge synthesis

- 'a continuing review of the literature' (Eisenberg and Small 1993, p.264)

Teaching and learning

- further work on 'how to teach individuals to become information literate' (Bjorner 1991, p.159)

- 'empirical research to validate attributes of information based education..., and to identify others' (Eisenberg and Small 1993, p.264)

- '... the evolution of a comprehensive theoretical classification scheme and to test that scheme...to identify the relationships among individual research attributes, the information bases of educational situations and other elements of learning events (particularly the attainment of learning objectives)' (Eisenberg and Small 1993, p.274)

- developing: 'a) a list of information attributes and associated character states, b) a tested data collection instrument for gathering data on the information base of learning events, c) a validated classification scheme for categorising the information bases of learning events' (Eisenberg and Small 1993, p.275)

- 'research...into ways that information literacy education can be integrated into all levels of education, including teacher education' (Recommendation 14 of the Jones' Report *Australia as an information society*)

Evaluation of teaching and learning programs

- research on the impact of information literacy and its programs (Kirk, in Booker 1992, p.168)

- research into the impact of resource based learning on information literacy (Breivik 1993, p.16)

The contribution of information literacy and information technology

- testing the assertions that information literacy contributes to lifelong learning and the development of an informed society (Kirk and Todd 1993, p.129)

- research into the impact on the individual of new information technologies (Palmquist 1992, p.32)

Developing understanding of important concepts and people's experience

- probing into serious questions about the nature, role and impact of specific attributes of information (eg information systems, resources, skills, and processes) in education (Eisenberg and Small 1993)

- researching 'information seeking behaviours and communication patterns of experts within different disciplines' (Arp 1990, p.48)

- 'extensive research on successful information seeking concepts and skills in different disciplines' (Arp 1990, p.49)

- studies into students' experience in the online information environment (Oberman 1991, p.194)

My study into tertiary educators' conceptions of information literacy is not one of the lines of research which has been recommended in the literature. Nevertheless, it does fall into the same domain as those recommended directions which suggest exploring the nature of concepts and people's experience, and it will contribute to thinking about how to teach information literacy. Although few researchers are questioning our present descriptions and understandings of information literacy, Dervin and Nilan (1986) call for research to improve our understanding of basic concepts in the information needs and uses arena. Information literacy is one of the concepts which needs to be understood, both more clearly and from different perspectives. It is necessary to understand more about people's experience of information literacy, and therefore something more about the nature of this phenomenon in order to address broader issues of, for example, how to teach information literacy or evaluating its impact.

My research does, however, address the existing agenda in the following ways:

- Seeking to understand people's varying experience of information literacy contributes to a better understanding of information related concepts (Dervin and Nilan 1986)

- A review of the literature of information literacy has been undertaken to substantiate the need for the study (Eisenberg and Small 1993)

- The study is likely to provide a useful alternative framework for information literacy education (Bjorner 1991)

Towards an alternate research approach: from describing attributes to describing people's conceptions

In this chapter I have portrayed the understandings of information literacy which have arisen from the work of researchers, and the research directions which have been established. These are researchers' contributions to our understanding of information literacy (Figure 4.1a), as seen through the outcomes of their studies and the assumptions about the nature of information literacy which they have adopted. In this section I will examine the implications of the approaches being adopted and argue for an alternative approach to information literacy research; namely, exploring people's conceptions (Figure 4.1b).

What are the problems associated with established approaches to information literacy research?

The few studies which have been conducted into information literacy have served to deepen and consolidate the views developed by opinion leaders and advocates since the mid 1980s. We now have a better understanding of the computer competence which, in a technology focussed view, is seen as integral to information literacy; we have a detailed picture of information processes and competencies; and a consensus view of a definition of information literacy and the attributes it involves. As these studies are either grounded in existing views

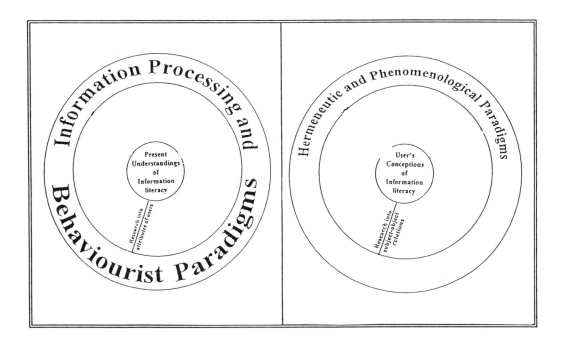

Figure 4.1a Researching information
literacy as attributes of people

Figure 4.1b Researching information literacy
in terms of people's conceptions

of information literacy, or draw further on the views of opinion leaders or other experts, the results are largely compatible with the dominant behaviourist and information processing based ways of thinking about information literacy noted in previous chapters. Until now, information literacy research has either continued to explore the views of opinion leaders and other experts, or has been based on assumptions about the phenomenon made whilst our understanding of it is still limited and subject to change. Such assumptions are not unquestioned in the literature:

> Typically, a list of attributes is postulated *a priori* by researchers and then used to describe particular situations or methods. The scheme has questionable validity and generalisability. (Eisenberg and Small 1993, p 267)

Other notable features of the body of information literacy research are:

- the number of studies in this area is extremely limited, despite its perceived importance

- available research outcomes have not led to any significant change in our understanding of information literacy

- no studies have been located which focus on the views of people other than information literacy researchers and scholars or information professionals

- researchers do not appear to be questioning existing understandings of information literacy despite confusion about the nature of information literacy and the questions   raised by some scholars

- researchers assume that information literacy is a transferable skill across discipline contexts and information problems

- research studies have not been context specific, assuming instead the generic nature of information literacy before examining the phenomenon in specific contexts

Finally, Kirk and Todd point to the fragmentary nature of these studies and its consequences:

> Available research is fragmented and piecemeal, without connection to prior research or sufficient concentration in one area to build a useful body of knowledge that can inform practice. (Kirk and Todd 1993, p. 129

Although there is a discernible trend towards studying the users of information systems, this is   not yet the dominant approach in information science/retrieval research generally.   Much information retrieval research has been conducted focusing either on 'components of information systems or on the intermediary, disregarding the complex behaviour of the end users' (Park 1993, p.347). The shift towards user based research oriented towards a 'second order perspective', that is user's views, rather that researchers' views, continues to be dualistic and cognitivist in approach. In other words, information users continue to be seen as separate from information systems, and continue to be described separately. Users are also described in terms of what may be 'in their heads'; the emphasis being on cognitive structures rather   than on relations between people and aspects of the world around them. Information literacy research, perhaps the newest subset of information needs and uses research has not yet begun to adopt a user oriented approach.

Maintaining existing directions in information literacy research will have a number of consequences. Firstly, it will lead to a continued recycling of the views of opinion leaders, probably in the form of more detailed processes or alternative process models, competency statements and attributes. Secondly, these directions do not accommodate the possibility of examining the views of information users in furthering our understanding of information literacy. Thirdly, research into the teaching and learning of information literacy will suffer from a gap in knowledge about information literacy if people's experiences of the phenomenon are not explored; that is such research will be based on assumptions which do not take people's experience of the phenomenon into account.

Moving towards a user oriented research approach for information literacy would be following the lead of researchers in the information needs and uses (Dervin and Nilan 1986), and more specifically in the bibliographic instruction domains (Kuhlthau 1988; Mellon 1986). Those studies from the more general field of information needs and uses which have researched users, however, have focussed on barriers to information use, rather than examined reasons for successful endeavours; they have also focussed on people as separate from their information environments, accounting for behaviour in terms of 'mental models':

> While many studies have documented the cause of search difficulties, fewer have identified the sources of search success. The most enabling endeavours have concerned user's mental models. (Huston 1990, p.693)

The move towards 'user' focussed research continues to separate people from other elements of the information environment. This is most clearly evident in studies seeking to develop user models; the need for such studies are regularly raised in the literature (Kemp 1990). User models are usually interpreted as 'mental models', such as those derived from studies into mental models associated with the use of online catalogues (Baker 1986; Borgman 1986) and Rubens' (1991) division of the world of information into the bibliographic and nonbibliographic domains. Kuhlthau's model of the search process, although not a 'mental model', is intended as a description of students as they move through the process, rather than as a description of the ways in which they relate to aspects of the world.

What changes are required in adopting a relational approach to information literacy research?

Describing higher educators' conceptions of information literacy, therefore, requires a third shift in the framework within which we attempt to understand the phenomenon. This is a shift from researching the views of information literacy advocates and other experts, to researching people's experiences or conceptions. Such a shift in knowledge interest requires a change in research approach. Important differences between a relational approach and the 'alternative paradigm' as it was described by Dervin and Nilan (1986) are presented in Table 4.2.

The change of knowledge interest goes beyond the impetus to study users to studying their conceptions of the world. This change will enable us to examine the varying conceptions of the phenomenon from the perspective of those who experience it. These ways of thinking revolve around the acceptance of the importance of understanding people's perceptions, views or experiences of a phenomenon.

Essentially, one of the most influential views underpinning current information needs and uses research is that the 'user' and the 'information system' are separate entities. According to such a model, the system has properties which users need to learn, and solving information problems involves bridging the gap between the user and the information system in problem solving (Rubens 1991, p.273-274). Taking a relational view of information literacy requires a reconceptualisation of this model to see whole phenomena, that is the user together with aspects of his or her information universe, in terms of the varying relations between them. In this alternative view we do not presuppose that users are physically or conceptually separable from their information universes, although indeed they may see themselves that way.

Adopting a relational approach to research also involves a shift in thinking about the nature of 'information'. A relational view of information is consistent with neither the traditional nor the alternative paradigm. The view of information in the alternative paradigm has been labelled 'constructivist', in that the user is the focus of attention. The user is regarded '...not as a passive receiver but as the centre of an active ongoing process of change' (Morris 1994, p. 22). In further describing a constructivist approach to information, however, Morris establishes a model which lends itself to a relational interpretation: '

> ...information triggers perceptual changes in the user, and changes in the user alter how the information is perceived.' (Morris 1994, p.22)

Table 4.2   Paradigms in information needs and uses research II

Relational paradigm	Alternative paradigm (Dervin and Nilan 1986)
Information is seen as experienced by human beings. It is an element of the information environment which may be conceived in varying ways. Both 'information' and the person engaged with it contribute to how it is interpreted	**Information is constructed by human beings.** It may be defined as: a) that which is capable of transforming image structures or b) any stimulus that alters the cognitive structure of the receiver
Users are seen as engaged with aspects of the world reaching out to and focusing on it in particular ways. There is a limited number of ways in which any phenomenon is conceived	**Users are seen as constantly constructing;** free within system constraints to create from systems and situations whatever they choose
Researchers focus on describing and understanding conceptions, the subject- object relations that constitute phenomena in the information environment	Researchers focus on **understanding information use in particular situations** and are concerned with what leads up to and what follows system interaction
Researchers focus on how the conceptions are delimited, searching for significant variations between them which illuminate how the conceptions differ in terms of structure and reference	Researchers focus on **how people construct sense** searching for universal dimensions of sense making
Research questions start with people's ways of conceiving aspects of the world. Neither the information user nor the elements of the environment are of *per se*; the relations between them are investigated	**Research questions start with the user.** The system is examined only as it is seen by the user
Researchers ask 'what' and 'how' questions eg *what* meanings are being attributed to the phenomenon, and *how* is that meaning being constituted?	**Researchers ask 'how' questions** eg how do people define needs in different situation, how do they present these needs to the system, and how do they make use of what the system offers them?
Information needs are defined in terms of a particular kind of relation between the user and a task eg a problem to solve, a decision to be made, a question to answer.	**Information needs are defined in terms of the users cognitive structures** eg a) a conceptual incongruity in which the person's cognitive structure is not adequate to the task, b) when the current state of possessed knowledge is less than needed, and c) when internal sense runs out.

The idea that information and people both participate in the construction of meaning fits well with the relational view. In this view the user would not be seen as the centre of focus. Rather both the user and 'information' are seen as constituting meaning.

When interpreted this way, Dervin's early definition of information as 'whatever an individual finds informing' (Dervin 1977, p.22) could be considered an early move towards a relational view; it establishes the need for a qualitative relation between a person and 'information'.

Dervin herself, however, does not move in this direction, but rather favours what she labels a 'communitarian' perspective (Dervin 1994).

The change towards researching conceptions, or the relations between people and their information worlds, remains within the qualitative tradition which has been increasingly adopted by information needs and uses researchers. It involves applying to information literacy research ways of thinking which have been extensively applied in educational research. The major reasons for adopting a relational view of information literacy have been discussed in chapters two and three. If phenomena can be understood usefully in terms of differing relations, or conceptions, between people and aspects of the world, and if teaching and learning can be understood usefully as being about changing those conceptions/ relations, then those very conceptions need to become the object of research. Beyond this, a relational approach to information literacy research is required to ensure internally consistent strategies for discovering the conceptions that will begin to form the hub of the information literacy wheel.

A preliminary research agenda based on the relational approach

Researching higher educators' conceptions or ways of experiencing information literacy, opens up a new and uncharted domain for information literacy research. As studies in the educational arena have examined conceptions of learning, conceptions of phenomena being studied, and conceptions of vehicles of learning such as lectures and essay writing and literature reviews, so in the information literacy forum we need to understand people's varying conceptions of information literacy, conceptions of phenomena which need to be understood in becoming information literate and conceptions of vehicles through which information literacy is expressed. Examples of phenomena which need to be understood may include, for example, the information life cycle, information problems, freedom of information, as well as specific elements of the information environment. Examples of vehicles through which information literacy is expressed could involve problem solving, and decision making.

A tentative field for future information literacy research could be mapped as follows.

Research into:

A   People's experience of information literacy, where people includes students, information professionals, researchers or any other possible group
1.   People's varying conceptions of information literacy
2.   People's varying conceptions of information literacy in specific contexts
3.   People's varying conceptions of specific phenomena which need to be understood in becoming information literate
4.   People's varying conceptions of vehicles through which information literacy is expressed, eg problem solving or decision making

B   People's experience of learning information literacy, where people includes students, information professionals, researchers or any other possible group
1.   People's varying conceptions of learning information literacy
2.   People's varying conceptions of learning information literacy in specific contexts
3.   People's varying conceptions of learning about specific phenomena which need to be understood in becoming information literate
4.   People's varying conceptions of learning about vehicles through which information literacy is expressed eg problem solving or decision making

C   Teachers' experience of information literacy, where teachers include, but are not limited to, those responsible for information literacy education
1.   Teachers' varying conceptions of information literacy
2.   Teachers' varying conceptions of information literacy in specific contexts
3.   Teachers' varying conceptions of specific phenomena which need to be understood in becoming information literate
4.   Teachers' varying conceptions of vehicles through which information literacy is expressed eg problem solving or decision making

D   Teachers' experience of students learning information literacy, where include, but are not limited to, those responsible for information literacy education
1.   Teachers' varying conceptions of learning information literacy
2.   Teachers' varying conceptions of learning information literacy in specific contexts
3.   Teachers' varying conceptions of learning about specific phenomena which need to be understood in becoming information literate
4.   Teachers' varying conceptions of learning about vehicles through which information literacy is expressed eg problem solving or decision making

If successful in terms of continuing to advance knowledge and contributing to professional practice the relational approach to researching information literacy could be applied to the broader field of information needs and uses research.

Towards higher educators' conceptions of information literacy

In making differing relations or conceptions the object of research, I am following the path of phenomenography, which has been developed as a branch of educational research since the mid 1970s, and continuing the tradition of conducting educational research in the information domain. The studies into the phenomenon of learning, from which phenomenography grew, were devised in response to a perceived lack of understanding of how learning appeared to people, in particular to students in higher education (Dahlgren 1984b, Marton and Saljo 1984, Saljo 1979). That problem is very similar to the problem of how information literacy is experienced by people, which I have chosen to investigate. Phenomenography's specialised interest in the variation in subject—world relations, the success with which the approach has been applied to problems within the educational domain, and the continuing international interest in and refinement of the research approach make it an ideal method to use in this study into varying experiences of information literacy.

To summarise, information literacy needs to be understood in terms of people's experience of this phenomenon rather as well as in terms of scholars' views. Such an investigation will contribute not only to our understanding of the phenomenon, but also to the teaching and learning of information literacy and to future information literacy research. For the reasons outlined above and in previous chapters, I have explored conceptions of information literacy amongst a group of information users who can be expected to influence the learning experiences of higher education students. The investigation of higher educators' conceptions of information literacy described in subsequent chapters also launches the research agenda described above. Its completion has provided an initial bench mark of understandings of information literacy which further research can confirm, refine and build upon.

The next chapter describes in detail the knowledge interest of phenomenography and the research methods it employs, in relation to my empirical investigation of the varying experience of information literacy amongst higher educators.

Chapter 5

Thematising conceptions of information literacy

Previous chapters have examined the different ways in which information literacy is presented in the literature by advocates and scholars, educators and researchers. It has also been shown that the picture of information literacy revealed in these writings is predominantly behavioural in character and expressed in terms of information processes or attributes of information users. Each chapter has then argued for taking a relational approach to information literacy, including information literacy education and research. Adopting an alternative view of information literacy, however, requires the availability of different pictures. We need to understand the phenomenon in terms of how it is conceived or experienced by people who make use of information. We need descriptions of information literacy, that are themselves relational, to provide a complete and internally consistent alternative framework for thinking about the phenomenon.

This chapter describes the empirical study which has provided an initial picture of information literacy as it is conceived by information users. In it, are discussed the choice of phenomenography as a research approach, key features of phenomenography including the meanings attributed to conceptions and phenomena, the form of the research outcomes, and details of how the study was implemented. Overall, the chapter explains how higher educators' conceptions of information literacy were thematised, or brought into focus and described. The following headings organise the discussion:

- Phenomenography: a research approach for understanding information literacy

- Conceptions and phenomena: the knowledge interests of phenomenography

- Categories of description and outcome spaces: findings of a phenomenographic study

- Thematising higher educators' conceptions of information literacy

- Trustworthiness of the outcomes

Phenomenography: a research approach for understanding information literacy

In the early stages of this research, phenomenography (Marton 1981a, 1981b, 1992, 1993) was one of three approaches considered for exploring information users' perspectives on information literacy. The other two approaches were empirical phenomenology (Giorgi 1970) and sense making (Dervin 1992). Both phenomenography and empirical phenomenology are well established in phenomenography and empirical phenomenology are well established in educational research, and sense making has emerged as an important qualitative approach in the information needs and uses domain. Empirical phenomenology and sense making, however, were less suitable for the study than phenomenography.

Although the sense making approach recognises that people see the world differently, it does not make this variation the object of study. Sense making is used to account for the reasons why information problems are experienced in particular ways and the processes through which people use information. It helps researchers understand how people bridge the gap between an information problem and the way in which they deal with that problem. Dervin, the founder of sense making defines it as:

> ...an alternative approach to the study of human use of information and information systems... (it is) ...an approach to studying the constructing that humans do to make sense of their experiences' (Dervin 1992, pp.67-68)

The sense making approach was not suitable because it operates on the assumption that information use should be studied in terms of information problems, information processes and gap bridging, and assumes a constructivist view of information. These assumptions are imposed on participants in studies to the extent that they must learn and adopt the 'sense making metaphor' in interview situations. This was problematic for the study which was re-opening the question of what it meant to be information literate with the intention of seeing the phenomenon from the user's perspective. Working from an established model of information and information use would have made it difficult to allow users' interpretations to emerge.

Empirical phenomenology (Giorgi 1970; van Manen 1990) also accepts as axiomatic that people experience the world in different ways. Phenomenological studies, however, do not focus on variations in conception; they seek the essences of phenomena through examining one or more individual's experiences:

> An essence would represent the deepest understanding available established on the basis of intersubjective agreement. (Alexandersson 1981, p. 8)

Phenomenography was finally selected because the object of study in the research approach was qualitative variation in conception, a focus which conformed with the overall relational perspective being adopted. Phenomenography is

> ... a research specialisation aimed at the mapping of the qualitatively different ways in which people experience, conceptualise, perceive and understand various aspects of ... the world around them. (Marton 1988a, p.178)

It is a qualitative research approach, which evolved during the 1970s at the University of Gothenburg, Sweden, in response to educational questions about the different ways in which people experience or conceive of learning. Since then it has been developed, refined and applied to a range of phenomena within the field of education and beyond. Today phenomenography is seen as both a *research program* aimed at describing people's conceptions and a *research tool* for the study of phenomena (Svensson 1994).

Phenomenographic studies over the last twenty-five years have influenced significantly interest in a relational approach to teaching and learning in higher education. Since the early 1970s, studies have illuminated how people learn, that is how they conceive of learning tasks such as reading texts (Marton and Saljo 1984; Marton, Carlsson and Halasz 1992), writing essays (Hounsell 1984; Prosser and Webb 1992, 1994) and literature reviews (Bruce 1992a, 1994b); as well as what they learn, that is how they conceive of aspects of the world as the outcome of learning, such as the concepts of force (Svensson 1989), number (Marton and Neuman 1990), or price (Dahlgren 1984b). Phenomenography has also been applied to uncovering conceptions of teaching (Dall'Alba 1991; Samuelovicz and Bain 1992) and a range of other phenomena such as computers (Nordenbo 1990) and political power (Svensson and Theman 1983).

Three important phenomena relevant to metalearning: skill (Svensson 1984), learning (Saljo 1979; Marton and Saljo 1984; Marton, Dall'Alba and Beaty 1993) and competence (Sandberg 1994) have already been interpreted relationally. Our deepening understanding of these phenomena, each of which is closely aligned to the idea of information literacy, has been a direct result of phenomenographic investigation. This suggested that an attempt to similarly reinterpret information literacy using the approach was likely to be successful.

Marton accounts for the strength of the phenomenographic approach in terms of explaining differences in the outcome of learning and notes the occurrence of a discrete number of conceptions of any one phenomenon as an established pattern

> People in general hold qualitatively different conceptions of the phenomena they are surrounded by... Such differences would constitute a highly potent source of explanation when it comes to the questions of how to account for ... qualitative differences in the outcome of learning. This is of course the basic idea of phenomenography, and it has been confirmed many times...again and again we find a limited number of qualitatively different ways in which the phenomena...are... apprehended. (Marton 1988a, p.189)

The continued development and use of the phenomenographic approach may also be attributed to the following advantages, which make it particularly attractive for use in describing people's differing conceptions of information literacy:

- it has the potential to provide us with direct descriptions of a phenomenon

- it aims to describe conceptions in a holistic and integrated way

- it has the potential to capture a range of conceptions due to its focus on variation in people's experiences

- its purpose is to produce descriptions of conceptions which are useful in teaching-learning contexts (Sandberg 1994, pp.48-9)

- it focuses on groups of people rather than individuals (Marton 1986a)

- its research outcomes are generalisable (Gerber 1993)

Conceptions and phenomena: the knowledge interests of phenomenography

The knowledge interest of phenomenography is in describing the different conceptions of a phenomenon which are present amongst groups of people in a particular context. At the heart of the knowledge interest is the nature of a conception. This is a concept which is central to phenomenography and needs to be clearly understood.

For many years, the nature of a conception was described, somewhat vaguely, by phenomenographers as a way of seeing or experiencing the world. The lack of precision in use of the term has been criticised by Bowden (1994, p.14). Common early descriptions of conceptions include: 'a way of thinking about a specific object..' (Lybeck and others 1988, p.83), and 'the relation between human beings and the world around them' (Marton 1988a, p.181). However the characteristics of that relation were not well defined. Furthermore the difference between *conceptions* and *conceptualisation* was largely disregarded, the two terms often being used interchangeably. More recently, however, the nature of conceptions has been the subject of attention. Svensson first distinguished between the terms concept, conceptualisation and conception within the phenomenographic domain. He described a *concept* as the abstract general meaning attributed to a phenomenon 'as it is present in a language'; a *conception* as the experienced meaning of a phenomenon and a *conceptualisation* as cognitive activity, 'the thinking through which a conception is constituted' (Svensson 1989, p.531).

The nature of conceptions themselves has also been formulated more precisely using language borrowed from Gurwitsch's theory of consciousness (Marton 1992, 1993, 1994) and Husserl's theory of intentionality (Sandberg 1994). As alternative ways of delimiting conceptions these two approaches are not incompatible because both draw on phenomenological theory. It will be seen that, in this study, the use of both approaches to interpreting conceptions was required to identify how the various conceptions were related to each other.

Sandberg (1994, p.52) describes a conception as denoting 'the basic meaning structure of individuals' experiences of a specific aspect of their reality'. That meaning structure, he argues, characterises the intentional relation between the individual and the object in the relation. In turn, the intentional relation may be described in terms of '...a conceived meaning and a conceiving act... the noema or noematic correlate for the conceived meaning, and the noesis or noetic correlate for the conceiving act' (1994, p.55). This means that a conception is constituted by a way of focusing on some aspect of reality (the noetic correlate) which leads to a particular meaning being conferred upon it (the noematic correlate). Both of these must be described to convey adequately the nature of the conception. In addition, each conception has a 'horizon which indicates the fringes or limit of the conceived meaning' (Sandberg 1994, p.56). The terms noema and noesis are here used to label what are usually referred to by phenomenographers as the referential and structural components of a conception.

Marton (1992), on the other hand, describes conceptions in terms of awareness, or consciousness. In this sense, a way of experiencing the world, that is a conception, is also equated with the internal relation between a subject and an object.

According to Marton, however, this internal relation exists because awareness is structured in such a way that 'certain things come to the fore whilst others recede to the ground' (1992, p.9). The object of focal awareness, as it appears to the subject is also referred to as the 'theme'. The internal relation, or way in which the object appears to people, is described as constituted structurally and referentially.

The structural aspect of the conception includes both an internal and external horizon. These are described as 'a way of delimiting the object from its context and relating it to the same or other contexts' (the external horizon) and 'a way of delimiting component parts of the (conception) and relating them to each other and the whole' (the internal horizon) (Svensson 1984, cited in Marton 1992, p.7). The structural aspect is seen as dialectically intertwined with the referential aspect, which is the meaning attributed to the phenomenon in question. In order to adequately describe the conception, both the structural and referential components of the internal relation between subject and theme (or object) must be specified; furthermore the thematic field (aspects of the world related to the theme), and the margin (aspects of the world not related to the theme) must be identified (Marton 1994, p.98). Thus a conception is described in terms of its internal structure and the way in which it is delimited in people's consciousness.

The actual forms that conceptions take in any one study are nevertheless derived from the empirical work rather than from any metaphysical position (Svensson 1994). There are, however, a number of general assumptions that can be made on the basis of multiple phenomenographic studies now completed. These assumptions are consistent with the views of conceptions portrayed by Marton and Sandberg:

- The most important elements of conceptions are the relations between subject and object. Thus any conception must have at least two related parts which together create meaning (Svensson 1994, p. 14; Svensson and Theman 1983, p. 4). The relation is sometimes labelled an 'internal relation'. (*Internal relation* means that meaning is constituted within the subject-object relation; *external relation* means that meaning is imposed from outside that relation, for example from a discipline framework.)

- Dialectically related structural and referential components characterise the internal relation (Marton 1992)

- Conceptions represent the organised content of thinking (Svensson 1994, p.17)

- Conceptions are dependent on both human activity and the world or reality external to any individual (Svensson 1994, p.14)

- The relation between thought and external reality.... is varying in character (Svensson 1994, p. 15)

- Conceptions are not entirely naturally given entities, neither are they totally subjectively constructed entities (Svensson 1994, p.15)

An important implication of these views of conceptions is that the outcomes of phenomenographic research, descriptions of conceptions, are not 'mental models' (Marton 1988b, p.43; Johansson, Marton and Svensson 1985, p.247; Svensson 1994). They also confirm that when seeking to uncover conceptions we need to adopt a second order perspective:

> ...we are not trying to look into the (person's) mind, but we are trying to see what he or she sees, we are not describing minds, but perceptions; we are not describing the (person) but his or her perceptual world. (Johansson, Marton and Svensson 1985, p.247)

Identifying conceptions as the knowledge interest of phenomenography points to the central importance of phenomena. Illuminating conceptions is the same as illuminating phenomena when a phenomenon is defined as the combination, or 'complex', of the relevant varying subject-object relations (Marton 1994, p.92). In many phenomenographic studies it has been discovered that there are logical relations between the various conceptions, which form a structural framework within which the various conceptions may be described. The focus on uncovering this structural framework has, in some cases, led to new understandings of the whole phenomenon under study (see, for example, Lybeck, Marton, Stromdahl and Tullberg 1988; Marton, Carlsson and Halasz 1992).

Most important, for the purposes of the study, is that it is possible, on the basis of the recent developments to phenomenographic theory described above, to specify what is meant by seeking to describe conceptions of information literacy. Describing conceptions of information literacy involves describing the differing internal relations between people and some aspect of the world around them, and the differing ways in which the various elements in that relation are thematised. It is also reasonable to expect that focusing on people's experience in this way will lead to new understandings of the phenomenon of information literacy. The specific strategies used to achieve this are described later in this chapter in sections dealing with the data gathering and analysis process.

Categories of description and outcome spaces: findings of a phenomenographic study

In a phenomenographic study it is important to differentiate between *conceptions and phenomena* and *categories of description and outcome spaces*. Failure to clearly distinguish between these is a major point on which phenomenographers have been criticised (Bowden 1994, p.14). Essentially, categories of description and outcome spaces are the outcomes of a phenomenographic study which serve as tools to capture and communicate the features of the conceptions or the phenomenon that they represent.

Outcome spaces are diagrammatic representations of the logical relationships between the different conceptions of a phenomenon. Marton describes this as the structural framework encompassing the categories of description which denote the conceptions:

> ...each category is a potential part of a larger structure in which the category is related to other categories of description. It is a goal of phenomenography to discover the structural framework within which various categories of understanding exist. (Marton 1986a, p.34)

More recently, he has argued that outcome spaces represent phenomena in the same way that categories of descriptions represent conceptions:

> The logically structured complex of the different ways of experiencing an object has been called the outcome space of the object. Outcome space thus turns out to be a synonym for 'phenomenon' (the thing as it appears to us, contrasted with the Kantian 'noumenon', 'the thing as such'). (Marton 1994, p.92)

The outcome space forms a 'map' (Saljo 1988) of the different ways in which information literacy is experienced amongst participants in the study. It is, therefore, a configuration of the set of categories, rather than being itself a representation of individual conceptions.

Laurillard identifies three types of outcome space that reflect different ways in which the structural relations between conceptions may be viewed:

- an inclusive, hierarchical, outcome space in which the categories further up the hierarchy include previous, or lower, categories
- an outcome space in which the different categories are related to the history of interviewee's experience of the phenomenon, rather than to each other
- an outcome space which represents a developmental progression, in the sense that the conceptions represented by some categories have more explanatory power than others, and thus may be seen as 'better'. (Laurillard 1993, p.45)

In this study of higher educators' conceptions of information literacy the outcome space proved to be developmental with each category revealing increasing complexity in the meaning structure of the conceptions. Some parts of the outcome space are also hierarchically structured. Of greater interest, however, is that the outcome space reveals structural relations at three different levels: in the meaning structure, in the structure of awareness and in the varying ways in which information is perceived. This will be explained fully in the first section of chapter six which presents the outcomes of the analysis.

Categories of description are not themselves the conceptions of information literacy, rather they represent, or 'denote' the conceptions, acting as the researcher's interpretation of others' experiences of the phenomenon (Johansson, Marton and Svensson 1985, p.249). They are 'tools used to characterise ways of functioning' (Marton 1981b, p.167). Categories of description have four primary characteristics. They are:

- relational, dealing with the intentional, or subject-object relation comprising the conception
- experiential, that is based on the experience of participants in the study
- content oriented, focusing on the meaning of phenomenon being studied
- qualitative or descriptive (Marton 1988a, p.181)

They are developed in relation to each other and in relation to the data from which they are derived. Categories of description are usually expressed 'in the form: something (x) is seen as something (y)' (Lybeck and others 1988, p.101). This expression labels, or names, the conception being denoted. The label is then elaborated with a description of the conception, including illustrative quotes from the data.

In this study conceptions of information literacy are described drawing on both Sandberg's and Marton's views in order to provide the fullest possible descriptions of the variation experienced. The descriptions allow others to see information literacy as it is experienced or conceived by the participants in the study, and inform them about the particular focus of attention which causes information literacy to be interpreted in that way.

All the categories, therefore, have a structural component and a referential component. They describe the meaning (that is, the referential component or *what* is conceived), and the figure ground relations between the elements of each conception as well as the focus of attention from which that meaning is derived (that is, the structural component or *how* it is conceived). The structural aspects of each category form the platform upon which the outcome space is built. The categories, presented in chapter six, are representations of higher educators' conceptions of information literacy discovered in the course of the study.

Thematising higher educators' conceptions of information literacy

The next section of this chapter deals with how the empirical study was implemented using the following headings:

- The pilot study

- The participants: higher educators

- Designing the data gathering instruments

- Data gathering strategies: conducting interviews and collecting written data

- Analysis: finding and describing conceptions of information literacy

To reiterate, the aim of this study was to identify variation in conceptions of information literacy that would be useful to the higher education community. Higher educators were selected as the group within which conceptions would be identified.

The pilot study

A pilot for the study was conducted between July and August of 1994. The purposes of the pilot were to trial data gathering instruments and data gathering strategies. While the details of the data gathering instruments and strategies will be discussed in the following sections, the preliminary work on which some decisions were based is presented here.

In the pilot study several questions were trialed in three different contexts: face to face interviews, email, and written responses during seminars. The original intention was to gather data, which would have equal weight in the analysis process, using all three data gathering strategies.

The 'questions' trialed during the pilot were:

1a) Describe a time when you demonstrated that you were (or were not!) information literate

1b) For you, what is involved in being an information literate person?

2a) Please describe your experience of being (or trying to be) an information literate person

2b) For you, what is involved in being an information literate person?

3a) How do you use information in your every day life and work?

3b)   What does it mean to be a competent information user?

4a) How do you keep informed about your professional or research interest?

4b) Describe your experience of being or trying to be an information literate person

4c) Describe your picture of an effective information user

Describe a time when you demonstrated that you were
(or were not!) information literate.

For you, what is involved in being an information literate person?

Your responses to these questions will contribute to our task today by revealing something of your own experience of information literacy. They may also assist me in designing data gathering questions for my doctoral study into qualitative variation in tertiary educators' experience of information literacy. Please return this sheet to me after the workshop if you are willing to share your response. Thank you, Christine Bruce.

Figure 5.1   Worksheet used for gathering written responses at an information literacy seminar

Written responses to 1a and 1b were obtained during a staff development seminar where participants devised desirable information literacy characteristics for graduates of their university (See Figure 5.1). Fourteen tertiary educators including librarians and academic staff from a range of disciplines such as nursing, education and engineering submitted their responses at the end of the session. Each person wrote a paragraph of between one and two hundred words in response to the two questions. While responses to the first question tended to be brief anecdotes, responses to the second question tended to be lists of characteristics. Responses to both provided limited insights into people's experience. Large numbers of written responses would have been needed if this had been used as the primary data gathering strategy, and different questions would have been required. Written responses obtained in seminar situations based on more suitable questions were used as supplementary data in the final study.

An attempt to use electronic mail interviews in the pilot study, using questions 2a and 2b failed. Three participants, two female, and one male, all of whom were avid users of electronic mail did not respond to the messages sent to them over a period of one month. Each of these participants had agreed to a personal request to participate in the pilot study before they received the initial electronic mail message. A copy of the message used appears in Figure 5.2. One of the two women claimed lack of time as the reason for not responding but agreed to be interviewed when that alternative was suggested. On the basis of this experience electronic mail was also not used as a primary data gathering strategy. I did, however use it to communicate with a small number of educators who accepted the medium readily. As no responses to questions were obtained via this medium, I included the second question in the set in the interviews which followed.

3rd August 1994

Dear (Colleague),

As you know I am looking for people who may be willing to talk with me about their experience of being, or trying to be!, information literate.

The purpose of the discussion is to try to discover the different ways in which tertiary educators (this includes you!) experience information literacy. I believe this is important because the ways in which educators mould students' experience of information literacy is likely to be shaped by their own experience.

As tertiary educators we also need to understand what it means to be an information literate person and what is involved in helping students at all levels to become information literate. If you would like to participate in my study, would you begin the conversation by responding to the following questions, by letter, fax or e-mail, in as much detail as possible:

 1) Please describe your experience of being, or trying to be!, an information literate person.

2) For you, what is involved in being an information literate person?

Would you please also indicate, if you are willing to respond to requests from me for clarification or further information?

With many thanks for your interest,

Christine Bruce, Centre for Applied Environmental and Social Education Research

Queensland University of Technology, Kelvin Grove Campus

Locked Bag No 2, Red Hill Qld 4059

Fax: 07- 8643986, E-mail: c.bruce@qut.edu.au

P.S. If you would prefer to converse with me face to face, instead of writing, please don't hesitate to ask.

Figure 5.2   Electronic mail message sent to colleagues who had agreed to correspond

Face to face interviews were conducted with one male, a senior lecturer in an engineering faculty and one female, a librarian providing information design and development services to academic staff, using the remaining three sets of questions. As a strategy the interview proved to be successful. Descriptions of experience were easily obtained with little prompting from the interviewer. The question *What does it mean to be a competent information user* required impromptu redesign. I paraphrased it as: *What in your view would be a competent information user?* This latter question, together with *What is your picture of an effective information user?* provided useful insights. The use of orienting questions, prior to asking these, were however, clearly necessary. By the end of the interview both participants were using the phrase information literacy in their responses, despite the fact that the phrase had not been emphasised in the questions. On the basis of this, the face to face interview was chosen as the primary data gathering strategy, and a final set of questions selected.

The participants: higher educators

Sixty higher educators from eight universities participated in the study. The core participants were a group of sixteen interviewees from the Queensland University of Technology and Griffith University, with a further forty-four supplying written data. Although details of individual participants are not provided in order to protect their identities, information about the character of the group, their gender, discipline backgrounds, occupations and universities, is presented in Tables 5.1, 5.2 and 5.3. Most details are in relation to the interviewees because suppliers of written data did not consistently provide the personal information requested.

Table 5.1 Participants' universities

Name and location of university	Number of Participants
Griffith University (Queensland, Australia)	15
Southern Cross University (New South Wales, Australia	1
Queensland University of Technology (Queensland, Australia)	20
University of Central Queensland (Queensland, Australia)	14
University of South Pacific (Suva, Fiji)	1
University of Queensland (Queensland, Australia)	4
University of Wollongong (New South Wales, Australia)	1
UMIST (Manchester, England	1
Other (not identified)	3
Total number of participants	60

Table 5.2 Gender and discipline backgrounds of interviewees

Griffith University		Queensland University of Technology	
Male (1)Commerce and Admin	Female (1)Commerce and Admin	Male (1)Engineering	Female (1)Business Education
(1)Higher Education	(1)Higher Education	(2)Psychology	(2)Higher Education
(1)Science	(1)Music		(1)Information Science
(1)Music	(1)Information Science		
(1)Environmental Eng			
Total Number of Interviewees: 16 (Number of participants appears in brackets)			

Table 5.3 Interviewees by occupation

	Griffith University (Number of interviewees)	University of Technology (Number of interviewees)
Lecturers	2	2
Librarians	3	1
Counsellors	2	2
Staff Developers	2	2
Total Number of Interviewees: 16		

Participants in the study were selected both on the basis of '...intended use of the research outcomes and ...the internal requirements of phenomenographic research per se' (Bowden 1994, p.4). At a general level, higher educators were the focus because conceptions of information literacy were being studied with the intention of influencing information literacy education in universities. It seemed reasonable to assume that their views of information literacy would be likely to influence their approaches to information literacy education. I also wanted to elicit the conceptions of experienced, rather than neophyte information users. Again, higher educators were a better choice for this purpose than, for example, undergraduates.

Specific individuals were invited to participate in interviews because they were known to have an interest in information literacy. None of them, however had written about information literacy or information literacy education, nor had they engaged in information literacy research. This was important because I was seeking conceptions from people who could be considered information literate but who were not themselves information literacy scholars or experts. (It will be seen later, however, that despite the extensive experience of information use that could be expected of *any* lecturer, librarian, staff developer or counsellor, several were confused about whether they would label themselves information literate.) Equal numbers of higher educators were selected from each stakeholder group and from each university as can be seen from Table 5.3.

Participants other than interviewees were 'self selected' in that they provided written responses either because:

- they communicated with me via email about information literacy and hence were invited to participate;
- they attended an information literacy seminar or workshop and accepted the invitation to contribute; or
- they had previously expressed an interest in information literacy to me and accepted an invitation to contribute.

In summary, participants were chosen to ensure that maximum variation was obtained from within the selected context. This strategy has been labelled purposive sampling:

> Purposive sampling is based on the assumption that one wants to discover, understand, gain insight; therefore one needs to select a sample from which one can learn most. (Merriam 1988, p.48)

Therefore the group included academics, information services staff with a direct involvement in teaching and learning, staff developers and learning counsellors. They were drawn from a range of discipline backgrounds. The stakeholder groups were predetermined because their professional interests require them to interact with the world of information extensively and because their conceptions of information literacy are most likely to impact on the experiences of students. Although none were 'scholars of information literacy', they had varying degrees of knowledge about, and interest in, the information literacy agenda. For some, the world of information and strategies for working within it had been the subject of formal study, whereas for others it had not. Others were actively involved in teaching information literacy.

In my study sixteen participants contributed to the core data, participating in interviews, while a further forty- four participants provided supplementary data in written form (see Table 5.4).

Table 5.4   Participant profile in relation to data gathering strategies

Strategy	Lecturers	Librarians	Staff Developers	Counsellors
Seminars (written)	7	24		1
Mail (written)	5	2		
Email (written)	2	1	2	
Interviews	2	4	4	4
Total participants	18	31	6	5

In any phenomenographic study, the number of participants should be sufficient to yield adequately rich descriptions of the varying conceptions which, together, comprise the phenomenon. It is generally accepted that approximately twenty participants will achieve this (Sandberg 1994, p.72).

Designing the data gathering instruments

This section describes the instruments at the heart of the procedure through which conceptions of information literacy were uncovered. As there are no standard procedures for gathering phenomenographic data, techniques have to be formulated for each study, taking into account the nature of the phenomenon under investigation and the data gathering principles which must be adhered to. Fundamental to the data gathering procedure, however, is the need for it to 'be sufficiently open to allow the subjects to express their own way of structuring the aspects of reality they are relating to' (Johansson, Marton and Svensson 1985, p.252). The data gathering procedure often involves tasks, direct questions (Saljo 1988, p.39), or a combination of the two.

In an ideal world the following cues: *What does information literacy mean to you?* and *Describe your picture of an information literate person* would be likely to be effective in ascertaining tertiary educators' conceptions of information literacy. From the pilot study, however, I discovered that some colleagues were not conversant with the term *information literacy* I had to find a way of orienting these colleagues towards the phenomenon, elements of which they regularly experience. The pilot also indicated that:

- the term *competent information user* had technological associations for some people, consequently the term *effective information user* was preferred

- asking people about times when they were not information literate was of little value, they ended in describing a phenomenon which was not of interest to the study

- asking people about how they kept 'informed' consistently oriented them towards sources of information, therefore the question was discarded.

The instrument selected included three questions (3a, 4b and 4c) from the pilot designed to reveal, in a detailed way, the manner in which information literacy was experienced by the participating higher educators. Before the participants responded to the questions, they were told that the study aimed to identify the different ways in which they experience, or see information literacy, and that they would be given time to reflect on the questions if they wished:

1) How do you use information in your every day life and work?

2) Tell the story of a time when you used information effectively

3) Describe your picture of an effective information user (or information literate person

4) Describe your experience of being (or trying to be) an information literate person

The first two were intended to orient the participants towards the phenomenon. Their roles were to encourage participants to focus on their own experience of information literacy. At this stage the participants began to describe their experience of using information using their own choice of context. Responses to the first question may not have reflected an emphasis on effective use of information, which was the focus of the remaining questions.

The third was intended to elicit reflected understandings of information literacy. It focuses directly on the participant's view of information literacy or effective information use. The term *information literacy* was used here only with participants who expressed familiarity with the phrase. The term *effective use of information* was considered an acceptable substitute because it potentially incorporated all the various ways in which information literacy could be interpreted; it did not encourage interviewees down any one particular path.

The fourth questions shifted the focus from the participants' picture of an information literate person back to their own experience of information literacy. Having discussed their picture of an information literate person, they were invited to describe their own experience of being, or trying to be, information literate. The term *information literacy* was used here with all participants in the study.

All the questions complied with the following criteria:

- they were open enough to embrace all current understandings of information literacy without drawing attention to any particular approach to the phenomenon

- they allowed the respondent to choose his or her own interpretation of the phenomenon

- they allowed me to put aside my own views of the phenomenon when asking questions

- they encouraged the respondents to take a describing orientation, suggesting that it would be possible to identify, from the responses, the ways in which information literacy appeared to the people whose views were being sought.

None of the questions in the final set took the form of a 'what is x?' question. Bowden (1994, p.8) suggests that *What is x* questions tend to work against the diagnostic purpose of data gathering. The questions were used in interviews and for gathering data in written form. Follow up probes (Prosser 1994a, p.33) were not designed after the pilot because participants' responses did not appear to be sufficiently predictable. Common questions, however, were used for requesting elaboration, including: Please explain? Tell me more about..? Can you explain that in a different way? Give me an example? (Bruce 1994c, p. 53)

Data gathering: conducting interviews and collecting written data

Conceptions may be expressed in different forms of action but they are most accessible through language' (Svensson 1994, p.16). For this reason, interviews are the most commonly used method for data gathering in phenomenographic research, while other sources have included written data, children's drawings and the product of people's work (Marton 1986a, p.42). The advantages of the interview, which are more extensive descriptions, and the ability to probe the subject's understanding in detail, often need to be weighed up against written responses from the respondent which are usually more focussed, containing less extraneous material. The study combined both these strategies in order to gain the benefits of each. Interviews were supplemented by written data obtained via electronic mail, normal mail and in information literacy seminars. Interviews were chosen as the primary strategy because the pilot study indicated this was the technique with which participants were most comfortable, and which provided the deepest, or most extended descriptions of experience. The combination of strategies also permitted efficient access to a geographically dispersed population.

Written data were collected for at least three recently published phenomenographic studies (Bruce 1994b; Marton, Carlsson and Halasz 1992; Prosser 1994b). Prosser (1994b, p.30) concludes that: '...logically related categories of description ... can be identified ... using ... written responses to open ended questions'. For this study, written data were collected in three contexts:

- at an Australian Library and Information Association seminar *Information literacy exploring directions for the 1990s,* in October 1994

- at an information literacy seminar for students in the Queensland University of Technology's Graduate Certificate in Higher Education

- via electronic mail

Conceptions of Information Literacy

Thank you for participating in this study into the different ways in which people experience, or conceive of, information literacy. Your responses will help me search for these differences. Understanding these differences will lead to better communication amongst people interested in information literacy and important insights into what is involved in teaching information literacy. Please answer the following questions in as much detail as possible:

Tell the story of a time when you showed that you were information literate
Describe your picture of an effective information user

.........................(Please continue over the page)

Thank you for your response. If you are willing please indicate 1. the name of your library, or other workplace.., 2) your discipline area................................., 3) your gender...

Please return this form to me after the seminar or send it to C. Bruce: CAESER, QUT, Kelvin Grove Campus, Locked Bag No.2, Red Hill, Q. 4059. Fax: 07 - 8643986

Figure 5.3   Worksheet used for the collection of written data

Providing written responses to the data was taken seriously by these participants. Some chose to forward their completed responses to me at a later stage giving them time to reflect on the task (see Figure 5.3 for worksheet used). The term *information literacy* was used in data gathering because the contexts suggested that it would not be unfamiliar. The request to 'tell a story' was intended to ensure that text book explanations of information literacy were not presented. Some of the participants found the writing task difficult, confirming the appropriateness of the decision to use interviews as a primary data- gathering strategy. Comments overheard during writing sessions, each of 20 minutes to half an hour, included:

- 'I am finding it hard to write about this, I need to talk about this.'
- 'I can't write - I need to draw.'
- 'I am having trouble thinking of a specific occasion when I was information literate — I am always information literate..'

Phenomenographic interviews are a specialised form of qualitative research interview (Bruce 1994c, p.47). At the most general level their purpose is to 'gather descriptions of the life world of the interviewee with respect to interpretation of the meaning of the described phenomenon' (Kvale 1983, p.174). Phenomenographic interviews also share the characteristics of the qualitative interview outlined by Kvale. They:

- are centred in the interviewee's life world
- seek to understand the meaning of phenomenon in (the interviewee's) life world
- are qualitative, descriptive, specific and presuppositionless
- are focussed on certain themes
- are open to ambiguities and change
- take place in an interpersonal interaction
- may be a positive experience. (Kvale 1983, p.174)

Phenomenographic interviews are distinctive from other qualitative research interviews in that their specific purpose is to seek variation in people's experience or understanding of the phenomenon in question. Furthermore their focus is on the relation between the person being interviewed and the theme of the interview, in this case information literacy. The interviewer's focus is neither on the person, nor on the theme, but rather on how the theme appears to, or is experienced by, the person being interviewed.

In my study, the aim of the interview was to uncover the structure of the experience of information literacy. Essentially, the goal was to try to see the phenomenon as it was seen or experienced by the interviewees. This was achieved through helping the interviewee to thematise the relevant aspects of their life world and probing to identify the internal and external horizons of participants' experience using the questions previously described. The need to understand the nuances in the figural gradations of awareness meant that interviewees had to be encouraged to elaborate at length on their experience of information literacy. Such probing and encouragement was achieved through the use of further questions based on the participants' initial responses to the questions identified previously. The interviews may therefore be appropriately described as semistructured.

Before the interviews were conducted, the intent of the study was explained twice to participants; Francis (1993, p.70) has raised the importance of interviewees understanding the focus of the study. The first time that they heard about the study was when I contacted them to find out if they were willing to be interviewed. At this stage I explained that I was interested in the different ways in which higher educators understood what it meant to be information literate. This was explained a second time as part of the interview using a handout (See Figure 5.4) which also included the questions we were going to discuss. I also explained, at this stage, my role in the interview, which I described as trying to see information literacy the way they did. For this reason, I said, I would probably ask them to explain their comments or to provide further examples to help me see better.

Higher Educators' Conceptions of Information Literacy

The intention of this interview is to discuss how you think about effective information use.

I will ask you to respond to the following questions:

1)   How do you use information in your every day life and work?

2)   Tell the story of a time when you used information effectively

3)   Describe your picture of an effective information user (or information literate person)?

4)   Describe your experience of being (or trying to be) an information literate person

---

Figure 5.4 Handout given to interviewees

Important characteristics of a phenomenographic interview have been identified by Svensson and Theman (1983, pp.7-8). As the interviews progressed it was possible to see how the elements they stress emerged.

Firstly, 'the interview represents a constant flow of changing opinion' (Svensson and Theman 1983, p.7). The following extracts from Interview Two show fluctuations in how the interviewee is thinking about information literacy. Much of the discourse to highlight his changes in thinking is omitted. In this part of the interview, the interviewee is talking about information literacy in relation to students he assists with study skills. He begins by explaining information literacy in two different ways, as external to the student, and as being about information use. He swings between these interpretations for some time, and has difficulty explaining what he means when saying that information literacy is 'out there'.

In the following extracts the interviewer's questions appear in bold.

> ... information literacy is out there. It's something that they have to contact and my role in the process is that of a facilitator.
>
> **So what is it you're actually trying to bring them into contact with?**
>
> Information using. I believe that our culture has a very very definite notion or construct of an information literate person...'
>
> **So you said that information literacy has to do with.....You reinterpret that as information using. Could you explain then what you mean by information using?**
>
> Information using, I think, has to be linked to a task. There's no point, I think, in becoming... if I can just give some examples. I meet some Singaporean students and their level of information literacy is just incredible, it's admirable and yet the capacity to use that information is... limited. (Int. 2, p.1, Learning Adviser, Male)

By the end of this extract this learning adviser is no longer seeing information literacy as information use. The students he refers to are information literate but are not skilled at using information. A question confirms this change in interpretation:

> **So, to what extent then is the use of information actually linked to information literacy. Are they the same or different?**
>
> They're different. They're different.
>
> **Could you talk a bit more through that? I'm trying to see your view of information literacy.**
>
> ...Information literacy, in our culture, I think, would be used as a tool to challenge ideas, to develop ideas, to offer new modes of presentation and a little just speculative learning, I think, as distinct to reproductive learning.
>
> **O.K. As you talked then, what are you actually referring to when you use the word information literacy?**
>
> I think information literacy is again, something, outside the student. Information use is something within the student ... (Int. 2, p.2, Learning Adviser, Male)

When I encourage the interviewee to explain what he means by talking about information literacy as 'outside the student', he reverts to describing processes of information use and knowledge:

> **O.K. I still want to push this question of then what is information literacy? What is this thing that is beyond the student?**
>
> Well, in terms of a definition of it?
>
> **A description of it.**
>
> A description of it. I think it's someone who's able to use information for a start. That's the first level and think it's a notion that needs considerable scaffolding 'cause I think the nature of information literacy is that it's developmental. It's constantly changing. It's just continuous so therefore I think our notion of the individual ought to be just continuous as well. I think it starts with someone who can use information. Secondly, someone who knows the information is useful, of its own accord. Someone who is able to distinguish between which information to use and which information not to use... (Int. 2, pp. 2- 3, Learning Adviser, Male)

Secondly, the interviews reveal 'constant following up and penetrating interrogation (which) is naturally exhausting for both the respondent and the interviewer' (Svensson and Theman 1983, p.7). This following up is described more specifically by Svensson and Theman as involving asking questions based on comments made by the interviewee at an earlier stage. I have chosen extracts from Interview Five to demonstrate this, and include the interviewee's final comment as a testimony to the demanding nature of the process. In the section of the interview immediately preceding what is recorded below, the interviewee has stated that the ability to tackle previously unencountered problems is one aspect of effective information use:

> **You said before that the first one was one aspect. Did you have other aspects in mind?**
>
> Did I say that?
>
> **Yes, you're allowed to change your mind (laughter)**
>
> Well, it's all just general decision making. (Int.5,p.6, Academic, Male)

A little later in the interview I again suggest a return to something said by the interviewee at the commencement of the interview:

> **...I want to go back to this thing you said when we started talking.**
>
> I wish you wouldn't do that.
>
> **We were talking about what information was and you said that well, there were different definitions of information depending upon the application...**
>
> Maybe that was wrong, maybe it's just everything on which we make a decision. (Int.5,p.8, Academic, Male)

Although these extracts are short they capture the flavour of the interview. The demands of being required to defend his remarks are made clear by the interviewee when he is asked, on completion of the interview, if he has anything to add:

> I've probably covered it, I can't think of anything else, you've drained me. (Int.5,p.11, Academic, Male)

Thirdly, 'the form of the interview puts a mental stress on the respondent and this sometimes results in an emotional reaction' (Svensson and Theman 1983, p.8). There were many occasions where the interviewees became confused, because they were confronted with what they perceived to be inadequacies or inconsistencies in their own thinking. Although this was useful in that it revealed that different ways of thinking were in fact being elicited, and that participants were being stretched to the limits of their experience, it was a stressful experience for them. As an interviewer, I was able to sustain the interviews through these stresses, probably because I had pre existing professional relationships with the interviewees.

One example of an occasion on which such stresses arose comes from Interview Four. The interviewee has previously described an information literate person as:

> ...anyone but me. It would be someone who could come in and switch onto the world over here and engage in wonderful trans Atlantic conversations...used all sorts of modem things...(Int. 4, p.6, Female, Staff Developer)

Since then, she has produced a second, and completely different picture of an effective information user. My challenge was to confront the interviewee with the difference, move through the distress phase and encourage her to continue her description:

> **But that has got nothing to do with the picture of the (effective) information user which you gave me before.**
>
> No. But that's an information user that I can understand and relate to. (in some distress)
>
> **Now is that an effective information user?**
>
> He doesn't seem to be short of information, does he?
>
> **No. Now if he wasn't using electronic networks in any way, would he still be an effective information user?**
>
> That's a trick question because I've already said no before in relation to me now in relation to him, I have to say it wouldn't matter in the slightest.
>
> **O.K. So wouldn't it matter. What is it that actually makes a competent information user?**
>
> I suppose it's the level of scholarship, isn't it. You have to be... and mental ability and..
>
> **Can you tell me more about that. I know you're just starting to explore it. You're just thinking about it yourself right now but can you try to think it through a bit more for me. Nearly over.**
>
> Well I suppose it's because here, using him again as an example, he has such a background of wide reading and deep reading and somehow he has the sort of brain that he can use as a filing cabinet which I can't do..

A third example comes from an interviewee who has expressed considerable difficulty in communicating her ideas. Comments such as 'I'm not being inspired at the moment', 'I can't think of anything Christine', 'I want to know Christine, I can't tell you. You tell me', suggest the stress that she is under. Despite these difficulties, the interviewee was able to talk through some examples which conveyed different ways of thinking about information literacy. It was not until towards the end of the interview that she finally indicated the reason for her discomfort. She felt that she was being asked to describe information literate people in her environment, when, in her view, these were a rarity:

> Only that, I mean, we see the worst here and I suppose you're asking me...all the things you want me to say are the positive things and its hard for me to find them, I'm sorry. (Int. 7, p.9, Female, Librarian)

This new insight allowed me to invite her to think about the question I had asked differently:

> **Perhaps attack it this way, in terms of where you would like your people to be?** (Int. 7, p.9, Female, Librarian)

After the interviews had been completed all data were typed in preparation for analysis. Interview transcripts were checked against tapes, and then sent to interviewees for confirmation. A covering letter thanked each participant for his or her involvement, invited them to make any additions or changes to the transcripts, and asked whether they would like to receive information about the outcomes. In January 1996, copies of a conference paper presenting preliminary outcomes were sent to all interviewees.

Analysis: finding and describing conceptions of information literacy

Data analysis in a phenomenographic study continues the process of exploring the subject-object relations begun when data gathering. It is directed towards uncovering the various conceptions and representing these in the form of categories of description. There are two main outcomes of the analysis: an outcome space representing the phenomenon of information literacy as it is conceived by higher educators, and descriptions of the varying conceptions found in that outcome space. The main aim of the analysis was to discover participants' conceptions of information literacy and to devise categories and an outcome space which would communicate these to researchers and practitioners interested in information literacy. As the nature of categories of descriptions and outcome spaces have been described already, the process through which they are constructed will now be reviewed.

Walsh (1994) argues that there are two views of the analysis process amongst phenomenographers. In the first view, analysis is seen as a process of construction, and in the second it is seen as a process of discovery. She also points to a range of possible consequences of each view. The most serious of these are that if the former view is held, researchers are in danger of imposing a logical framework which is not justified; and if the latter view is held, they are in danger of bypassing the analytical process (Walsh 1994, pp. 22- 23). I have interpreted the 'analytical process' to mean the identification of the structural components of the conceptions and how they are connected in the broader framework which is the outcome space. The two points of view are captured in the idea that 'conceptions are discovered, categories of descriptions are devised' (Johansson, Marton and Svensson 1985, p.250). The analysis process involves both of these activities, which, although we can conceive of them separately, in practice usually occur simultaneously.

The dilemma which Walsh presents may be resolved by viewing the analysis process as *both* process of construction and a process of discovery. In the same way that we see conceptions as being constituted in the relation between perceiving individual and appearing object (both are active in constituting the conception), so we may see the categories of description as being constituted in the relation between the researcher and the data (both are active in constituting the categories). It is a process of discovery because the conceptions reveal themselves through the data and it is a process of construction because the researcher must identify and describe these conceptions in terms of referential and structural elements. Constant and demonstrable iteration between the construction of the categories and the data (Svensson and Theman 1983), together with an appreciation of the character of conceptions and categories of description, was the approach used in my study to achieve the required balance. Evidence of reference to the data is provided in the categories in the form of illustrative quotes.

Detailed procedures for engaging in the analysis process are not available. Those writing about the phenomenographic analysis usually emphasise that it is a 'discovery process' (Saljo 1988, p.45), a 'nonalgorithmic discovery procedure' (Marton and Saljo 1984), or that it is not possible, or indeed desirable to prescribe techniques for use in a phenomenographic study (Prosser 1994a, p.32). Rather, the analysis process is guided by the researcher's understanding of what is being sought, the variations in conception that are captured in terms of structural and referential components. What happens in any one study is therefore an interplay between the researcher's understanding, the nature of the phenomenon being studied and the style of the available data. Procedures used are intended to facilitate 'catching the essence of people's world of thoughts' (Dahlgren and Fallsberg 1991, p.152). During the analysis the procedures remain subservient to this intention; they are not rigidly adhered to.

Various ways of proceeding, however, have been suggested, together with indications of what the researcher should be looking for throughout the process. The latter are fundamentally related to directing the reader towards the structural and referential components of the subject-object relation which lie at the heart of the conception. The way of proceeding which I followed draws on descriptions of the analysis process provided by Marton and Saljo (1984), Saljo (1988), Marton (1986a), Marton (1988a,b), Bowden (1994), Dahlgren and Fallsberg (1991) and Sandberg (1994). Although it is portrayed in a linear fashion, the actual implementation was recursive, and often drew simultaneously on more than one phase of the analysis. The procedure is framed within Sandberg's (1994, p.86) five phases of phenomenographic analysis:

- becoming familiar with the transcripts
- the noematic level of the intentional analysis
- the noetic level of the analysis
- the intentional constitution of the conception
- establishing the outcome space of the conceptions (Sandberg 1994, p.86)

Becoming familiar with the transcripts   The first step in the analysis process was to become familiar with the transcripts of the interviews and other data gathered. The purpose of reading the material was to identify the conceptions of information literacy 'that seem to underlie the statements made by the respondents'(Saljo 1988, p.41). This is an active process on the part of the reader which is helped by asking questions such as How does the respondent construe the phenomenon?, What concepts does he or she use to explain it? and What types of similarities with other phenomena are introduced? (Saljo 1988, p.41). During this phase it became possible to identify sections of the discourse which demonstrated significant differences in conception. (I have already provided examples of how changes in thinking were evident in interview transcripts in the previous section). Dahlgren and Fallsberg (1991, p.152) refer to this process as 'condensation', Marton and Saljo (1984) refer to it as identifying 'pools of meaning' which then need to be grouped and classified according to their similarities and differences. The sections of discourse were marked within the transcripts to ensure that it was always possible to refer to the context within which particular statements were made.

The noematic level of the intentional analysis   In this second phase, the referential, or noematic element of the conception was the focus of attention. During this phase extracts from the interviews were coded with coloured flags according to the significantly different meanings being ascribed to information literacy. It was essential in this phase to realise that it was the meanings underlying participants' statements rather than the statements themselves which were being grouped:

> The content is...not primarily considered in terms of meanings of linguistic units, but from the point of view of expressing a relation to parts of the world. Furthermore, fundamental characteristics of the relation are focussed on.... This makes the specific form of language used, although the basis for analysis, subordinate to their expressed content. What counts as the same conception may be expressed in many linguistically very different ways and what counts as different conceptions may be expressed in similar language. (Svensson 1994, p.19)

The major questions applied to the data during this phase were: 'In what ways is this person experiencing information literacy? What would be the most appropriate ways, on the basis of this data, to complete the phrase: Information literacy is seen/experienced as.....'. Thus this level of analysis became the first step towards devising categories of description.

The noetic level of the analysis In the third phase the structural, or noetic, element became the focus of attention. In this phase I compared the statements from which the conceptions of information literacy were identified, 'to find sources of variation or agreement' (Dahlgren and Fallsberg 1991, p.152). I was' looking for the essential, the most distinctive, the most crucial structural aspect of the relation between the individual and the phenomenon' (Marton 1988a, p.182). The primary question applied to the data was: 'What does the participant focus on, in order to experience information literacy in this particular way?' In relation to theory of awareness, this may be rephrased: 'What is figural to the participants in their differing experiences of information literacy?' Another way of asking the question was 'What is the meaning structure underlying the conception?'. As a result both meaning structures and awareness structures were available in formulating the outcome space. This third phase of the analysis often happens in parallel with the second phase; Marton links the two in his description of the search for the structural component of the conceptions:

> When reading and classifying descriptions of a phenomenon, we are not merely sorting data, we are looking for the most distinctive characteristics that appear in those data....structurally significant differences that clarify how people define some specific portion of the world. (Marton 1986a, p.34)

During this phase of the analysis, 'information' was identified as the object in the 'subject-object' relation. Therefore, various ways in which the object appeared in the different categories were examined also.

The intentional constitution of the conception This fourth phase involved drawing together the referential, or neomatic elements, and the structural or noetic elements of the conceptions, to describe the subject- object (intentional) relations which comprise the different conceptions. The description of the relation, that is a meaning structure and an awareness structure, together with the label naming the conception, forms the 'category of description' which was devised to denote each one. In this way the fundamental differences between each category were made clear. This process was similar to Dahlgren and Fallsberg's (1991, p.152) phases of labelling and contrasting the categories, in which finally, 'the obtained categories are compared with regard to similarities and differences'. Due to the recursive nature of the analysis, draft categories of description were actually constructed early in the process; these were progressively revised as the noetic and noematic elements of each conception were clarified through regular consultation with the transcripts.

Establishing the outcome space of the conceptions The final step involved identifying the ways in which the categories were related to each other. This was done through examining the internal structure of the conceptions as expressed in the meaning structure and the awareness structure for each one. The relations between the categories were 'examined from the point of view of logic' (Marton 1981b, p.167), making the ordering of the categories 'purely a logical question' (p.167). Constructing the outcome space was highly dependent upon an adequate analysis of the two types of structure. In fact it was necessary to revisit the earlier stages of the analysis several times to confirm or adjust the descriptions in the process of constructing the outcomes space. In constructing the outcome space a three tier approach was taken using the meaning structures, the awareness structure and the varying ways in which information was perceived. All three contributed to the structural framework within which meaning was attributed to information literacy. The meaning structure and the awareness structure, however, were the key elements in positioning the categories within the framework.

Trustworthiness of the outcomes

Lincoln and Guba (1985) suggest that the trustworthiness of studies with naturalistic underpinnings should be established through addressing their credibility, transferability, dependability and confirmability. Phenomenographic research is usually described as interpretative, rather than naturalistic. Nevertheless phenomenographers also need to establish trustworthiness within a phenomenological, rather than a positivist framework. Criticisms of phenomenographic research on the basis of lack of validity, lack of predictive power, researcher bias and denial of the voice of the individual through categorisation (Bowden 1995, p.145), have led to increased attention being paid to the need to establish the trustworthiness of the outcomes (Bruce 1994c; Bowden 1995; Gerber 1993; Sandberg 1994, 1995a, 1995b). The trustworthiness of the outcomes of this study, the descriptions of variation in the conceptions of information literacy, is based on approaches established by Saljo (1988), Gerber (1993) and Sandberg (1994, 1995a). The thinking of each of these researchers contributes to an understanding of what is required to ensure sound outcomes of a phenomenographic study. Outcomes of a phenomenographic study could be said to be sound where:

- there is a demonstrable orientation towards the phenomenon of information literacy through the process of discovery and description
- they conform to the knowledge interest of the research approach
- they are communicable

The trustworthiness of this study was established through meeting the above criteria.

Demonstrable orientation towards the phenomenon of information literacy through the process of discovery and description

In a study designed to interpret and understand people's conceptions of some phenomenon, such as information literacy, strategies need to be put in place which will safeguard against unfaithful representation during the course of the whole study:

> ...the strength of good qualitative studies (is) that they maintain a consistent level of truthfulness across the stages of the study, rather than using (reliability or validity measures) as a checking mechanism towards the end of the study (Gerber 1993, p.49)

Gerber (1993) and (Sandberg 1994) rely heavily on the application of phenomenological theory throughout the research process to ensure faithful, or truthful, representation. This strategy has also been adopted. Its application to the study is described below.

The main criterion for the acceptability of the outcomes of this study is that the different conceptions of information literacy have been described faithfully; this was achieved through the adoption of the phenomenological principle to *'the things themselves'* in order to make the descriptions possible (Sandberg 1994, p.62). The 'thing itself', or people's lived experience of information literacy, was uncovered during the interview process through the application of the phenomenological reduction in the design of the data gathering tools and the implementation of the strategies. The phenomenological reduction, in this context was used both during data gathering and analysis, to ensure, as far as possible, that I came to see the phenomenon through the eyes of the participants. I applied the following features of the reduction as described by Ihde, which have already been successfully adopted for phenomenographic studies. This involved

- an orientation towards the appearance of the phenomenon
- a describing orientation
- a horizontalisation of all phenomena
- looking for structural features of the phenomenon
- using intentionality as a correlational rule. (Sandberg 1994, p.67- 9, Ihde 1986)

As the application of the phenomenological reduction is applicable throughout the research process I could check its application in four stages of the study:

- The research question itself was demonstrably oriented towards the phenomenon; in this study I was seeking the different ways in which information literacy appears to higher educators. I was also able to ensure that the phenomenon was allowed to unfold through the data gathering process without undue interference on my part. I had to ensure that data gathering questions did not direct respondents towards particular appearances of the phenomenon.

- The pilot study was used to test whether or not the data gathering tools tapped the lived experience of the phenomenon, that is they were tested to check that the respondents adopted a describing orientation.

- During the interviews I attempted to put aside my own views of the phenomenon, and treat all responses equally, thus abiding by the rule of horizontalisation.

- During the analysis it was necessary to strive for a describing orientation, and to seek the structural components of the conceptions. (adapted from Gerber 1993, p.45)

Essentially all elements of the study—the pilot, data gathering and analysis—were guided by its aim, and the interview questions were carefully crafted to ensure that participants' constructions of the phenomenon were elicited (Bowden 1994, p.7). Further, participants all understood the contribution they were making and indicated a willingness to cooperate. Adults, and even children are able to grasp easily the idea that people see things in different ways, and that my intention as an interviewer is to understand how they see 'x' (Bruce 1994c, p.54).

Conformity to the knowledge interest

Although the above strategies served to ensure faithful descriptions of the conceptions, it was also necessary to demonstrate that the structural features of the conceptions were identified. As the construction of the outcome space depends upon the identification of the structural features of the conceptions, the very availability of an outcome space serves to affirm the descriptions devised:

> Another source of verification of the appropriateness of a set of categories is the internal logic of the categories themselves. (Saljo 1988, p.46)

Another indication that the structural features of the conceptions have been identified is the possibility of describing learning about information literacy in terms of changes in conception:

> A further aspect of the internal structure of categories that depict different conceptions of a phenomenon is that learning can be described as the change from one conception within this structure to a different one. (Saljo 1988, p.46)

The increasing complexity of the conceptions in the outcome space and the possibility of using them to influence and describe learning in information literacy education are analysed in detail in the following chapters.

Communicability

Sandberg (1995a, pp.7-8) identifies three phases in which communicative validity is relevant to interpretative research: during the interview, in conducting the analysis, and in testing reaction to the results. The last phase which establishes that the categories of description themselves are communicable is stressed by both Saljo (1988, p.45) and Sandberg (1994, p.62).

During data gathering communicative validity is established by generating data through dialogue (Theman 1983, cited in Sandberg 1995a, p.7). The core data for this study were collected through interviews, a context which allowed me to check, where possible, that the interviewee was being correctly interpreted.

Clarification of meaning was also possible when obtaining responses via email, but less easy where written data were collected in seminars or workshops. The problem with written data was minimised by asking questions that asked for experiential responses, in the form of a story, and by making the written data 'supplementary' in status. The categories of description were constructed initially using the interview transcripts, after which the data pool was broadened to include the written data.

In the analysis phase the quality of the research outcomes is dependent upon how the researcher interacts with the data (Sandberg 1995a, p.8). To ensure that the descriptions were faithful to the text meant retaining the context of all sections of data that were selected for consideration throughout the analysis. The transcripts and typed versions of written data were not physically dissected at any stage. Specific sections of discourse were only physically extracted from the data in the final stages of preparing the full versions of the categories of description. The heavy reliance on quotes from the data to provide evidence in support of the descriptions was another strategy used to ensure that the analysis was faithful to the text. This strategy had the further benefit of allowing participants' 'voices' to be heard in the categories.

Finally, the categories must be understood and interpretable by other researchers and the educators for whom they are intended. I have verified the communicability of the categories through workshops and seminars. On the first occasion the outcomes were used by a group of postgraduate students studying a subject called *Information user instruction*. Part of the subject introduced theories that would influence teaching and learning in information and information technology contexts, and the idea of information literacy was one of these. Students were invited to examine the various categories of description in relation to how they conceived of information literacy, and in relation to how they would wish their clients to conceive of information literacy. The possibility of adapting the research outcomes to a practical application partially establishes communicability. Further practical applications which have not been trialed are suggested in chapter seven.

On the second and third occasions I presented preliminary outcomes of this research, including the categories of description and the outcome space, to colleagues interested in information literacy and the broader field of information needs and uses research. One seminar was conducted at a local, one day event focussed on library research. The other was conducted at the Second Australian National Conference on Information Literacy held in Adelaide, in December 1995. The interest in, and general endorsement of the outcomes by researchers and practitioners suggests there is a movement towards acceptance by a group of significant others of the quality of the work. Sandberg (1995a, p.8) points out that this acceptance is part of an ongoing negotiation of meaning and relies on intersubjective judgement at various stages of dissemination.

In the final chapters the outcomes of the study are presented, the descriptions which will serve as an initial core for a relational model of information literacy. Also examined are the new pictures in relation to those previously available, and implications for information literacy education and further research.

Chapter 6

Descriptions of conceptions of information literacy

This chapter describes information literacy as it is conceived amongst the higher educators who participated in my study. The descriptions are outcomes of the data gathering and analysis strategies reported in chapter five. Taken together they represent the phenomenon of information literacy as it has been uncovered in this investigation. Marton (1994, p.92) identifies a phenomenon as the appearance of a 'thing', rather than the 'thing itself'. Also following Marton (1995), we can say these outcomes form a description of the 'anatomy of awareness' of information literacy amongst the group. This means that the categories describe information literacy as it is conceived (seen, experienced or understood) by people.

Altogether seven conceptions of information literacy were identified:

- The information technology conception—information literacy is seen as using information technology for information retrieval and communication. (Category one)

- The information sources conception—information literacy is seen as finding information. (Category two)

- The information process conception—information literacy is seen as executing a process. (Category three

- The information control conception—information literacy is seen as controlling information. (Category four)

- The knowledge construction conception—information literacy is seen as building up personal knowledge base in a new area of interest. (Category five)

- The knowledge extension conception—information literacy is seen as working with knowledge and personal perspectives adopted in such a way that novel insights are gained. (Category six)

- The wisdom conception—information literacy is seen as using information wisely for the benefit of others. (Category seven)

The names given to the conceptions serve as labels for the categories of description.

They have been created to communicate quickly, but perhaps also superficially, the meanings attributed to information literacy by the participants in the study.

In the previous chapter it was pointed out that any phenomenon can be described as a set of qualitatively different subject-object relations. In the case of an abstract phenomenon like information literacy, the nature of the object in the relation needs to be discovered through the analysis procedure. Here, the analysis has revealed that the 'object' part of the subject-object relation is *information*. Thus, the phenomenon of information literacy may be described as a series of varying relations between people and information. These relations are the conceptions of information literacy.

Each conception is described in one category. Within each category, the conceptions are described in terms of their structural and referential components. Structure and reference are of course intertwined. The referential component is the global meaning associated with the conception. This is described primarily through the category labels, eg *Knowledge construction conception* and the statements describing how information literacy is seen, eg *information literacy is seen as.....* The structural components illuminate the meaning further by showing how that meaning is constituted through a particular arrangement of parts of the conception. They are captured in the structure of awareness, the meaning structure and the distinctive feature associated with each category. The most distinctive feature in each case is also the focal element of the structure of awareness.

The outcomes of the analysis are presented in two parts

- the outcome space, describing the phenomenon of information literacy amongst higher educators; and

- the categories of description, describing the individual conceptions of information literacy which together are structurally related to form the outcome space.

The outcome space

The outcome space presents a graphical depiction of the structural relationships amongst the various conceptions of information literacy uncovered in the analysis. It will be seen in what follows that the outcome space of the phenomenon of information literacy needs to be described in three parts:

- the varying meaning structures

- the varying structures of awareness

- the varying ways in which information is perceived

These parts were used to reveal the structural relationships amongst all the categories. Describing the varying ways in which information is perceived in the different categories is not essential to demonstrating the structural relationships between the conceptions. However, I have chosen to do so because the views of information confirm the place of each category in the structure. Also as information is the 'object' in the subject-object relation, the way in which that object appears is sufficiently important to be included in the analysis of the outcome space!

The variations to be analysed in the outcome space, therefore, are each part of the internal relations between the person and information which constitute information literacy in each category. To put it another way, they are about the character of working with information which is experienced as information literacy. All three are integral to the understanding of each category, and of the structural relationships which bring the categories together in the form of an outcome space. The place of each category in the outcome space remains fixed irrespective of which aspect is being examined.

The varying meaning structures

The first graphical depiction of the relationships among the categories is based on their *meaning structures* (see Figure 6.1). Each category has a meaning structure. Describing the meaning structures was one approach to describing the internal relations between the subject and the object components of the conceptions. These meaning structures establish the essential parts of the meaning being attributed to information literacy in each category. They also specify how these parts are combined to form a whole. Details of the meaning structure are explained in the second part of this chapter. Here I will focus only on those parts which show the relationships between the categories.

The elements of the meaning structures show the relations between categories five, six and seven. These categories are hierarchically related. An important, shared element of the meaning structures for these categories is the idea of a 'knowledge base'. The relative places of categories five, six and seven are based on the varying attributes of this knowledge base. In category five, the knowledge construction conception, a personal knowledge base is considered to be the outcome of the experience of information literacy. This knowledge base is an individual's construction of existing knowledge in the field of interest. The knowledge bases in categories six and seven differ from that in category five. They are *enhanced* knowledge bases, including considerable personal experience as well as a mastery of the field(s) of interest. For this reason categories six and seven appear 'higher' in the hierarchy than category five. Categories six and seven appear on the same level because they are mutually exclusive in that 'wisdom' is not a concern in category six; similarly 'insight' is not a concern in category seven

The places of categories one, two, three and four cannot be explained in relation to their meaning structures. Their places in this structure are based on the variations in the structures of awareness. The analysis of the relationships between these categories based on their awareness structures will show that they are easily related. On the other hand categories five, six and seven share the same awareness structure. I have treated them as separate categories however, because the precise nature of the focal element in each is different, and the meaning structures, as I have already shown, reveal important variation. The focal elements of each category link these meaning structures to the awareness structures. They appear *underlined* in Figure 6.1.

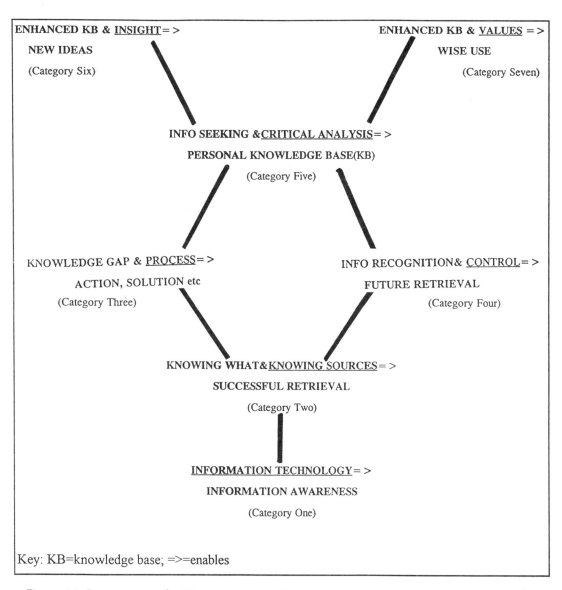

Key: KB=knowledge base; =>=enables

Figure 6.1 Outcome space depicting meaning structures

The varying structures of awareness

The structures of awareness developed for each category are simplified to portray the critical differences between the conceptions. Thus, each structure includes three major elements which the analysis showed to be key parts of the experience of information literacy. These three elements include *information use* and *information technology* in all cases, and one other element which is idiosyncratic to the conception concerned. The varying structures of awareness are portrayed together in Figure 6.2.

A cursory inspection of these structures will show that it was possible to arrange them to depict the progressive changes in the place of *information use* and

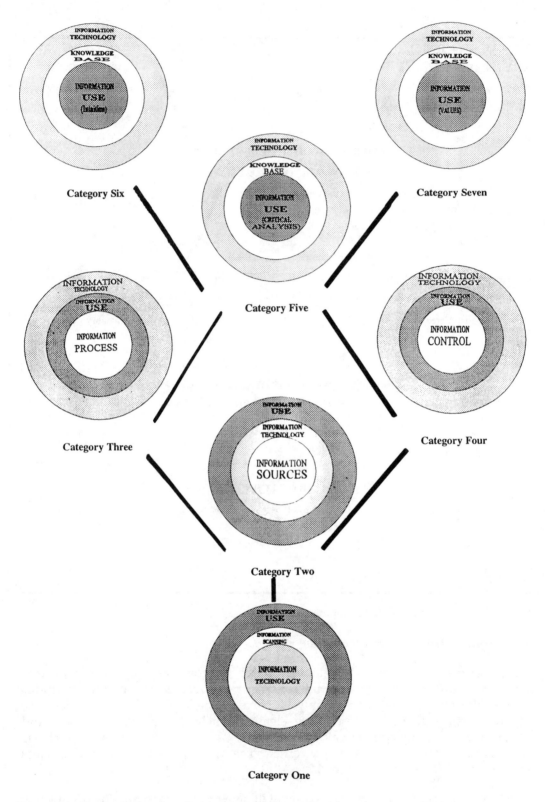

Figure 6.2   Outcome space based on structures awareness

information technology across the categories. In category one, the information technology conception, information technology is focal; that is it is central to awareness. *Information use* however, is marginal, it is at the outer edge of awareness. In the latter categories the respective places of these two elements are completely reversed. *Information used* becomes the focus of attention and *information technology* appears in the margins of the experience of information literacy. Categories two, three and four show the third element in awareness as being focal with *information use* and *information technology* taking varying places depending upon the particular conception in question.

To summarise the differences in the awareness structures, *information use* moves from being marginal to focal across categories one to seven, and *information technology* moves from being focal to marginal across the same categories. The most distinctive element in each category is the focal element in the awareness structure.

Categories five, six and seven, which, at first glance appear to have similar awareness structures, differ, already shown, in relation to the meanings attributed to both information use and the nature of the knowledge base which forms part of the experience. I have included, from the meaning structures, the distinctive element of information use which distinguishes these three categories in the graphics portraying them. These elements (critical analysis, intuition and values) reflect the structural linkages seen in the meaning structures.

The varying ways in which information is perceived.

Previous sections have described variation in the structures of awareness and in the meaning structures across the set of categories. There is also variation across categories one to seven in relation to how information appears, or is perceived. This variation is summarised in Table 6.1

Table 6.1 The varying ways in which information appears

Category	Appearance of information
Categories one and two	objective part of the external environment knowledge is required to access it
Categories three and four	objective-contextualised part of the external environment knowledge is required to access it
Category five	subjective an object of reflection internal to the individual
Categories six and seven	transformational in character able to be transformed able to transform

In categories one and two information is viewed objectively. Information is considered to be part of the external environment, and particular kinds of knowledge are required in order to access it. In category one this is knowledge of information technology, and in category two it is knowledge of information sources.

In categories three and four information is also viewed objectively and as part of the external environment. In these categories, however, information is seen within the context of particular purposes for which it will be used. Personal strategies in the form of information processes or information control mechanisms are implemented to bring useful information within the user's sphere of influence. In these categories information is not subject to any change as a consequence of having being manipulated by the user.

In category five information appears subjectively. It is regarded as an object of reflection and, as a consequence, a particular way of interpreting that information becomes a part of the information user's knowledge base. Information is no longer seen as part of the external environment, rather it is seen as internal to the individual. This is a significant change in how information is viewed when compared with categories one to four.

In categories six and seven information is viewed as having a transformational character. In these categories information is no longer seen as an object of reflection, rather the knowledge base is a personal resource which is drawn upon in the process of reflection. Information is transformed, in the sense that new insights are gained, and knowledge extended, in category six, the knowledge extension conception. In category seven, information, when used wisely, has the power to transform people.

Summary
To summarise, the outcome space which depicts information literacy as conceived amongst higher educators in this study is comprised of seven categories of description. These categories are related to each other by way of their respective awareness structures, meaning structures and views of information. Each category describes a particular way of interacting with information. The descriptions capture the experiences of information literacy or the conceptions, which, taken together, comprise the phenomenon, that is information literacy as conceived in this community. The individual categories are described in detail in the remainder of this chapter.

The categories of description

The categories of description describe the critical features which make each conception distinguishable from the others. The conceptions described by these categories can be identified in the discourse from members of all participating groups. In all the categories the subject component is the information user and the object component is information. For each category the subject-object relation which constitutes the conception is described in terms of a referential (or meaning element), and a structural element. The former identifies *what* information literacy is conceived as, and the latter identifies *how* it is conceived. For example, in the first category we see that information literacy is seen as using information technology for information retrieval and communication. This is the referential element, or the meaning of information literacy, when conceived this way. The focus on information technology is the most basic unit of the structural element. Both structural and referential elements are integral parts of the whole. The structural elements of the categories are then further analysed in terms of their awareness structures, meaning structures and the views of information associated with them. In this framework information technology is that part of the experience which is focal for the participants when they are conceiving of information literacy this way. It is the distinguishing feature of the category, central to both the awareness and meaning structures. A detailed explication of the category follows, supported by evidence from the data in the form of quotations.

All quotations are accompanied by a statement, in brackets, indicating the section of the data from which they are extracted; for example: (Int. 4, p.6, Staff Developer, Female). This means that the extract is from interview number four, on page six, and that the interviewee was a female staff developer.

Category one: the information technology conception

Information literacy is seen as using information technology for information retrieval and communication.

At the heart of this category lies the importance of information technology for information access and personal networking information technology is the focus of attention and information is viewed objectively, as something outside the individual. One of the major roles of technology is to make that information accessible, or to bring it into awareness. Technology also plays a vital role in allowing the information user to stay informed and to manipulate information that has been located.

In this sense the relation between people and information may be described in terms of depending upon technology to enhance access to information. For some people this is achieved; for others information technology forms a barrier to information access. Accessing information in this category is seen as random scanning of the information environment—a 'just in case', rather than a need driven approach.

Within this category varying orientations to information technology give rise to two subcategories:

- Information literacy is seen as using information technology effectively: *an achievable goal* (Subcategory A

- Information literacy is seen as using information technology effectively: *an unachievable goal* (Subcategory B

The structure of awareness

The importance of information technology is the *distinguishing feature* of the conception. This is because the lack of use of information technology signifies ineffectiveness or information illiteracy. Therefore, both the focal element in the structure of awareness and the meaning structure are centred on information technology. People's ability to retrieve information and communicate using technology are key benefits; these are therefore represented in the next level of awareness under the label of 'information scanning'. Information use is in the periphery of awareness because the way in which information is used is not a primary concern, rather it is the potential of technology for enhancing information access and communication which is seen as important. These elements will be analysed in more detail in the descriptions of the two subcategories. Although none of the participants explicitly discuss their view of information, the emphasis on information scanning in this category reveals the objective, external view of information itself.

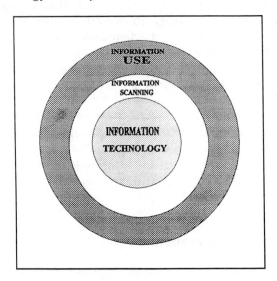

Figure 6.3   The structure of awareness as experienced in the information technology conception

The meaning structure

The various elements of the category described so far form part of the meaning structure. The meaning structure is a way of capturing, in linguistic form, the essential meaning of the conception. In this category it is:

Using information technology is essential for information awareness

Information awareness is the outcome of the experience. This meaning structure is also central to both the subcategories. In each one, however, there are additions to the meaning component which lend distinctiveness. The meaning structure of the first subcategory is:

Using information technology is essential for information awareness: this is achievable within a community of users.

The meaning structure of the second subcategory is:

Keeping up with information technology is essential to information literacy; this is the responsibility of individuals, therefore information literacy is an impossible goal.

Information literacy is seen as using information technology effectively: an achievable goal. (Subcategory A)

Information literacy in this subcategory means being comfortable with technology and being able to keep up with new developments rather than be distressed by them. Successfully using information technology. however, is seen as a socially shared responsibility, dispersed within a community of users, rather than the responsibility of any one individual. This way of conceiving of information literacy is described by participants as part of their own experience or someone else's. In the following extract the interviewee is describing her ideal information literate person, a view which differs substantially from her own experience. The importance of being comfortable with using information technology, and the desire to randomly seek information, are both highlighted. It is important to note in this extract that it is not communication which is considered to be the core of information literacy, but rather information technology which forms a particular medium for communication:

> Researcher: Describe your picture of a competent information user.
> Interviewee: Well, it's anyone but me. It would be someone who could come in and switch on to the world over there *(waving at the PC in the room)* and really engage in wonderful trans-Atlantic conversations... It would be someone who thought they'd go down for half an hour to the library bottom floor and just play around with the indexes *(CDRoms),* see what they could find. It would be someone who used all kinds of modem things... (Int. 4, p.6, Staff Developer, Female)

Another interviewee describes her view of information literacy also in terms of using computer technology. Needless to say this is only one of her views of information literacy. Her statements are powerful because she has been trying to explore her own views of what constitutes information literacy. She has just been describing someone who is heavily involved in research in the humanities and social sciences, but who does not use computers:

> in terms of information literacy he is hopeless. He is not very comfortable with electronic means of communication....I tend to see an information literate person as someone who has competency in computers and networking and those sorts of skills... (Int. 10, pp.6-7, Librarian, Female)

A third description of an information literate person, in this case also of someone known to the interviewee, focuses on the importance of using electronic tools and constantly seeking new information; a description which also reflects the view of information as objective and external. The information scanning in this case is conducted using world wide web browsers such as Mosiac or Netscape. It is not the information sources, but the commitment to scanning which is the emphasis of this comment:

> She is a person who is keeping up to date with her field academically, and is actively using information sources. She is a person who is actively out there spending time above and beyond the call of duty...seeking interesting new sources of information. (Int. 14, p.9, Librarian, Male)

The fundamental importance of information technology is bluntly described by one leader of a research team:

> These days there is a standard set of electronic tools (within the technical university sector anyway) that everyone (all competent people) uses to a greater or lesser extent. (Email 1, Researcher, Male)

He also describes, as part of his own experience, browsing or scanning for information 'just in case'. His description illustrates the difference between searching for specific resources and what I am here labelling as *random scanning*:

> Periodically I run CDRom searches of a few relevant databases. But mostly these are looking for something specific. At these times I generally throw in a few general searches anyway just to see. Sometimes I just browse the Internet using the package Mosaic which can now browse and search www and gopher sites and then retrieve files using ftp. Often I come across interesting information and can keep up with the developments. (Email 1, Researcher, Male)

This same researcher provides a clue to how it is that effective use of information technology is possible. It seems that thinking about information literacy as using information technology, and being able to do so successfully, means recognising that this is not a solitary experience. Keeping up with information technology involves being part of a community, each member of which assists others with the use of technology:

> It is hard in isolation. You need people to help. Then everyone becomes expert in slightly different aspects and is available to help and teach the others.(Email 1, Researcher, Male)

For those who focus on information technology, the world is seen as very different, and that difference is mainly noticed in terms of electronic communication. The ability to communicate with and receive information from colleagues all over the world results in being part of a global network:

> I've moved into a very different world, a world of networks and all of that information. (Int 8, p.7. Librarian, Female)

Information literacy is seen as using information technology: <u>an unachievable goal</u> (Subcategory B)

In this subcategory information literacy in seen as something which is not achievable, it is described by participants as being constantly beyond their grasp. As they see it, they are constantly working at keeping up with the changes in information technology which are required for effective access to information. Information technology remains the focal element of the conception, but it is seen as a barrier to achieving information literacy. This conception is represented by statements, such as like the following, which attend to the elusiveness of the phenomenon:

> I'm assuming that information literacy is out there.... information literacy is out there, you can't really touch it because the minute you think you have it, it's developed again and it's escaping your grasp at every turn. (Int. 2, p.1, Learning Adviser, Male)

This interviewee has been talking about helping overseas students attain information literacy. The evidence for a particular view of technology being responsible for this view of information literacy comes from his comments about students' ability to use computers immediately prior:

> ..the most that they've ever done (with computers) is some very basic word processing and they consider themselves to be quite information literate. (Int. 2, p.1, Learning Adviser, Male)

Another interviewee likens information literacy to 'infinity'. He also attributes this characteristic to constant change in information technology, that is the 'mode of delivery'. Interestingly, for him, this movement also results from change in the subject or information user:

> So information literacy for me, is a process. It's not something you achieve; it's like infinity. You're approaching it but you never quite get there. You can never say, 'I am now information literate...because information is always changing, its modes of delivery are always changing. You as an individual are always changing, so you must always be moving. (Int. 14, p.3, Librarian, Male)

The idea of change is a recurring one in this view, appearing in many of the fragments of conversation which illustrate it, for example:

> ...the nature of information literacy is that it is developmental. It is constantly changing. (Int. 2, p.1, Learning Adviser, Male)

This particular subcategory is probably the least formed in the data. Although it emerged in more than one interview it was difficult to probe. In the case of the interviewee who returned to it often, questions asking for further explanation led to an immediate slip into a different kind conception, expressing a different kind of experience.

The fragmentary nature of data is not uncommon, however, in phenomenographic research. Marton, Dall'Alba and Beaty (1993, p.285) comment that their data contain 'expressions which reflect only fragments of the complete conception.

In this case it may be possible to enhance our understanding of this subcategory by comparing it with its partner. Both have the same essential meaning structure, and both have information technology as the focal point of awareness. It is likely that information use, not mentioned at all in the few conversations illustrating this conception, is in the background of awareness. We can also infer, as there is no evidence to the contrary, that the perceived difficulties in keeping up with technology arise from a perceived need to independently master it. This would be the logical opposite of the notion that information technology is useable when its mastery is seen as a social, rather than an individual, responsibility.

Summary

To summarise, category one identifies a way of experiencing information literacy that is dependent upon the availability and useability of information technology. Information literate people, when viewed this way are those who scan the information environment to attain a high level of information awareness. It is possible to experience information literacy, according to this view if one is a member of a community which supports the use of technology (Subcategory A). Where the ability to use information technology rests with individuals, information literacy becomes an unachievable goal (Subcategory B). In the next category, the attention of the information user shifts from information technology to information sources.

Category two: the information sources conception

Information literacy is seen as finding information located in information sources.

In this category information sources are the focus of attention. As in the previous category, information is viewed as something outside the individual, contained within the sources. It is knowledge of information sources which makes it possible to retrieve the information which is contained within them. The sources may be in a variety of media, including electronic. In this category different orientations to the problem of information retrieval give rise to three subcategories. The relation between the information user and information can be described in terms of knowledge of information sources (Subcategory A), independent use of sources (Subcategory B), or the willingness to use an intermediary to access sources (Subcategory C). The three subcategories are:

- knowing information sources and their structure (Subcategory A);

- knowing information sources and using them independently (Subcategory B);

- knowing information sources and using them flexibly, either independently or via an intermediary (Subcategory C).

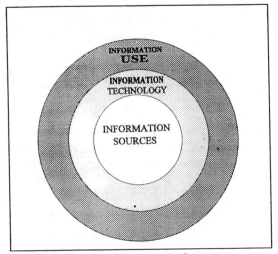

Figure 6.4   The structure of awareness as experienced in the information sources conception

The structure of awareness
The importance of information sources is the *distinguishing feature* of the conception. This leads to information finding being focal in the awareness structure, and an important element of the meaning structure. Information technology has varied emphases in the conception depending upon the particular subcategory being examined. Although *what* information is required is important, the way in which the information will be used is of little interest. *Information use* is therefore in the outer edge of awareness. This awareness structure is shared by each subcategory.

The meaning structure

The key elements of the conceptions described so far form part of the meaning structure of this category

Knowing 'what' is required + knowledge of information sources = successful information retrieval

The emphasis on knowing *what* is required is a distinctive part of the character of this experience. It is revealed through the use of phrases such as 'knowing what you want' or 'knowing what they want'. This need to know what is required is very different from the information scanning, 'just in case' approach which is part of the character of the information technology conception.

The meaning structure of the first subcategory is:

Knowing 'what' is required + knowledge of information sources = successful information retrieval

The meaning structure of the second subcategory is:

Knowing 'what' is required + knowledge of information sources + independent use = successful information retrieval

The meaning structure of the third subcategory is:

knowing 'what' is required + knowledge of information sources + locating independently or via an intermediary = successful information retrieval

Information literacy is seen as the ability to find information *due to knowing information sources and their structure* . (Subcategory A)

In this subcategory, knowledge of information sources is seen as characterising the experience of information literacy. The personal knowledge of sources, their content and structure are emphasised, with such knowledge making it possible to retrieve specific information required. Information literacy requires a knowledge of available resources; these may or may not include electronic sources, but usually do include library resources. The sources may also be people, that is human sources. This kind of experience of information literacy is described by an academic who is reflecting on the importance of being able to find information when preparing for lectures:

> What can I recall that I might have seen which might be interesting?...you get to know the materials that are available and the sources and the journals in which that material will be. (Int. 6, p.1, Lecturer, Male)

His emphasis on knowledge of sources was confirmed when, shortly after making the above comments, I asked him what was involved in being an effective user:

> Well, it was identifying the sources of information of course, and mostly the sources of information I use are not electronic sources...its simply getting to know the resources, getting to know the library that you've got at hand...so that you can go instantly to the library and in many cases, without ever having to go to the catalogue you can identify what you need. (Int. 6, p.2, Lecturer, Male)

Knowing what sources may be found where, includes being familiar with the holdings of libraries in other institutions. Various catalogues are searched based on knowing what kind of materials would be held in the collections:

> I do searches of (electronic library catalogues) simply because I know that a particular institution has certain specialities or special interests,... for example I might go to Monash University Library for ethnic music. (Int. 6, p.2, Lecturer, Male)'

This experience of information literacy was also described by librarians in the group. The need to know, or become familiar with, what is available is seen as important for both librarians and academic staff in being effective information users:

> When you come into a new library, you really don't know what's there, and you have to spend a bit of time to become familiar with it. (Int. 7, p.2, Librarian, Female)

Strategies are implemented for enhancing this type of knowledge, for example the compilation of lists of subject resources for circulation amongst clients and for raising the awareness of library staff.

The point that information technology has varying status in this conception is brought home by this interviewee's comment that it is knowledge of sources, rather than ownership of a personal computer that makes for information literacy:

> ...everyone thinks that the answer to being information literate is to have a computer on your desk, and then you'll all of a sudden become it. I would rather see them looking at what we already have here (in the library).. .(Int 7, p.2, Librarian, Female)

Knowledge of sources includes an understanding of types of sources, for example journal articles, books, conference papers. Such knowledge enables the information user to interpret bibliographic citations in order to successfully retrieve information:

> some of them don't even know how to interpret a reading list...in order to do that they have to recognise a journal article or a book or whatever it is...(Int. 7, p.2, Librarian, Female)

Knowledge of sources may be important for personal use, as in the case of the academic earlier, or in order to assist clients:

> I really do have a lot of knowledge that allows me to access information I need and the information others need(Written Transcript B2, Librarian, Female)

Another librarian describing her experience of using information this way, stresses the importance of maintaining her knowledge of sources in order to be able to refer patrons to them:

> I'm conscious all the time of trying to keep up, just so that I'm not caught letting a student down. (Int 10, p.3, Librarian, Female)

The inclusion of knowledge of human sources of information in this category is justified by participants who include these sources in their discussions. These sources were noted as important by both librarians and academics. In the following quotation a librarian points to the importance of the human network of sources.

She has just been asked to describe her picture of an information literate person:

> someone who knows what they want... it's the identification and the knowing who could put them in touch with things that is a mark of competence. (Int. 10, p.5, Librarian, Female)

Another participant's description of using what he calls 'the colleague system' is also a clear example of a focus on knowing human sources of information. For this lecturer, asking colleagues for information is a substitute to accessing print information sources. Knowing the human source is thus a direct parallel of knowing the print or electronic source. What is critical is knowing whom to ask:

> If I can think quickly of a colleague who's done that or who knows someone else, that's the way I think engineers work. (Int. 13, p. 5, Academic, Male)

This interviewee's focus on knowledge of human sources is illustrated when he requests that we play a game during the interview. I was asked to name a technical topic to demonstrate that he could nominate the appropriate information source:

> We'll just play a little game for a sec; if you tell me a technical topic, I'll tell you who I would ring up. (Int. 13, p. 5, Academic, Male)

Information literacy is seen as the ability to find information _due to knowing information sources and using them independently_. (Subcategory B

This view of information literacy is similar to the one described in the previous subcategory, except that the information user must be able to independently use the relevant sources. Again, these sources may be print, electronic, human or may appear in some other media. Information technology is relevant to this subcategory only in that some sources maybe electronic. To put it another way, information technology is not the focus of the conception, it just happens to be the package through which some information must be accessed. The importance of being able to use the information source to access information, however, is pointed out as a critical element of information literacy by a number of participants. In the following examples the ability to use the source is specifically stated in addition to describing knowledge of sources:

> ...being an information literate person is not only knowing the sources of information but also being able to access the information sources. (Written transcript C8)

> ...Knowing what sources are available to find information when needed. How to use the sources. Recognising when more information is needed and what type of information. Being able to locate various sources of information (independently). (Written transcript C2)

> From a librarian's perspective...it is someone who is able to identify what they want and is able to locate and use it. (Written transcript B18, Librarian, Female)

As though to emphasise independently accessing information, one respondent writes:

> Effective information user—probably one that library staff have had little interaction with. (Written transcript B18, Librarian, Female

There is also experiential evidence in the transcripts to support respondents' reflective statements about information literacy. For example, one female describes her approach to dealing with an offer from a stockbroker to purchase her shares:

> ...to make an informed decision I realised I needed information. I identified the sources concerned...checked how many people had been selling ... and for how much etc. (Written transcript B17, Librarian, Female)

Support for describing information literacy in terms of knowing how to use sources also comes from participants who describe themselves as not being 'fully literate' on the basis of not knowing:

> I'm not fully literate because there are some areas which are too huge (Internet) to know how to access fully. (Written transcript B2, Librarian, Female)

> I was not information literate recently when I realised I did not know much about using the Internet ... I did not know the process of getting the information or how to use it once I had it. (Written transcript C10, Librarian, Female)

One of the benefits of being able to access information independently is that it speeds retrieval. It is worth noting here, that the view that independent access speeds retrieval is paralleled in the third subcategory by the view that using an intermediary for access speeds retrieval. In the following quote the interviewee describes information literacy as being able to 'get hold of' information rapidly:

> somebody to me who is information literate, would be much more at home in libraries and with the electronic technology, ...(it) probably takes me twice as long to get hold of (information) because I wonder who can help me. (Int. 16, p.6, Staff Developer, Female)

Another interviewee describes his view of an information literate person. He supports his description with an explanation of his own need to attend regular workshops to maintain his own skills in information location:

> An effective information user...(is) an effective information finder...up to date with where to find information in the first place and able to go and find it. (Int. 11, p. 5, Learning Adviser, Male)

In this view the need to be able to use information sources independently is also naturally a feature of learning to be an information literate person. Students are described as having to know about useful sources and needing to be able to search them:

> ...the process has been understanding their topic,...being able to know where the resources are that they need,... and its not much use saying to them this database is full of wonderful stuff if they don't know how to search. (Int. 10, p.4, Librarian, Female)

Independence in using information retrieval tools, from this perspective, is also considered a characteristic of an information literate library clientele. One librarian describes the characteristics she would like to see in her clients:

> I would like them to be able to use a catalogue efficiently... I'd be delighted if they could just not come to the desk and ask us to look it up in the catalogue. (Int. 7, p.9, Librarian, Female)

This interviewee has expressed the same view earlier in her interview, when describing her picture of an information literate person:

> ...someone who is prepared to try themselves to find information rather than always come and ask you to do it for them. (Int. 7, p.6, Librarian, Female)

One result of information literacy from this perspective, is a reduced need to ask for help:

> ...a lot of information literate people don't need to go to the reference desk and ask, because they know where to go themselves, and I guess that is the ultimate aim.(Int. 7, p.5, Librarian, Female)

Information literacy is seen as the ability to find information due to knowing information sources and using them flexibly, either independently or via an intermediary. (Subcategory C)

In this subcategory it is the adoption of a flexible approach to information retrieval, either doing so independently or asking for help, that differentiates it from the other two. Knowing what is required is still an important component of the experience, and so is knowledge of potential sources, but the information may be obtained either by the person requiring it, or by a third party. The information user who obtains information via a third party is considered information literate. This is in contrast with the character of the second subcategory in which it is only independence which indicates effectiveness. In this subcategory, however, the willingness to use a third party is considered an essential feature of information literacy.

One lecturer, discussing the importance of being able to access information for the preparation of new units and research, stresses the need to use other people for assistance. Although she sees the effective information user as needing to identify what information is required, she does not see that person as needing to be capable of independently locating the information. The effective information user can obtain support from appropriate personnel:

> I don't think that people have time to sit down and learn every new package that comes out, and I think that you should be able to use the personnel that have that experience. (For example) I got quite a lot of help from our librarian in terms of looking for new books in the field...when you try to do that yourself you could probably spend a day trying to do that yourself for instance. (Int.1, p. 5, Academic, Female)

Shortly after she made this response I asked this interviewee what it meant to use information effectively. She restates the importance of being able to use the expertise of others:

> It meant... getting people to help you in terms of finding where the resources were, and there were quite a lot of library personnel involved in that. (Int. 1, p.6, Academic, Female)

Another interviewee expresses the need to have help available when using library resources:

> I've always asked one of the librarians to start me off and then work my way through it. That was in the days when I had more time to do that sort of thing. (Int. 4, p.11, Staff Developer, Female)

The combination of elements in this subcategory, *knowing what is required and being willing to use others* in the retrieval process, is illustrated by an academic describing the experience of writing an entry for a *Dictionary of biography*. He offers the illustration in response to a request to relate an anecdote about a time when he used information effectively:

> I hired a student to do some searches for me... I sent him off with some very specific resources to track down, to do some very specific kinds of searches...the important thing was having a kind of native intelligence in knowing what you're going to need and where it's likely to be, and what you're going to have to look for. (Int. 6, p, 5, Academic, Male)

The element of being able to rely on others is also expressed by librarians:

> An effective information user ... knows what they want if not how to get it, and is not afraid to ask to find an answer- will ask people who do know. (Written transcript B3, Librarian, Female)

> I see a competent information user as someone who knows what they want, can identify what they want, knows where to get it,...then they either have the skills to get it themselves or they've got someone on hand who can get it for them. (Int. 10, p. 9, Librarian, Female)

Independence in accessing information is clearly not a necessary component of this subcategory:

> Being information literate is to know when the need for information exists, and to be able to do something about it—whether it be approaching someone else about where to find information or locating it yourself. (Written transcript C10)

Summary

To summarise, in category two information literacy is experienced in terms of knowledge of sources of information and an ability to access these independently or via an intermediary. The sources may be human sources. It is different orientations to the problem of information retrieval which produce the subcategories. In the third category information processes become the focus of attention.

Category three : the information process conception

Information literacy is seen as executing a process

In this category information processes are the focus of attention. Information continues to be viewed objectively, as something outside the individual. Its usefulness, however, is shaped by the information problem that contextualises it. The subject-object relation is constituted in terms of the information process through which the user solves the problem. The information process, when executed, makes information accessible to the user.

The structure of awareness

The importance of information processes is the *distinguishing feature* of this conception. For this reason, both the focal element in the structure of awareness for the conception and the meaning structure for the conception are centred on information processes. Information processes are those strategies implemented by information users confronting a novel situation in which they experience a lack of knowledge (or information). As the way in which the information is to be used is very much a consideration in this experience, information use forms the next level of awareness.

Information use is not the primary consideration because the required information must be obtained before it can be used; however the acquisition of information is part of the overall process of problem solving or decision making experienced. Information technology is not an important feature of participants' descriptions of this experience. It is therefore located in the outer field of awareness (See Figure 6.5)

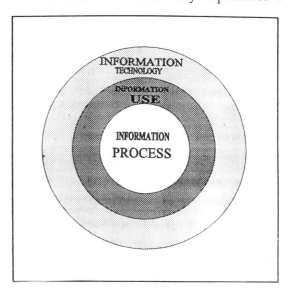

Figure 6.5   The structure of awareness as experienced in the information process conception

The meaning structure

This way of conceiving of information literacy can be expressed in more detail as follows: information literacy is seen as the ability to confront novel situations, and to deal with those situations on the basis of being equipped with knowledge of a process for finding and using the necessary information. The precise nature of the process, however, varies from person to person. In this category, therefore, the meaning structure is:

Knowledge gap or novel situation—implement process- action, solution or decision.

Effective action, problem solving or decision making is the outcome of the experience. The three elements of the process: the knowledge gap, implementing the process, and the outcome of the experience are examined in detail below.

The knowledge gap

The following description of an effective information user illustrates this way of conceiving of information literacy. Early in the description we are presented with the notion of a *novel problem* being encountered, and an associated *knowledge gap*:

> ...I think that most staff would be effective information users in that any of us would be able to tackle a new problem which we've had no past knowledge of, and be able to chase it up and follow it through. For example, a colleague was asked to provide some advice about (an engineering structure). He'd never looked at that type of structure before in his life but he was able to chase it up and find out the structural implications of what was going on and discuss it with the rest of us. (Int. 5, p. 6, Academic, Male)

The element of *no past knowledge*, which here means no, or limited, personal knowledge of the problem at hand, is the starting point of the experience. The information user experiences a problem which is recognised as an information problem. Various processes are then implemented to achieve the desired result.

Implementing the process

The nature of the process may include knowledge of information sources as described in category two; this is however a relatively minor part of the experience. Different people describe the process differently, but typically it includes several elements, representing a series of steps or stages in the procedure. Here the process is likened to problem solving techniques:

> The first thing has to be to define what the problem area is... so an effective information user will be able to narrow down the problem. Having narrowed down the problem that would lead to, or would provide an indication that there needs to be more information gathered in certain areas around that problem; so the effective information user would be able to identify where the additional information is needed or where the gaps are. I guess a small but vital part of it is to be able to gather that information from whatever sources are available and to analyse it; and then based on that make a decision or solve the problem or whatever... It's almost like basic problem solving techniques. (Int. 5, p. 10, Academic, Male)

A similar process is described by a lecturer who has recently completed a literature review for her doctoral thesis. She summarises the process as involving:

> 1) location of data, 2) interpretation of data, 3) acting on the data, in this case by allowing it to produce an alternative conceptual viewpoint. (Written transcript A2, Lecturer, Female)

The problem to which the process applies may come from personal as well as academic life. One respondent who details a similar process provides the following example for clarification:

> I wonder what it would cost to put an awning over the window? Information needed:
> 1) who supplies awnings?
> 2) what is their phone number?
> 3) how much does an awning x X y cost?
> 4) it costs $z-; an evaluation is now made to decide
> 5) OK lets buy it—or no, this is too expensive.(Written transcript B2, Librarian, Female)

For one respondent at least the process is not as straightforward as it appears in the descriptions. Having outlined the process of location, analysis and action, he goes on to describe it as a 'creative art' (Int. 5, p.10). The process is implemented differently by different individuals in different contexts.

In this way of experiencing information literacy, the 'problem to be solved' may itself be the identification of appropriate information resources. This sounds similar to the previous category (the Information Finding conception). In that category, however, information finding relies upon knowledge of sources, whereas in this category the identification of sources relies upon knowledge of process. A reference librarian who describes her experience of finding information based on the execution of a process, rather than on knowing specific sources, provides an illustration. This respondent has just described an occasion on which she located an international treaty using the Internet for a client, because that treaty was not available in the library. She is able to do so, even though she is not familiar with legal resources or the discipline of law, because of her ability to execute certain processes:

> Even though I was not familiar with the subject or content of the request I was able to use processes associated with the location of this type of resource. This is something that happens quite often. I am not using my knowledge of content but my knowledge of process to find information. (Written transcript B16, Librarian, Female)

This respondent provides a typical example of the need to look beyond words used to the meaning expressed, by taking into account previous and subsequent statements made. In an earlier sentence she used the phrase: 'I used my knowledge of information sources to look up the treaty'. A superficial treatment of the data would have led to this statement being included in the previous category dealing with information finding and knowledge of sources. The passage as a whole indicates that her phrase 'knowledge of sources' should be interpreted as 'knowledge of process'

This is confirmed by the respondent when she disclaims knowledge of law and legal resources. She further generalises: 'if you can apply a process of finding information it is very effective for use in any discipline'.

The outcome of the experience

The descriptions of the 'processes' above all include elements of being able to resolve an initial problem. There is a strong implication, for example, that the academic asked to provide advice about an engineering structure was able to do so. Similarly the female academic writing a literature review was able to develop an alternative conceptual viewpoint, the purchaser of awnings was able to decide whether to buy the product or not, and the reference librarian was able to meet her client's information need. These 'endpoints' of being able to do something practical in consequence of the process appear to be fundamental parts of the character of the conception.

Summary

To summarise, in category three information literacy is experienced in terms of the ability to implement information processes. Information literate people are seen as those who can recognise a need for 'information', and who can use the information they access to meet the original need. This need is usually stated in terms of problem solving or decision making. Although there are no subcategories here, there is variation amongst individuals in terms of how the process is experienced. The next category is the last of the group of four which share an objective view of information. Like the third category it is neither information technology, nor information use which is focal in awareness, but an element idiosyncratic to the category, that is information control.

Category four : the information control conception

Information literacy is seen as controlling information.

In this category information control is the focus of attention. Information itself continues to be viewed objectively, as something outside the individual. The information to be brought within the information user's controlling influence may appear in any form: journal article, electronic mail message, etc. The subject object relation is constituted in terms of specific strategies for establishing control. There are three specific tools which are seen as useful for controlling information, leading to three distinct subcategories:

- Information literacy is seen as controlling information *using filing cabinets* (Subcategory A).

- Information literacy is seen as controlling information *using the human brain* (Subcategory B).

- Information literacy is seen as controlling information *using electronic databases* (Subcategory C).

In each subcategory the character of the relation varies as follows:

- Subcategory A: control of information is established using filing cabinets

- Subcategory B: control of information is established using the brain or memory via various forms of links and associations

- Subcategory C: control of information is established using computers to allow storage and retrieval

The structure of awareness

The importance of information control is the *distinguishing feature* of this conception. For this reason, both the focal element in the structure of awareness, and the meaning structure for the conception are centred on information organisation. Information organisation, in this context, is about storing information, usually documents, in a fashion which ensures easy retrieval. All the information is selected on the basis of its likely value for future use in research or teaching, for example. In this sense

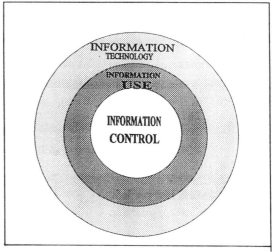

Figure 6.6   The structure of awareness as experienced in the information control conception

information is again seen as objective, but is selected within a particular context. Use of information, however, is not the primary concern of this conception, the concern is rather bringing it under the controlling influence of the user. Information use, therefore, forms the second level of awareness. As with category three, information technology is not a critical feature of participants' descriptions of this experience. Although used by many of the participants, it is not an essential part of the character of the experience; technology is therefore located in the outer field of awareness.

The meaning structure

In this category the meaning structure is:

> *Recognising/obtaining useful information—storing/organising the information—being able to retrieve and use the information when required.*

Because each element of the meaning structure is significant in this category, the full character of the experience comes from the presence of all three elements. The organising element is the one which makes descriptions belonging to this category easily recognisable. The meaning structure of the various subcategories include some details about the medium used for organisation. This is because the interviewees focus on the various media as contrasting elements. In Subcategory A the meaning structure is:

> *Recognising useful information—storing/organising the information using filing cabinets being able to retrieve and use the information when required*

In Subcategory B it is:

> *Recognising useful information—storing/organising the information using the brain - being able to retrieve and use the information when required.*

133

In the Subcategory C it is:

Recognising useful information—storing/organising the information using electronic databases—being able to retrieve and use the information when required.

Information literacy is seen as controlling information _using filing cabinets_. (Subcategory A)

In this conception the trusty filing cabinet is seen as a tool for storing and controlling information for retrieval. Control, as in the other subcategories, is imposed by the information user. The specific ways in which information is organised in this subcategory may be related to the structure of research interests. Projects being undertaken influence the structure of organisation. In this way links are created between items of information and particular aspects of the project. This is illustrated by an interviewee's description of how she decides where to store a document

> it relates to x or something so I stick it in the file and it's there if I need it. (Int. 4, p.5, Staff Developer, Female)

The same interviewee describes her own experience of information literacy by focusing on the need to manage vast quantities of information related to daily work routines and research projects. She makes these comments in response to a request to describe a time when she was an effective information user:

> I daresay it would be in the project when we had massive amounts of stuff to process and I consider we did that very effectively...I thought: 'we need to get a piece of information from (organisation).' I rang them up and I said please send me that report which they did. I read it...put it in the right file, then when the chapter was being written, I took it out of the file and used it.(Int. 4, p.6, Staff Developer, Female)

This respondent's decision to extract and use information from the report in question was closely related to the structuring of her own report. It was imperative that her material be organised to reflect that structure.

Another interviewee describes the same kind of experience of effective information use in relation to collecting, storing and retrieving journal articles. The feature of recognising what is relevant is present as well as deciding to store it, then being able to retrieve it. As with the previous interviewee, there is no perceived need to recall the information from memory, it simply gets stored in an appropriate place:

> I scan the journals every week...if I see an article that looks like it will be of interest to me, I'll...read the abstract. If it's still of interest I'll photocopy it.... having photocopied it, I don't feel any obligation to read it through. I tend to bring it back and file it in my system (of filing cabinets) here. (Int. 12, p.2 Staff Developer, Male

Importantly, the interviewee is able to retrieve the material he has gathered when it is required:

> ...when there's someone who comes in and wants something on a particular topic...I've got a file there with articles relevant to it.(Int. 12, p.2 Staff Developer, Male)

One reason for using filing cabinets is that the interviewee does not wish to use his or her brain in this way: 'there's only so much the brain can absorb'. (Int. 4, p.6, Staff Developer, Female).

Information literacy is seen as controlling information <u>using the human brain</u> (Subcategory B)

At the heart of this conception lies the human brain as a vital tool for storing and controlling information for retrieval. This particular way of conceiving of information literacy tends to be described by participants as part of the experience of colleagues, rather than part of their own experience. One respondent who described her own experience in terms of storing information in filing cabinets, describes a colleague as using his brain where she would depend on the structure of her files. She makes this reply after a request to describe someone she sees as information literate

> What makes him competent is what he's got in his ruddy head. He *knows*. He's seen something there, 1968 somebody said that, and he *knows*, and he knows where to go and get it. (Int. 4, p.9, Staff Developer, Female)

After describing an episode in which such competence is demonstrated, this interviewee goes on to develop the importance of being able to organise and retrieve information using the brain as a tool. In doing so she contrasts this strategy with her own approach of using filing cabinets:

> Well,...somehow he has the sort of brain that he can use as a filing cabinet which I can't do. I use my filing cabinet as my brain. His things are filed in his brain and he knows exactly where to get them...it's a reverse process. (Int. 4, p.9 10, Staff Developer, Female)

This subcategory differs from the first, because its focus is different. The focus is on using the brain, or memory, rather than the filing cabinet for organising and storing information. It is also seen, by respondents, as a qualitatively different experience:

> I can manage (my pieces of paper) and access them in a fashion; I can't actually pull them out of here! (pointing to her head)...that's something I just cannot do. (Int. 4, p.10, Staff Developer, Female)

Another interviewee describes a colleague as an effective information user because of that person's ability to remember, that is store, information about people:

> ...one of the reasons she is an effective information user is that.... she seems to be able to remember people, to remember what they are doing, to have a life story attached to each person she ever meets. (Int. 9, p.4, Staff Developer, Female)

She goes on to describe the ability to retrieve information from the memory as being made possible though a series of mental associations or links. It is important to remember here that these links are part of the conception of the interviewee, they represent the interviewee's way of conceiving of information literacy, not the view of the colleague she is describing:

...it's because she's linking the information to a person, and that helps somehow to access the information. So that when a topic comes up, she not only has in a sense one reference point, she has two, and they are linked, so that she is able to retrieve that information. (Int. 9, p.4, Staff Developer, Female)

She then provides an example of a situation in which the information is retrieved. This example is intended to provide some evidence for the linking of 'life stories' to individuals described previously:

...a number of times when things come up she'll say 'so and so would be a good source of information on that', or' you could go and ask so and so because that person did such and such'. (Int. 9, p.4, Staff Developer, Female)

This element of creating links was also evident in the 'filing cabinet' subcategory. Although the interviewees describing the database subcategory do not explicitly mention it, databases are usually constructed with the deliberate intention of linking records through shared elements such as authors, titles and subject headings.

Information literacy is seen as controlling information <u>using electronic databases</u> (Subcategory C)

In this subcategory the tool for storing and controlling information for retrieval is neither the filing cabinet, nor the brain, but database software. Filing cabinets and memory are both considered inappropriate strategies for information control by participants who conceive of information literacy this way. 'Filing cabinet' style organisation is described as 'dead hole ish' (Int. 14, p.1, Librarian, Male); and another participant confesses to not knowing what information he has access to, even on his own shelves (Int. 13, p.1, Academic, Male). Evidently this academic does not see himself as using his brain as a medium for information control!

One illustration of this experience comes from an academic who describes his need to select and control information belonging to a particular area of professional interest:

When I was a lecturer I had the need to collate material (about x) from time to time... I found the best way to get all the material together was to prepare this database... we inputted all the magazines and conference proceedings up to a certain point in time, and then we kept it up to date since then. (Int. 13, pp.6 7, Academic, Male

This database, apart from being distributed all over the world, is also of value to its creator, making it possible for him to retrieve material when required:

I've had people ring me from all over Australia wanting information on something... I use it privately for preparation of lectures. (Int. 13, p.7, Academic, Male)

Conceiving of information as establishing control electronically is expressed by another respondent. The interviewee, a librarian, describes his view of information literacy by drawing on his own experience and that of his students.

Like one of the other interviewees, he depends on abstracts rather than reading whole documents:

> ...what I'm getting in many cases is the abstract of the information. I'm not finding the time to chase up the ...full article...the abstract is fine. That gives me the information I need to know... (Int. 14, p. 1, Librarian, Male)

In relation to students, they are described as using technology to store relevant information. Information is 'controlled' in the sense that available software allows students to search the data entered based on selected keywords. This allows the students to retrieve information they did not know they had:

> They wouldn't be queuing up for the photocopier. They would be able to scan relevant parts of i t (the document) straight into their computer. They would analyse it with their software, and they would be able to keyword search. Now where was that reference about such and such? It's in these three articles. Well, I didn't know it was in that article! (Int. 14, p.11, Librarian, Male)

In relation to himself, the interviewee describes his dependence on the databases created by others for maintaining control, rather that producing his own. This quote also contains an explicit reference to the 'external' nature of information noted in this category:

> ...I'm not the proud owner of Endnote or Procite or some nice little package that I can put all this information into and then readily retrieve it myself. In a sense I don't need to do that because I perceive that the information is still out there and I can always retrieve it, and I try to promote the same notion to students and staff when they're using a database. (Int. 14, p. 11, Librarian, Male)

Summary

To summarise, in category four information literacy is experienced as controlling information. Information literate people are seen as those who can use various media to bring information within their sphere of influence, so that they can retrieve and manipulate it when necessary. Information continues to be regarded as external to the user although it may be brought within organisational boundaries for use within specific projects. The next category to be described, category five, the knowledge construction conception, is the first of a triad of categories that are somewhat different from the first four. Information is no longer viewed objectively in these categories. Emphasis is placed on the nature and role of personal knowledge bases in information literacy, and information use becomes focal in the structure of awareness.

Category five: the knowledge construction conception

Information literacy is seen as building up a personal knowledge base in a n e w area of interest.

In this and subsequent categories, information use becomes the focus of attention. In previous categories, information has been seen as external to the individual, and apparently as having a 'constant' or 'objective' character. Information, in this category, becomes an object of reflection and it appears to each individual user in a unique way. Information takes on a 'fluid' or 'subjective' character. As an outcome of the experience, 'information' is internalised, it becomes a part of the user; it is no longer external. We can say that the relation between the user and information is constituted in terms of meaning construction and interpretation. Such meaning construction requires active participation on the part of both elements of the subject object relation. The information user is involved in evaluation and analysis, whilst the information presents itself uniquely to the user.

Information, therefore, is used in this category for knowledge construction or developing a knowledge base. The idea of a knowledge base in this category goes beyond that of a store of information; it involves the adoption of personal perspectives. This is achieved through critical analysis of what is read. Most importantly, the knowledge base of the discipline is not changed or added to in any way.

The structure of awareness

Critical information use, for the purpose of constructing a personal knowledge base is the distinguishing feature of this conception.
Knowledge base is a term used by respondents to describe the intent of their information seeking, for example: '...building up a knowledge base in the field' (Int. 4, p.2, Staff Developer, Female).
Critical analysis, as an

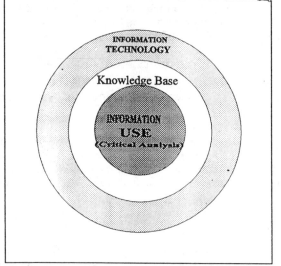

Figure 6.7 The structure of awareness as experienced in the knowledge construction conception

important feature in the process of knowledge construction, is an essential part of the character of this conception. The ability to weigh and analyse the relative worth of information is described repeatedly by participants. Information technology is in the margin of this experience, because for these respondents technology is not essential; it is used by some, while for others it can be a barrier.

The meaning structure

Although the structure of awareness is similar for this and the remaining categories, their meaning structures are very different. This is why they have been described as separate categories. In this category the meaning structure brings together information seeking and critical analysis, with meaning construction or the building up of a knowledge base as the outcome:

Information seeking + critical analysis = personal knowledge base.

Information seeking, in this category, does not refer to conventional information retrieval methods, certainly 'knowledge of sources', such as appear in the information finding category is not important. The approach described by respondents, as will be seen further on, is serendipitous. The knowledge base, which is the outcome of this category, becomes a prerequisite for categories six and seven.

Those respondents who conceive of, or experience, information literacy in this way, describe the experience in detail. It will be seen from what follows that they are concerned with adopting a *particular orientation* towards what they are learning about. Another feature common to these experiences is that the individuals are highly selective about the information with which they choose to work. Although the respondents describe different sources of information, precisely where the information comes from is irrelevant. What is important is that the information comes from an appropriate source (a feature consistent with the emphasis on evaluation in the category). Information may come from Internet discussion groups, reading documents, listening to the radio, talking to people in a public place, or using electronic databases. Three critical elements of the conception: building the knowledge base, critical analysis and challenges presented by information technology are analysed below.

Building the knowledge base

The most detailed description of building the knowledge base comes from a respondent talking about the use of printed material. She describes her experience as a 'selection process'. It is an experience with which many scholars are familiar, that of starting with known items of interest and tracing further sources of interest through references:

> ...well I read a book because I'm interested in the topic and the book might have a very useful quote from another author. I then turn to the back of the book and find the reference and then I go to the library catalogue and look it up, order it, get it off the shelf, read it, in turn, that will refer me on to yet another bibliography at the back of another book and so on and so on. (Int. 4, p.2, Staff Developer, Female)

Secondary, or tertiary sources of information, such as indexes and abstracts are only used towards the end of the process if the respondent considers it necessary:

> ...at the end of that process, if I find I still have holes in the information that I've gathered and that I need to go further, then is when I would consult the indexes that would tell me all the other things that are available and which might be of interest, and I'd access which ones of those I thought would be of use. (Int. 4, p.2, Staff Developer, Female)

This process described is anything but mechanical. It depends upon the ability to analyse critically material read. This leads to the adoption of personal perspectives which influence further development of the work being undertaken:

> ...What's happening in the process is that I'm able to say, 'oh, well he says that about it because of the way he's approaching the subject or because of his previous experience or his expertise in that particular area of the field. She's approaching it from here. Where do I stand in relation to those two? I prefer that way of looking at it'. O.K. So I'll follow some of that person's references rather than, I know the sort of vibes or prejudice or whatever this person is going to bring to it,

and I'm not really interested in that, so I will build up......It's a fairly selective way of doing it but at the same time you remain aware of both prongs of the fork if you like... (Int.4, p. 2, Staff Developer, Female)

This need to take a position in relation to what others are saying is also pointed out by other interviewees. The following interviewee has been using the 'information stream' metaphor to describe becoming conversant with an area of interest:

...I see effectiveness as being able to get in and out of the stream and getting in is the most important issue, but when you're in, being able to get back out, if only to adopt a, not a disinterested perspective, but in fact to be able to take a position... (Int. 12, p.3, Staff Developer, Male)

Interacting with people is another significant way of building a knowledge base. Interacting with people also requires the person gathering information to be very clear about his or her purpose, and to have the ability to select according to those purposes. The ability to see the relevance of information may be a consequence of a link being made by other people. For this to happen the information user must communicate his or her professional interests or research projects. Making this communication is a conscious act on the part of the effective information user:

...when I do (tell people about what I'm doing), then I find that other people try to relate what I'm doing to what they're doing; and this helps me see a relationship I might not have seen before. (Int. 9, p. 1, Staff Developer, Female)

Just as when working with printed material some interaction is required between the reader and the content of the documents, so interaction is required between individuals:

It really is an interaction...if you don't give information you won't get any! (Int. 9, p. 1, Staff Developer, Female)

The importance of developing personal perspectives arises later in the interview:

...the potential is there for giving my view and then learning from other people what their views are; and, you know, that enables me to revise mine and maybe move in a different direction. (Int. 9, p. 7, Staff Developer, Female)

Interaction with people may also occur via electronic networks. A respondent needing to write a conference paper on how people use the Internet discovered that the most appropriate way to obtain the information required was to send out a query via mailing lists. She was able to use the replies, and continues to build her knowledge of the area by maintaining contact with the people with whom she established communication:

....these people now, contact me to say 'how's it going? and, you know, we write to each other. (Int 8, p.2, Librarian, Female)

Actual strategies for gathering information from which the knowledge base is constructed are dependent upon the user's approach to the task, or information style. The descriptions provided above indicate that individuals have different approaches to gathering information. One respondent explicitly reflects on this.

In doing so he contrasts what he calls the 'classical approach' to information gathering with his own. The classical approach he labels the 'salami technique'. His own is referred to as the 'cast the net approach':

> ...here's your topic, salami technique, you know, slice it up into little bits, do each little bit so that it's not overwhelming...all that sort of stuff...but my own personal style would be over reading, over gathering, but I'm not an instrumental task oriented person, I'm a more intuitive, reflective type person. Maybe that information style suits me. ...I want to...flip around a bit...the 'cast the net and see what's out there' approach.. (Int. 14, p.5, Librarian, Male)

Critical analysis

The second distinctive feature of this category is the emphasis on a critical, analytical approach to information. This critical stance is qualitatively different from being able to identify information relevant to particular interests. The whole process of developing a knowledge base is dependent upon critical analysis and this is recognised by the interviewees:

> ... an information literate person must always be a critical information literate person...without that element of critical evaluation I don't think it's worth very much at all. (Int.4, p.12, Staff Developer, Female)

> ...to be an effective information user you have to be able to analyse the information... (Int. 5, p. 2, Academic, Male)

> ...I think it all boils down to the ability to look at that information critically and sift the wheat from the chaff. (Int. 5, p. 8, Academic, Male)

Several examples are provided by respondents which explain what they mean by critical analysis. One of the engineering academics explains critical analysis as *involving identifying gaps in knowledge, recognising conflicting schools of thought and assessing the reliability of research* . He provides the following response when asked what is meant by critical analysis, and later relates this to his own research activity as well as that of research students:

> ... I think there are a couple of areas that are important. .... to identify gaps in the current knowledge and searching through the information to find out where there is conflict between various groups of researchers or schools of thought or whatever it might be; and also searching through to see where there's just been a simple blunder which may appear through preparing results from different people. So I guess those three things are important there. It's not good enough just to read and say, yes, Smith and Jones said this, and Brown and Jackson said that and whatever. You have to be able to look at them and say, 'why did they say it, what's the basis on which they've made their observation and perhaps why is that different from what Smith and Jones have said?' (Int. 5, p. 3, Academic, Male)

An outcome of critical analysis identified by participants is the adoption of personal perspectives on the area of interest. Descriptions of the process leading to the adoption of personal perspectives shed further light on the meanings attributed to critical analysis. For example, participants describe it as a 'process of clarification' (Int. 2, p.8, Learning Adviser, Male) and 'researching your own thoughts' (Int. 9, p. 10, Staff Developer, Female).

Critical analysis is also described as evaluating the usefulness of information and presenting 'a cohesive discussion on which aspects are stronger than others'. This includes developing 'supporting arguments...rather than reproducing what they (students) consider to be the ultimate truth'. Specific strategies for critical analysis include flow charting, concept mapping and developing matrices (Int. 2, p.4, 6 7, Learning Adviser, Male).

Fourthly, respondents describe experiences of critical analysis when they discuss the importance of being able to assess the scholarly value of documents. This is discussed both in relation to conventional documents and electronic sources:

> ...I just needed the key works that would tell me what it was all about.. (Int. 4, p.4, Staff Developer, Female)

> ...one of the problems that people are finding with dealing with the network is: just how scholarly are those opinions...? (Int. 8, p.3, Librarian, Female)

Challenges presented by information technology

When information literacy is conceived of, or experienced in this way, information technology can pose some significant challenges. These challenges are likely to be in:

- the development of the knowledge base, or

- in determining the quality of information accessed

The development of the knowledge base Information technology poses problems in gathering information for those people who approach the development of their knowledge base using a 'selection process'. This process was described earlier in this category under the heading of building the knowledge base. The same respondent who described her use of print resources for arriving at an understanding of a new field also describes the impossibility of using this selection process with electronic sources. She considers that the volume of information, the quality of information, and the medium itself pose problems (Int. 4, p.4, Staff Developer, Female).

The medium is problematic because the 'blue striped paper' used for computer print outs 'hurts the eyes' (Int. 4, p.4, Staff Developer, Female). The volume of information generated is a problem because the 'acres of information' accessed make a *discard process* necessary rather than a *selection process*. This is a completely different way of approaching knowledge acquisition as well as being more time consuming: 'it takes more time to do the discard process than the selection process' (Int. 4, p.4, Staff Developer, Female). Finally, the quality of information in bibliographic databases is perceived as wanting. Decisions must be based on:

> ...the tiniest bit of information, maybe a paragraph on the printout, whereas if you're looking at it as a physical book, you can actually browse and see and think, 'oh well, chapter five might be O.K., but that's about it in that book.' This little bit of information won't tell me that chapter five is O.K. So I'm missing stuff. That's very traditional, conservative, old hat way of approaching information literacy... And if they ever closed the library stacks down, like they have in many places, I would be sunk.   (Int. 4, p.4, Staff Developer, Female)

Determining the quality of information accessed Using networked information makes it difficult for those without sufficient expertise to ascertain the quality of

Determining the quality of information accessed Using networked information makes it difficult for those without sufficient expertise to ascertain the quality of information accessed. Problems also arise in terms of needing to understand precisely what has been accessed and how to treat it within the arena of scholarly discourse:

> ...I mean a published article you can cite and you can refer back to, and ... because it's been refereed or whatever...; but if somebody just says, well this is what I think, and they're Joe Blow from downtown Kansas. I mean it's a very very difficult area to pin down. (Int. 8, p.4, Librarian, Female)

At present, individuals need to find strategies for dealing with these problems whilst the conventions develop. The same respondent makes the following comments when asked how she deals with the difficulties:

> ...At the moment, probably by not pretending that it's a scholarly article and just by basically being as honest with citing it, and as correct with citing it as I can, and I think there are now resources around that say the correct way to cite an electronic news group, or whatever, and basically if I'm giving a paper or writing something and I'm using somebody's opinion then I say that that's what I'm doing. (Int. 8, p.4, Librarian, Female)

Summary

To summarise, in category five information literacy is experienced as the ability to develop a personal knowledge base in a previously unfamiliar area of interest. The information literate person can use strategies which, when accompanied by critical analysis or reflection, allow personal perspectives to be adopted. In this category information is seen as subjective; it is an object of reflection. In subsequent categories describing information literacy information becomes 'transformational'. This is first evident in the sixth category, the knowledge extension conception.

Category six: the knowledge extension conception

Information literacy is seen as working with knowledge and personal perspectives adopted in such a way that novel insights are gained.

As foreshadowed in category five, information use remains the focus of attention here. Information use, however, is no longer aimed at knowledge construction, but rather at knowledge extension. A capacity for intuition is seen as necessary for allowing information to be used in this way. The knowledge base differs from that in the previous category in that it includes knowledge gained through personal experience.

In this category the view of information differs from those noted previously. Information in earlier categories was seen as objective and external to the individual, as well as subjective and able to be internalised. Here information is seen as being part of the person and as being changed (transformed) by the person. Information itself is not an object of reflection. Instead it is drawn on in the process of reflection; it becomes part of a pattern of reflection linked to the nature of creative insight. The relation between the information user and information can be described as constituted in terms of creative insight and subsequent knowledge extension. Although the need for such creative insight is recognised by the interviewees, they do not understand how it works.

The structure of awareness

Information use, involving a capacity for intuition, or creative insight, is the distinguishing feature of this conception. Such intuition or insight usually results in the development of novel ideas or creative solutions to problems. The knowledge base is recognised by participants as being an essential part of this way of conceiving of, or experiencing, information literacy. As has been previously mentioned, the character of the knowledge base differs in this category; this will be explained further in what follows.

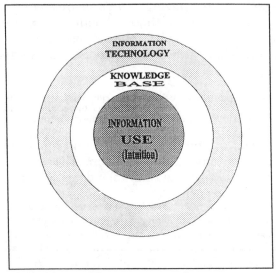

Figure 6.8   The structure of awareness as experienced in the knowledge extension conception

Information technology is again in the margin of this experience. It will be seen that participants do not see information technology as essential to information literacy when it is conceived of in terms of knowledge extension. Information technology may speed the process but has little else to contribute.

The meaning structure

The meaning structure of this conception begins with an enhanced knowledge base. It is enhanced in that it is derived from both scholarship and personal experience. Also included are the elements of creative insight, or intuition, and knowledge extension. All these elements may be combined to express the meaning of the experience as follows.

Enhanced knowledge base +   creative insight = novel ideas or solutions.

Novel ideas or solutions, that is knowledge extension, are the outcomes of the experience. These elements of the meaning structure differ from those in the previous category although, on the surface, the structure of awareness is similar.

Interviewees who conceive of information literacy in this way provide examples illustrating their view from their own experience and their observation of others. Overall the experience seems to be closely related to the process of research and writing. Although elements of the other categories may be present, the qualitatively different element of creativity is the foundation of the conception. Each of the main parts of the category, the enhanced knowledge base, intuition or creative insight and the role of technology are described below.

The enhanced knowledge base

The knowledge base in this category is the foundation which allows creative insight to occur. It is acquired through scholarly reflection and personal experience. The element of scholarly reflection is described in terms of 'wide and deep' reading and the opportunity for reflection and analysis. This suggests that this element of the knowledge base is equivalent to that described as the outcome of the previous category. Specific comments illustrating this character of the knowledge base include:

> It's the level of scholarship isn't it...and mental ability. He has such a background of wide and deep reading. (Int.4, p. 9, Staff Developer, Female)

> It's an activity that is affected by how much prolonged time you get to be quiet to concentrate on something for a while, which allows you to reflect, analyse and so on. (Int.14, p. 9, Librarian, Male)

The importance of personal experience in developing a knowledge base is described by an interviewee who uses his son as an example of a neophyte who has no experience to draw on:

> ... information (is) gathered almost subconsciously over a lengthy period of time and I'm conscious of this because (my son)'s got his learner's permit and I'm having difficulty because, things that I would just do naturally, he doesn't do because he hasn't built up that knowledge base of what to do... (Int. 5, p.1, Academic, Male)

The role of subconsciously gathering information through experience is returned to later in the interview when he describes problem solving in a professional context. Having a knowledge base to draw on in this context is described as requiring experience:

> I guess it goes back to the driving a car thing again, you gather these things almost subconsciously as you go along, extracting that information... (Int. 5, p. 7, Academic, Male)

The importance of the knowledge base to creative insight is explicitly noted by this respondent:

> The inspiration is probably a subconscious reaction to a broad knowledge base that you've got stacked away anyway (pointing to head)...I wouldn't have the inspiration if I didn't have the information. (Int. 5, p.9, Academic, Male)

Intuition or creative insight and knowledge extension

Creativity, or intuition, is about *how* novel insights are gained. Although most participants describe this as a mysterious process which they cannot explain, some describe it as an activity of the mind. The way in which it is explained by participants probably depends upon their own world views. What is more important is that 'new knowledge or information' is recognised as the outcome, and intuition is recognised as the contributing factor to effective information use. This part of the category is clearly linked to the view of information in this conception.

The following is an example of information literacy which illustrates the emphasis on generating new information and the creativity which makes it possible. This interviewee is describing someone she considers to be information literate:

He has an idea, so the creative thought... he does lots of literature surveys, has a look to see what the literature surveys suggest and then he would try and research to try and find out how close the literature source is to the experience in business and then he would put a paper out on that, so it's a new creative thought. So he uses information to create more information. (Int. 3, p. 6, Learning Adviser, Female)

This emphasis on generating new information has already been evident in the same interview. Here the interviewee is replying to a question about what is involved in being an effective user of information. She replies in relation to her own experience of using information in the research context:

I think it actually involves new information. Actually being able to bring a new perspective, something that has never been done before, to either extend an argument beyond where anybody has ever extended it, see something in a totally different light, be able to perhaps put in research that would support it and actually add to the information list. (Int. 3, p. 3, Learning Adviser, Female)

Another interviewee describes a colleague as information literate on the basis that she is able to use information to 'create her own thing':

...she incorporates the stuff she's found in a very forward thinking way...it's not looking back a t what she's read she's actually creating her own thing. (Int.8, p.12, Librarian, Female)

The whole emphasis on new information is summarised by an interviewee who comments that 'there is a sense of changing that information' (Int. 12, p. 8, Staff Developer, Female).

The creative element of the experience is elaborated by other respondents as a mysterious, intuitive process:

...it's a subconscious thing that's built up from experience over time. You get this sort of funny feeling... (Int. 5, p.8, Academic, Male)

...Now, things have come to me as a flash. ...after peering in the screen for some hours you get very...,' blow this, I'm going to go and lie down.' So I did. And then suddenly I jump up with this great inspiration and rush down and pound the keyboard. You don't.........no idea (how). Subconscious sort of says 'do these things'. (Int. 5, p. 8, Academic, Male)

At first the respondent is uncertain whether intuition is part of effective information use, then concedes:

I guess if it's not.......I think it has to be. I think it has to. (lengthy pause)   One never knows what happens if you don't have the inspiration. There's no way of looking at the alternative path. Maybe I haven't had enough flashes of inspiration either. So we don't know. That's difficult, isn't it..... (Int. 5, p. 9, Academic, Male)

Another lecturer, also describes the process of creating new information in terms of creativity and intuition. In this case the lecturer is concerned with making connections between previously 'unconnected pieces of information

I think there's a creative relationship really....You can stuff yourself full of information and only be capable of regurgitating it, but actually to synthesise and relate it to other things...I find that just happens spontaneously, you make connections...I still find it a rather mysterious process, you start to see the connections, the relationships. (Int. 6, p. 3, Academic, Male)

The peripheral role of technology

The role of information technology is to release time and energy to the mental activity required for creative insight/intuition:

> If the computer is really liberating us in terms of time, then what it is liberating us from are the bodily aspects of information gathering no longer do I have to flip pages, no longer do I have to write lots and lots of information, I can point click and download. Much more time has been liberated for the mind oriented thing. (Int. 14, p.10, Librarian, Male)

Another one of the respondents who focussed heavily on the role of intuition in his experience points out that he does not see information technology literacy as important to information literacy. He replies to a question asking whether technological literacy is necessary to being an effective information user:

> I don't think it's essential. It sure makes it easier. I don't think you need to be technologically literate provided you have other sources of gathering that information which may be using people who are technologically literate. Yes. I don't think it's an essential ingredient for the individual but it sure makes it easier...I'm sure there must be plenty of people who are quite computer illiterate who are good information users (Int. 5, p.11, Academic, Male)

This respondent also points out that the primary role of technology is to release individuals from expending time and physical energy:

> I mean, it surely enables one to be able to do it much more quickly than without it. If you're relying on not being able to use modern computer techniques, I think you can do it, but it'll take a long, long time, much, much longer. You might have to rely on other people with those computer skills. ...And I guess more and more information is becoming readily available... we can now dial it up from here. We don't even have to physically walk to the library which saves, you know, ten minutes a trip and you always run into somebody and talk. (Int. 5, p.11, Academic, Male)

The role of technology in this conception differs from that in the previous category; in the knowledge construction category information technology was seen as a potential barrier, requiring very different approaches to the process of knowledge construction. Although here information technology is seen as contributing to the possibility of knowledge extension, its role is not as important as it is in the information technology category.

Summary

To summarise, information literacy is experienced as knowledge extension. The information literate person relies heavily on personal knowledge, experience and insight in order to use information creatively. The element of intuition is an important distinguishing feature. As information is used creatively it is 'transformed' or new knowledge is produced. In the seventh, and final category, information literacy is seen as the wise use of information.

Category seven: the wisdom conception

Information literacy is seen as using information wisely for the benefit of others.

Information use, the focal point of the knowledge construction and extension conceptions, remains the focus of this category. The view of information in this category is similar to the view in category six in that information is seen as being a part of the person (the information user). Here, however, information transforms people (when used wisely), rather that being itself transformed. Information is, in this category also, subject to a process of reflection which is part of the experience of effective information use. The subject-object relation in this category is constituted in terms of wise use of information.

Information use, therefore, is understood in terms of making use of information wisely. A consciousness of personal values and ethics is needed to enable information to be used in this way. Wisdom is a personal quality brought to the use of information. The knowledge base underpinning information use is the same as in the previous category.

The structure of awareness

Wise use of information, involving the adoption of personal values in relation to information use, is the distinguishing feature of this conception. Wisdom is related to ideas such as social responsibility. The knowledge base is also an important part of this experience or view of information literacy. Participants recognise the need to draw upon their scholarship and experience in dealing with the academic and professional contexts in which information is used.

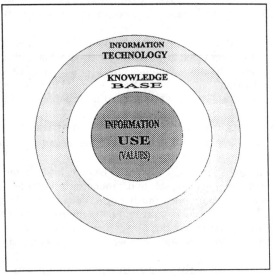

Figure 6.9   The structure of awareness as experienced in the wisdom conception

The knowledge base is therefore the second level of awareness. Information technology is again in the margin of this experience. For some respondents information technology was considered to be a negative influence on the experience of information literacy.

The meaning structure

In this category the first element of the meaning structure is the enhanced knowledge base; that is the knowledge base built up through processes of scholarship and personal experience. This is the same element that is present in the knowledge extension category. Further elements of 'personal values' and 'wise use of information' complete the meaning structure:

Enhanced knowledge base + values = wise use of information.

Personal values are critical and wise use of information is the outcome of the experience, providing the category with a distinctive meaning structure despite the apparent similarity in the structure of awareness with categories five and six.

This view of information literacy is summarised by one of the respondents in the latter half of his interview. He points to the relative insignificance of information access (and consequently information technology), the importance of wisdom and personal values in making use of information:

> Accessing information doesn't really come into it... I would like to think the information is not simply utilitarian...there's some kind of wisdom in the way its used...people have values and those values are brought to the using of information. (Int. 15, p. 10, Learning Adviser, Male)

Each of the three areas, values, wise use of information and information technology are examined in turn below.

The knowledge base supplemented by values, attitudes and beliefs

In this category the knowledge base as described in the previous category continues to be important. When information literacy is described as the capacity to use information wisely, however, that knowledge base is supplemented by an awareness of values, attitudes and beliefs which influences the use of information. One interviewee points to the important elements of an effective information user as follows:

> ...and that's to actually appreciate your own role as a user...A good information processor, I think, has a strong sense of their own beliefs and values and attitudes and how those beliefs and attitudes frame what they are doing. (Int. 12, p. 6, Staff Developer, Male)

Another interviewee describes his knowledge base as incorporating 'my culture and my values' (Int. 15, p. 4, Learning Adviser, Male). Information, he says, should 'remain subservient to the ethical domain of our lives:

> ...we all have, I think, larger responsibilities and have values which we may or may not be aware of at the time, but that they inform a lot of what we do whether it is in our work or in our personal relationships or in the way in which we relate to other people and that I see as the kind of ethical domain of our lives, and that information should remain subservient to that rather than being the goal in itself.' (Int. 15, p. 10, Learning Adviser, Male)

Wise use of information

Wise use of information occurs in a range of contexts including exercising judgement, making decisions, doing research. Using information wisely presupposes a consciousness of personal values, attitudes and beliefs as described above. Wise use of information involves placing the information in a larger context, seeing it in the light of broader experience, 'seeing the information historically, temporarily, socioculturally and so on' (Int. 15, p.9, Learning Adviser, Male).

When information is seen 'within a larger context and with one's own life experience' (Int. 15, p.5, Learning Adviser, Male), information is then used in qualitatively different ways. New information is not created as in the previous category; rather it is used to the benefit of the information user, colleagues or clients. One example is provided in relation to counselling clients in a sexual harassment case. The interviewee explains the situation as one in which his knowledge indicates that the case should be reported. His experience of the larger context of such situations, however, indicates that this would not be a wise option:

> ...is there any point in the person actually telling anyone about it?...it may be an option and it maybe that it would be the thing to do, but it is not necessarily a wise thing to do in terms of the pain involved. (Int. 15, p.3, Learning Adviser, Male)

This interviewee provides another illustration of wise use of information. In this case he is the 'recipient' in the interaction. He describes a colleague as being able to use her knowledge 'to elicit in me a deeper understanding of phenomena (Int. 15, p.13, Learning Adviser, Male).

Another interviewee similarly describes effective information use in terms of using information wisely, for the benefit of people. In this case the interviewee is describing someone he considers to be effective, rather than himself:

> ... she knows the best way to be able assist those people. ... she works in a public contact job where what she knows has an impact on what happens in those people's lives... So the decisions that she makes about people in her job actually affects, has an effect on their lives. (Int. 11, p.6, Learning Adviser, Male)

Using information may also be for personal benefit, rather than for the benefit of a client. An illustration of using information for personal advantage comes from an interviewee who used information to decide to curtail his involvement in an area of professional interest:

> I wasn't (benefiting) so I stepped out...I was getting information about the cost to me of being involved and for me to continue to ignore that information would have made my position...highly problematic. (Int. 12, p.5, Staff Developer, Male)

The peripheral role of technology

In this category information technology, although used by the participants, is not seen as making a contribution to information literacy. The respondent who describes this view of information literacy in most detail actually suggests that there may be an inverse relationship between effective use of information technology and information literacy. He leads into this comment by describing two acquaintances, the first he considers to be an effective user of information technology, the second an effective user of information:

> I don't know if he was a good information user or not. I do know he knows how to access information electronically... (She) has probably never used a computer...and to me she was a person who I would regard as being a good information user because she was able to be wise with that information...(Int. 15, p. 13, Learning Adviser, Male)

> ...there's a danger that there's an inverse relationship between being a good technical person and being a good information user when one construes information as something which needs to be related to knowledge and to wisdom. I shouldn't say there's an inverse relationship because I don't know, but one might well discover ... that there really is no relationship... (Int. 15, p. 14, Learning Adviser, Male)

Why information technology should be regarded as being quite outside the experience of information literacy, when viewed this way, is explained by another interviewee. This respondent is also concerned with the need for information to be subject to the 'beliefs and values and attitudes' of the information user. This is a role for human beings not information technology:

> The computer knows nothing. It's not a knower, that computer over there, it's simply a machine. I can get information from it. I can look up my files, open up to email, I can do those sorts of things but it is not knowledge. (Int. 15, p. 6, Staff Developer, Male)

Summary

To summarise, in category seven information literacy is seen as the wise use of information. When information is used this way, information is not transformed, as in category six, but people benefit. In this category, as in the previous two, information use is in the focus of awareness. Information technology, although present in awareness, is not just peripheral; it appears to be regarded with some scepticism, indeed very negatively. Most significant is the nature of the knowledge base that makes this experience possible. The knowledge base of wise information users is supplemented by values, attitudes and beliefs that they are explicitly aware of and that they affirm in their use of information on a day to day basis.

These seven categories of description reveal the different ways in which higher educators experience information literacy. The categories provide pictures of real people working with information in real situations. Their thinking about information use reflects their own experiences of trying to use the information available to them as effectively as possible. It is these pictures that form the centrepiece of the new model of information literacy, the *relational information literacy wheel*, proposed in the first chapter.

We can conclude from these varying conceptions, that information literacy is not a linear process, nor is it necessarily technology driven as is often suggested in the literature; it is also not readily definable as a set of skills. Instead people's experience of information literacy is an intricately woven fabric, revealing different patterns of meaning depending on the nature of the light cast upon it.

How do these new pictures of information literacy compare with those which we have already used in the past? How should they influence teaching and learning? How can we bring students into the experience of developing personal knowledge about unfamiliar fields? What do we need to add to the existing research agenda to continue to explore information literacy this way? In the final chapter these categories are examined in relation to other contemporary descriptions of information literacy and discuss their implications for information literacy education and research.

Chapter 7

New directions for information literacy

In the second, third and fourth chapters of *The Seven faces of information literacy* directions in, and influences on, our understanding of information literacy, information literacy education and information literacy research were examined. The framework presented was based on the literature available in early 1994. It was also argued that researching information literacy in terms of the varying ways in which it is conceived, or experienced, in the higher education community would lay a foundation for adopting a relational view of information literacy and information literacy education. Such an investigation was intended, too, to support the establishment of a line of information literacy research devoted to uncovering varying relations between people and relevant aspects of the world. This new relational model for information literacy, as opposed to the existing behavioural one, has been made possible as a result of the implementation of this study. Both the old and new models are presented graphically in Figure 7.1.

Drawn together in these figures are the three elements of information literacy scholarship: descriptions of information literacy, information literacy education, and information literacy research. In the behavioural model, descriptions of information literacy are made in terms of attributes of persons; information literacy education is seen as making possible the acquisition of these attributes; and research is conducted into the desirable attributes of information users.

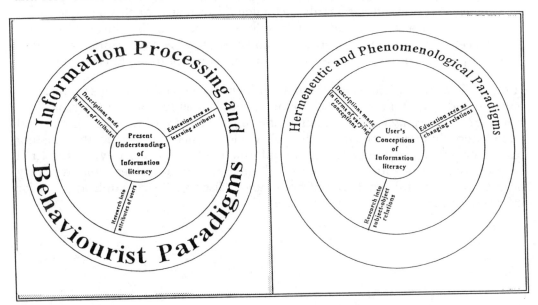

Figure 7.1a Information literacy—a behavioural model

Figure 7.1b Information literacy— a relational model

In the relational model, however:

- descriptions of information literacy are made in terms of conceptions

- information literacy education is seen as learning to conceive of effective information use, that is information literacy, in new and increasingly sophisticated ways

- research is conducted into conceptions of information literacy and related phenomena

At the heart of the behavioural model are the many personal attributes required for information literacy which have until now dominated the literature. An initial core for the relational model consists of the outcome space for information literacy.

Discussed now are the outcomes of this study, which lie at the heart of the new relational model, in order to explain their contribution to information literacy theory. Analysed are these findings in the light of the literature available prior to the implementation of the study. Also analyses is how they compare with thinking about information literacy and information literacy education as it has continued to emerge while this study was being undertaken. Then examined are the implications of the findings for information literacy education and research. The following headings will organise the discussion of the three spokes in the *relational information literacy wheel*

- How may the outcomes of the study be interpreted?

- How does this study contribute to our understanding of information literacy?

- How does this study contribute to information literacy education?

- How does this study contribute to information literacy research?

How may the outcomes of the study be interpreted?

The results of this study have revealed the varying ways in which information literacy is experienced by higher educators. It is important to restate at this point that the results are not descriptions of people, nor are they descriptions of the object of experience. Instead they are descriptions of the ways in which higher educators relate to aspects of the world in their experience of information literacy, or of effective information use. In other words *we now have a picture of information literacy* as it is seen, experienced, and understood by people who are effective users of information, but who are not themselves scholars of information literacy. We have begun to be able to see information literacy from a second order perspective. A summary of the picture available can be presented through the category labels.

These identify the meaning attributed to information literacy as it is experienced:

- information literacy is seen as using information technology for information retrieval and communication (The information technology conception)

- information literacy is seen as finding information (The information sources conception)

- information literacy is seen as executing a process (The information conception)

- information literacy is seen as controlling information (The information control conception)

- information literacy is seen as building up a personal knowledge base in a new area of interest (The knowledge construction conception)

- information literacy is seen as working with knowledge and personal perspectives adopted in such a way that novel insights are gained (The knowledge extension conception)

- information literacy is seen as using information wisely for the benefit of others (The wisdom conception)

This picture of information literacy not only represents the views of one community of information users, it also *identifies significant variation in experience* amongst members of that community. That is not to say that some members of the community experience information literacy one way and others experience it another way. Rather, there exists a set of varying kinds of experiences and we can expect that members of the community would experience any subset of these at different times. The range of experiences of individual members will depend upon what they have learned to focus on when they use information. Marton (1995) describes such a picture as 'a reflection of the collective anatomy of awareness'. This means that the study of information literacy has involved discovering the structure of people's experience in the same way that the study of the anatomy of animals or plants involves seeking an understanding of their structure. Most importantly the structure we now have access to portrays the 'anatomy of information literacy' amongst a group of people rather than amongst a series of individuals. None of the categories represents any one individual; taken together they reveal how information literacy is conceived amongst the whole group.

Variation in experience is not only identified, it is described in a particular way; in terms of *varying subject-object relations which constitute information literacy* in the higher education context. This means that the analysis has revealed that there are varying ways of experiencing information literacy and, more specifically, that these experiences are about the different ways in which an information user (the subject), relates to information (the object). At the commencement of the study it was not possible to predict what the 'object' component of the relation would be. During the course of the analysis, 'information', a complex phenomenon in its own right was discovered to be the object component in each of the categories of description. Although, at a very basic level, information was discovered to appear differently in the various categories, this study sought to identify varying conceptions of information literacy, not information. The analysis, therefore, also uncovered the variations in the subject- object relations which revealed the differences in what it meant to use that information effectively. Thus we have complex layers of variation, both in how information is used effectively and in how information appears to the person using it. These variations are captured in the three levels of the outcome space, including the meaning structure, the awareness structure and the depiction of the varying ways in which information appears.

Examining people's experiences of information literacy has also revealed that there are changing emphases on information technology and information use in the varying conceptions; and that the emphasis on technology in people's experience is inversely related to the emphasis on how the information is being used. This means that although information technology is part of people's awareness in all the categories it is of minimal, or peripheral, interest in those categories where information use is thematised. Conversely, information use is not the focus of attention where information technology is thematised. Some participants expressing views involving a focus on information use in fact had a negative view of the influence of technology on information use. These shifts in the structure of awareness between categories suggest that some forms of information use, such as are found in the knowledge extension and wisdom categories, require information technology to recede to the outer edges of awareness. When information users are engaged in meaning construction, or using information in innovative ways, they are not focusing on any information technology they may be using, if indeed they are using it at all.

The picture of the varying ways in which information appears to people in the varying conceptions also deserves comment. On the basis of the data gathered in this study, information appears as objective in the first four categories, as subjective in the knowledge construction category, and as transformational in the knowledge extension and wisdom categories. Whereas the 'objective' and 'subjective' appearances are part of the conventional wisdom about information, the interpretation of information as transformational as it appears in this study is novel. It is particularly unusual because it is not the information user, the 'subject' component in the relation, who is transformed. Rather, it is the person with whom the subject is interacting who is transformed in the wisdom conception and information itself that is transformed in the knowledge extension conception.

There is one final aspect of the outcomes that must be discussed, and that is the somewhat vexed question of whether or not some conceptions in the group are 'better' or 'more desirable' than others? The first point to be made is that none of the conceptions is wrong. Each is simply a different way of conceiving of the phenomenon of information literacy and each can be used appropriately in particular contexts. For example, where information scanning is important, the information user may be well advised to attend to information technology that would aid this.

The second point to be made, however, is that some of the categories are indeed more complex and more powerful than the others. On this basis it is possible to claim that the categories do become more sophisticated as we move from the lowest level of the outcome space, the information technology conception, to the topmost pair, the knowledge extension and wisdom conceptions.

What evidence is there to support this claim? As a starting point we can note that the meaning structures reveal differences in the degree of sophistication of the knowledge base, a component of three categories which have 'information use' as a focal element. In the knowledge construction conception the knowledge base is simply a personal synthesis of existing knowledge about a particular discipline or field of interest. In the knowledge extension and wisdom conceptions that knowledge base is enhanced by the presence of life experience related to that discipline or field of interest. As a result, qualitatively different ways of using information become possible. In the knowledge construction conception information use stops short at developing that knowledge base, whereas in the other two conceptions information use involves working with that knowledge base to make social and intellectual contributions.

Further evidence is found in how the idea of information use is interpreted across the categories. In the information technology conception, information use involves becoming aware of existing information or knowledge; in the information sources conceptions information use is centred on location and retrieval; in the information process and control conceptions information use involves recognition and organisation or problem solving. In the remaining categories, information use ultimately involves the transformation of people, circumstances or information itself. It is clear from this that the knowledge extension and wisdom conceptions encompass more powerful forms of information use than do the others. It is not unreasonable, therefore, to claim that the categories do become more complex as the outcome space is traversed from the information technology conception to the topmost pair. This 'hierarchical' view of the outcome space would be particularly important in information literacy education, as it suggests that the conceptions at the lower levels represent inadequate educational outcomes.

What are the strengths and limitations of the picture that has emerged?

The picture of information literacy that has emerged from this study has a number of strengths. Firstly, it is a picture of information literacy as it is understood by information users and not scholars. In this sense the study has opened another window through which to view the experience of information users. These new views of the phenomenon allow us to consider new directions in thinking about information literacy, information literacy education and research. Each of these areas, including the importance of the user oriented approach, will be explored in the next parts of this chapter.

Secondly, the research outcomes conform to the rigorous requirements of the phenomenographic approach adopted. All the categories identified have each of the characteristics identified by Marton (1988a, p.181); that is, they are relational, experiential, content oriented and qualitative. Also in adherence to the requirements of the research approach, the structural relations between the categories have been successfully identified. The whole structure that has emerged is elegant; relationships between the categories are identifiable in the outcome space.

Thirdly, the categories belong to a specific context, the higher education sector. This makes the categories particularly useful within that context. The categories can be used to enhance communication between stakeholders regarding their intentions in the area of information literacy education. They can also be used as staff development and curriculum development tools. Because the categories have been generated within the higher education sector, stakeholders may be expected to readily identify with them. The value of the outcomes to higher educators will be discussed in detail later in this chapter when their contribution to information literacy education is explored.

Limitations of the outcomes obtained are also identifiable. Although the specific context within which the study was undertaken lends a useful focus to the outcomes, it also reveals the incompleteness of the picture of information literacy which has emerged. This is a picture of information literacy as it is seen in the Australian higher education sector, amongst a group of academics librarians, staff developers and learning counsellors who are part of the university system in the western world. The existing picture may be deepened through replication or broadened at a number of levels. For example, we must note that studies into other phenomena have been enriched as a result of cross cultural research (Marton, Watkins and Tang 1995). Further studies of conceptions of information literacy in higher education, undertaken in other cultures, may lead to the establishment of what Marton (1995) refers to as 'a supracultural outcome space'.

Also within the higher education sector, we have as yet no picture of information literacy as it is experienced amongst students. This is a significant gap in a picture which is intended to influence information literacy education. Although we can compare classroom observation of students' experience of information literacy against that of their teachers, we do not yet have documented descriptions of the varying experience of neophytes. Each participant in this study, by virtue of their professional contributions, would have to be described as an expert user. Students' experience of information literacy will need to be explored, through further research, to strengthen any curriculum developed and to help in the diagnosis of learning difficulties. Their ways of seeing may differ from those of educators.

Outside the higher education sector the picture of information literacy could be developed to encompass experience in other educational sectors and in the workplace. The former is important to understanding how information literacy education can articulate across sectors; the latter to understanding the post education experience for which students must be prepared. As the very concept of information literacy was originally tied to the importance of effective decision making and problem solving in the workplace, the importance of the latter cannot be overestimated. It cannot be assumed that the experiences of higher educators match those of information users in other workplaces. These and other limitations are discussed further in my analysis of possible directions in information literacy research in the final part of this chapter.

How does this study contribute to our understanding of information literacy?

The outcomes of this study influence our understanding of information literacy in a number of ways. Firstly, they establish a way of thinking about information literacy in terms of varying relations between an information user and information. Information literacy has, until now, been considered in terms of attributes of persons, rather than in terms of ways in which people relate to the information.

Secondly, they provide a picture of varying structures of awareness which constitute people's experience of information literacy. We now have an understanding of how people are aware of various aspects of the world around them when they are experiencing information literacy in particular ways.

The third, fourth and fifth outcomes follow from the two just described. Thirdly, the study brings to light elements of information literacy which are not being considered in contemporary discourse about the phenomenon. These elements are:

- ways of thinking about information (that is the view of information having a transformational, subjective or objective character)

- the importance of intuitive aspects of information use evident in the knowledge extension and wisdom categories

- the very existence of the knowledge extension and wisdom conceptions in the outcome space, neither of which has a significant place in the current information literacy literature

- the notion of information literacy incorporating the capacity to transform information (in the sense of extending or generating new knowledge) and to transform people (that is to transform those with whom the information user interacts rather than empowering the information user)

- the social as opposed to the individual nature of information literacy

Fourthly, the outcomes improve our understanding of the relationship between information literacy and 'learning to learn', thus endorsing the rhetoric that regularly aligns the two. The categories of description substantiate the close relationship between information literacy and the ability to learn at many levels. For example, the information technology conception highlights the relationship between information literacy and maintaining awareness of ongoing developments. The knowledge construction conception highlights the relationship between information literacy and the ability to learn independently about a field of knowledge. The knowledge extension conception demonstrates that information literacy includes the ability to transform or extend existing knowledge.

Fifthly, they change our view of the role of information technology. The same emphasis is not placed on information technology by effective information users in higher education as it is by some information literacy scholars. According to the conceptions uncovered in this study, there is a need for information technology to recede from the foreground of attention to enable effective information use.

Clearly significant differences have been uncovered in ways of thinking about information literacy, resulting from setting out to describe conceptions or experience. To understand the significance of the change more fully we need to revisit the different ways in which information literacy is described in the literature. Before doing so, recent trends in describing information literacy are identified. The differences in the meaning attributed to information literacy between scholarly descriptions available before the study and the categories of description are examined, before an analysis of more recent contributions.

What have been recent trends in the description of information literacy? The concept of information literacy continues to generate interest all over the world (Ford 1994; Rader 1995). In the literature that has appeared while this study was being conducted there appears to have been no shift from the view that information literacy is best described in terms of attributes of people, irrespective of whether these attributes are information technology skills or the ability to implement processes of information use.

General directions that have been taken in the literature can be summarised as follows:

- increased emphasis on information technology and its role (Fitsimmons 1995; McClure 1994; Moran 1995; Sutton 1994; Wilson 1994)

- continued interest in the information skills interpretation of the phenomenon, which focuses on the processes of information retrieval and use (Doyle 1994; Cheek and others 1995; Todd 1995)

- interest in technology related literacies, such as 'network literacy' (McClure 1994)

- emerging interest in the importance of information literacy to the world of business management (Kanter 1995; Kiely 1994)

- descriptions of information literacy which continue to add to the lists of attributes previously compiled (Colorado Department of Education 1994)

- a more explicit interest in constructivist learning theory (Colorado Department of Education 1994; Todd 1995, 1996)

- chronological descriptions of information literacy development (Behrens 1994); and emerging interest in the creative aspects of information use (Gevers 1995).

How do the categories of description compare with the descriptions available in the literature?

The descriptions of information literacy available in the literature before this study was conducted are compared with the categories of description in Table 7.1. This table shows that there are ways of thinking about information literacy that appeared in the literature that do not form part of the experience of higher educators in this study. There are also ways of thinking amongst higher educators that were not identified in the literature. We can see from Table 7.1 that there are two meanings attributed to information literacy in the literature which have strong parallels with the categories identified. These are the definitions of information literacy which focus on the ability to use information technology, and the processes of information use often called 'information skills'.

Table 7.1 Comparison between scholarly description of information literacy and higher educators experience of the phenomenon

Descriptions from the (1990-93) literature	Descriptions of experience-labels
Information literacy as a way of consuming information	
Information literacy as using information technology	**Information literacy is seen as using information technology for information retrieval and communication**
Information literacy as a combination of information and technology skills Information literacy as including library and computer literacy	
Information literacy as a process (ie information skills)	**Information literacy is seen as executing a process**
Information literacy as an amalgam of skills, attitudes and knowledge	Information literacy is seen as controlling information
Information literacy as the ability to think like a searcher	*Information literacy is seen as finding information*
Information literacy as the ability to learn	*Information literacy is seen as building up a personal knowledge base in a new area of interest*
Information literacy as the first component in the continuum of critical thinking skills	Information literacy is seen as working with knowledge and personal perspectives adopted in such a way that novel insights are gained
Information literacy as part of the literacy continuum	Information literacy is seen as using information wisely for the benefit of others
Key: Normal font indicates no correlation, *Italics* indicate weak similarities, **Bold** indicates strong similarities	

The definitions of information literacy which focus on ways of consuming information, and on the combination of information and information technology skills have no parallels in the categories of description. Neither do those definitions of information literacy which draw together skills, attitudes and knowledge or which place the phenomena on continua of literacy or critical thinking.

knowledge or which place the phenomena on continua of literacy or critical thinking.

The remaining definitions have weak links with some of the categories identified. These are the definitions of information literacy which equate the phenomenon with the abilities to think like a searcher and to learn. Thinking like a searcher which entails knowledge of the bibliographic universe is similar to the information sources conception; the conception as portrayed in the category is focussed more on knowledge of specific sources than on how those sources are arranged, or mapped, in the world of information. Focus on the ability to learn forms part of the character of the knowledge construction conception. The category of description, however, considers learning in the very specialised sense of building a personal knowledge base in a previously unfamiliar area. The last categories in the information literacy structure, the knowledge extension conception and the wisdom conception, are not reflected at all in the literature of the early 1990s.

Overall, there is also a generalisable difference between most of the categories of description and contemporary thinking about information literacy; many authors tend to treat information literacy as the responsibility of individuals, whereas most of the categories suggest that information literacy is a social responsibility. In the information technology conception, for example, information literacy is achievable when responsibility for information technology skills are shared, or distributed, within a group. In the third subcategory of the information sources conception, information literacy involves a willingness to allow a third party to contribute to information location.

Similarly, in the triad of categories which thematise information use, other members of the community are appropriated in areas where the information user lacks specific skills. There are only two instances where the idea of shared responsibility is seen as unacceptable. The first is in the information technology conception; here in the second subcategory individuals must be able to use technology themselves. The second is found in the remaining information sources subcategories; the first of these requires individuals to be familiar with information sources and their structure; the second requires people to be able to use these sources themselves rather than via an intermediary. This difference suggests that the adoption of a relational model will require scholars and practitioners to think in terms of communities of information users rather than individuals. It also suggests that for libraries and other information services, programs of information use instruction cannot be seen as reducing the need for programs that offer direct assistance to users.

Recent literature shows that scholars are opting for interpretations which emphasise one way, or a limited number of ways in which people experience the phenomenon, rather than embracing the full range of experience. Many of these papers lean in the direction of the information technology conception. In one, for example, information literacy is defined as

> ...a convergence of traditional literacy, computer literacy, network literacy and media literacy used in the process of solving information problems. (McClure 1994, p.118)

Here information technology achieves prominence in the form of network literacy, computer literacy and media literacy, while 'the process of solving information problems', or information skills, becomes a domain to which information literacy is applied. Sutton, drawing on McClure (1994) and Kwasnik (1990), also leans towards the information technology approach. He combines information technology skills with information skills, describing information literacy as being able to read and write fluently as well as:

- use the computer effectively as an instrument in the creation, storage and management of information bearing products of the intellect;

- use the powerful post print media's effective tools of expression through their integration into information bearing products

- use the emerging National Information Infrastructure as an effective means of accessing, acquiring, managing, and manipulating information regardless of its geographic location or medium (Sutton 1994, p.14)

Similarly, Kanter (1995) locates information literacy within the information technology domain. He argues that information literacy involves an understanding of information processing, the ways in which an organisation's information systems support the work process and the need for 'an overall information architecture' that supports communication both within the organisation and without. Australian authors are also focusing on information technology. Wilson (1994), for example, equates information literacy with information seeking and retrieval, including the ability to handle technology. Even more markedly, Moran (1995, pp. 18-22), in her report on the role of information technology in higher education teaching and learning, equates information literacy with information technology literacy.

The trend towards a focus on information technology is not universal. Some significant documents which are likely to influence the Australian higher education arena do not highlight information technology at all in their approaches to information literacy. Todd (1995) and Doyle (1996), for example, continue to describe information literacy in terms of information skills, whilst Cheek and others (1995) focus on processes with no special emphasis on technology. That is not to say that information technology is considered irrelevant, rather it is not thematised and is treated as one amongst many elements of the information environment.

Bruce (1995, 1994d, 1994e) includes information technology use amongst a set of characteristics of an information literate person. In this description, use of information technology is present as one of a series of qualities, none of which is more significant than any other. The information literate person:

- engages in independent, self directed learning

- uses information processes

- uses a variety of information technologies and systems

- has internalised values that promote information use

- has a sound knowledge of the world of information

- approaches information critically

- his or her interaction with the world of information (Bruce 1994e)

The inclusion of the adoption of a personal information style is an addition in this portrait which differs from the earlier literature. Other major additions to the list of attributes required for information literacy include network literacy (McClure 1994), group skills and a system of ethics for using information and information technology (Colorado Department of Education 1994).

Pettersson (1994) draws together the information technology and information skills models, combining them with an emphasis on 'learning to learn'. His thinking, heavily influenced by Breivik, embraces a broader range of the conceptions identified in this study than is evident in other writing. Despite this, his interpretation of information use does not involve the more complex understandings of information use. Pettersson emphasises the need for people to be able to comprehend and 'repackage' (p.96) information. He also expresses a concern for people to be able to locate 'objective' information (p.92). This reflects the insight, captured in the categories of description, that ways of thinking about information literacy which do not thematise information use are associated with an objective view of information. Alternatively, a focus on information use accompanies a shift in thinking towards subjective and transformational views of information.

Of greater interest are those descriptions which move in the direction of the knowledge construction and knowledge extension conceptions. Kiely (1994), writing in support of the need for business and senior IT executives to be information literate, describes information literacy as 'the ability to distil meaning from data'. This ability is seen as critical to maintaining a competitive edge, ultimately differentiating corporate 'winners' from 'losers'.

Similarly, Candy, Crebert and O'Leary, in their report *Developing lifelong learners through undergraduate education*, do not thematise information technology. For them information literacy includes:

- knowledge of major current resources available in at least one field of study
- ability to frame researchable questions in at least one field of study
- ability to locate, evaluate, manage and use information in a range of contexts
- ability to retrieve information using a variety of media
- ability to decode information in a variety of forms: written, statistical, graphs, charts
- diagrams, tables;
- critical evaluation of information (Candy, Crebert and O'Leary 1994, p. 43)

Although most aspects of this description resemble earlier descriptions, 'the ability to frame researchable questions' reflects the knowledge extension conception. Framing researchable questions would require the knowledge base and creative insight, which characterise that category.

Gevers (1995) argues that people need an existing knowledge base (or an informed mind) to benefit from the world of information that is now upon us. For .Gevers, more important than retrieving information, or using new technology, is the way in which information is used. He describes this as the 'ability to see connections where these are not obvious, to be stimulated into insight by distant analogies and to develop unique understandings of particular problems or fields' (1995, p.4). Intriguingly, he comments on the difficulties caused by technology for those who wish to experience information literacy this way. His comments resemble those made by participants in this study who spoke disparagingly about the role of technology in effective information use:

> This creative way of working is better supported by the habit of browsing through conventional journals than by struggling with rapidly repeating printouts of the last 50 abstracts captured by key words, or even by the full articles themselves. It is not easy to browse on the monitor of a PC, and the conversion of edited and refereed journals into packets of information targeted to particular users may destroy some feature of our scientific creativity. (Gevers 1995, p.4)

How does this study contribute to information literacy education?

In chapter three it was argued that a picture, or map, of ways of experiencing information literacy was required to enable the development of a relational approach to information literacy education. It is now possible to begin to develop such an approach. Although considerably more research needs to be undertaken in this area, we have the 'target conceptions' which teachers and students can use in learning situations. The availability of the relational information literacy model provides a framework within which to:

- develop new outcome statements/objectives for information literacy curriculum

- devise new teaching approaches

- evaluate existing curriculum

- facilitate staff development for higher educators

The most important elements of the new model for information literacy education are the categories of description and the view of learning as coming to see effective information use in new and more complex ways. Adopting the relational view will overcome some of the difficulties associated with the skills based approach to information literacy education, such as the ever growing lists of skills which need to be incorporated into curricula. It is not, however, a panacea which will solve all difficulties. Educators and researchers will need to consider how to implement effectively a relational approach, and study the outcomes of such an implementation. In the following section, examined first are recent developments in information literacy education and the relational approach to teaching and learning. Then the possible influence of the new model on each of the four areas listed above are explored. The need for further research will be discussed in the third and final part of this chapter

What have been recent trends in information literacy education?

Recent writing about information literacy education demonstrates the following trends

- limited ongoing interest in distinguishing between library instruction bibliographic instruction and information literacy programs (Murdock 1995)

- continued variation in curriculum content and processes (Booker 1995)

- continued advocacy for the integration of information literacy education into university curricula (Bruce and Candy 1995; Candy, Crebert and O'Leary 1994; Loomis 1995; McNally and Kuhlthau 1994)

- continued advocacy for emphasis on resource based learning and information skills (Bruce, Doskatsch and others 1995; Todd 1995)

- continued interest in teaching new technologies, particularly use of Internet resources CAUL 1995; Fjällbrant 1995; McClure 1994)

- increased attention to staff development for information literacy education (Bruce and Candy 1995; Bruce, Weeks and Crebert 1995; Commission on Higher Education 1995

- early interest in workplace information literacy education (Fisher and Bjorner 1994; Kanter 1995; Kiely 1994)

- using the World Wide Web for delivering instruction (Fjällbrant 1995)

- emerging interest in the outcomes of phenomenographic research into learning for instructional design (Fjällbrant 1995, p. 2)

Policy makers all over the world continue to endorse the need for information literacy education. The Association of Supervision and Curriculum Development in the United States advocates that 'information literacy should be part of every student's educational experience'; and in South Africa a report prepared by the Ford Foundation recommends an 'information literacy pilot project to promote economic development...' (Ford 1995, pp.100-101). In Australia, the Candy report, *Developing lifelong learners through undergraduate education*, lists information literacy as one of the key characteristics of lifelong learners and one of the significant elements of undergraduate curriculum (Candy, Crebert and O'Leary 1994). Accrediting agencies are also being encouraged to attend to the issue of information literacy education (Hawes 1995), with the Middle States Commission on Higher Education continuing to provide strong leadership in this area in the United States (ACRL and Middle States Commission on Higher Education 1995).

While policy makers recognise the importance of information literacy, curriculum initiatives still reveal the various ways in which educators interpret the phenomenon. Some developments in this area closely reflect initiatives that were established in the early 1990s and others reveal change Murdock (1995), for example, advocates removing the emphasis on information location and retrieval from teaching programs altogether, while Pettersson (1994), linking information literacy to the development of learning organisations, calls for an emphasis on metalearning, or learning to learn, not only in the academic environment, but in the workplace. In high schools and in higher education increased emphasis on 'high technology' has led to calls, not for resource based learning, but for 'high technology resource based learning' (Mendrinos 1994 ; Moran 1995). Ford raises questions about the bias towards instruction in the use of technology when she writes:

> Technology improves physical access to information but does not necessarily improve intellectual access...the time to read, think and write cannot be reduced. (Ford 1995 , p. 100)

Most programs, however, continue to emphasise information technology and use of information sources.

In Europe, collaboration between university libraries has enabled the development of an ambitious World Wide Web based program. The objectives for the EDUCATE course in information literacy demonstrate a strong emphasis on information technology and information sources/retrieval, as well as leaning towards information processes and information control. The information use categories, however, are not represented at all, a point which is reinforced by description of the course as involving 'instruction in information retrieval'.

> The objectives of the EDUCATE course in information literacy are that you should:
> - be able to develop a systematic method of searching for information in connection with your studies—project work, writing a literature survey etc
> - be aware of the wide range of sources available for finding information and select sources which best meet your needs
> - be aware of appropriate indexing and abstracting services and databases and understand the principles of their use
> - develop your database searching techniques for accessing both online and CDRom databases
> - be able to use current awareness methods to keep up to date with the published literature after your initial search
> - be able to use citation indexes to find information
> - be able to use the international academic networks for getting information
> - be able to compare and evaluate information obtained from various sources
> - be able to cite bibliographical references in your project reports or theses
> - be able to construct a personal bibliographic system (Fjällbrant 1995, pp. 3-4)

The list above does not appear to include emphasis on constructing a personal knowledge base through critical analysis, knowledge extension or wisdom in using information. The Swedish EDUCATE program is, however, drawing on insights into learning resulting from phenomenographic research, particularly the concepts of deep and surface learning. It is not as yet, at least explicitly, adopting an approach to teaching and learning which focuses on changing conceptions, or students' experience of phenomena.

In Australia, university libraries with strong information literacy initiatives, such as Queensland University of Technology, University of Queensland and Griffith University (CAUL 1995) closely reflect the content of the Swedish program described above, if not the medium through which it is delivered. The Griffith University information literacy modules combine this content with a strong computer literacy component. The Griffith model is of considerable interest because of its vision for fostering information literacy using multiple strategies including staff development, curriculum development, extra-curricular strategies and a core strategy. Its teaching modules however, like the Swedish program, stop short of focusing on information use. In addition, there appears to be a further gap in the lack of emphasis on information processes. Many of the other 'information literacy' initiatives described in the CAUL paper are library instruction programs presented under a new name, or information technology literacy initiatives. Indeed one university library describes its information literacy program under two headings, library skills and computing skills. A different approach is taken by a team from South Australia in preparing an information literacy text for Open Learning students. Their book (Cheek and others 1995), *Finding out: information literacies for the 21st century*, draws together introductory material on information skills, study skills, library skills and media literacy.

Alongside the curricula which have been developing, are a range of other initiatives targeting the broader university community. The roles of the many stakeholders in information literacy education are being considered (Bruce 1995, Bruce and Candy 1995) and some strategies are being put in place to empower educators to assume responsibility for information literacy education in collaboration with other members of the university community. For example, the Griffith University Information Literacy Blueprint mentioned above identifies academic staff development as an important component. Amongst others, this strategy establishes the following directions:

- to provide opportunities for all staff to regularly update their own knowledge and skills
- to raise awareness of the nature of information literacy and the need to include information literacy education in academic curriculum
- to encourage and enable all staff to design and use teaching/learning strategies which target information literacy
- to implement programs which foster sustained interest in information literacy education
- to encourage staff to apply for funding (teaching or research grants) and publish in relation to information literacy education (Bruce 1994e, p. 18)

Specific staff development practices have been implemented in other universities. In particular, a document entitled 'Developing information literate graduates: prompts for good practice' (Bruce and Candy 1995), has recently been developed, and teaching staff responsible for Graduate Certificates in Higher Education are attempting to model information literacy education in their programs (Bruce, Weeks and Crebert 1995).

The above review of developments in information literacy education since 1994 reveals accelerated interest all over the world. Now reviewed are developments in the relational approach to teaching and learning followed by analysis of the possible contributions of this study to information literacy education.

How has the relational view of teaching and learning developed?

Up until the early 1990s advocates of the relational view described learning as a change from one conception, or way of experiencing a phenomenon, to another. This way of thinking about learning is underpinned by the idea that some conceptions are more scientifically acceptable than others, and that these are preferred 'outcomes' of learning. Svensson and Hogfors (1988) point out, however, that ideally students should not only learn the 'correct conception, but that they should also learn why the alternative conceptions are inappropriate. Nevertheless, although they have recommended that the whole framework of conceptions be used in the teaching-learning process, only one of these is to be preferred, and students should understand why this is so. The idea that one conception is somehow better than the others is not always easy to maintain.

Shirley Booth (1992), in her doctoral thesis examining students' conceptions of programming noted that programmers need to have access to a complete range of conceptions of programming, and need to be able to be able to adopt the conception or set of conceptions most appropriate to a given circumstance. She moved away from describing learning as a change in conception to describing learning as:

> ...gaining access to views of further faces (or conceptions of a phenomenon) and developing an intuitive relationship with the object so that an appropriate face or set of faces is seen in appropriate circumstances (Booth 1992, p.262

The first component of this description is consistent with the view that students need to understand the varying ways of experiencing a phenomenon. The second component acknowledges that, in relation to some phenomenon, the varying conceptions are neither right nor wrong, but are used in different circumstances. That some conceptions remain more powerful interpretations of the phenomenon is not inconsistent with this approach.

Recently, this view has been emerging in writing by phenomenographers discussing aspects of teaching and learning. Dall'Alba (1994, p. 86), for example, describes learning as '...a change from one way of understanding to another, qualitatively more complete one'. Her use of the term 'complete' is interesting; it allows the reader to interpret learning as developing a broader repertoire of conceptions. Marton (1995) endorses this view when he writes that learning can '...be characterised as an individual's successive growing within the complex of different understandings'. Such 'growing' would necessarily include awareness of the quality of the different understandings, and awareness of if, and when, it might be appropriate to use each one.

How can the research outcomes contribute to future directions?

On a general level, the categories described strengthen the argument for continued integration of information literacy education into curriculum through:

- illuminating the relationship between information literacy and learning to learn

- making concrete the somewhat abstract claim that information literacy is a key characteristic of self directed life long learners

More specifically the picture of the phenomenon which has emerged can begin to contribute to curriculum development and staff development for information literacy education.

Developing new outcome statements for information literacy curricula

The picture of information literacy derived from this study allows learning information literacy to be redefined in terms of coming to conceive of effective information use in new and increasingly complex ways. From this starting point there are two main ways in which descriptions of higher educators' conceptions of information literacy can influence the content of curriculum. Firstly, they allow curricula to be designed to emphasise conceptions, that is experience or content of thinking, about information literacy. Information literacy is no longer a series of attributes which a learner must acquire. Secondly, they provide a framework within which to ensure that the full range of conceptions is encompassed. While the categories could enhance existing curricula they could also be used to restructure teaching and learning in accordance with the relational approach.

Developing outcome statements in accordance with the relational approach to teaching and learning will, therefore, result in an emphasis on conceptions and experience rather than on skills and attributes of individuals. Such statements would be constructed recognising that ways of thinking about what it means to use information effectively are more fundamental to information literacy than skills and knowledge. This does not mean that students will not acquire skills and knowledge, but rather that these are secondary to conceptions; students will learn skills and knowledge within a broader framework of learning to conceive of effective use of information in different ways. As a result the product of information literacy curriculum is no longer 'measurable'. Instead the information literate person is one who experiences information literacy in a range of ways, and is able to determine the nature of experience it is necessary to draw upon in new situations.

Following are learning outcomes that may result if the categories of description were to be used as basis for framing outcome statements. The first set is based on a holistic understanding of the phenomenon derived from the outcome space; the second set is based on the individual categories which portray the conceptions:

Outcome statements targeting the need to learn about the phenomenon as a whole. Students will:

- conceive of information literacy in a variety of ways

- use information effectively in a range of contexts

- discern the ways of thinking about effective information use which apply to new information problems they encounter

- conceive of information as subjective and transformational in character

- appreciate the socially distributed nature of information literacy

Objectives targeting the need to learn about specific faces of the phenomenon. Students will:

- use information technology for information retrieval and communication

- find information, either independently or via an intermediary

- use information processes

- control information

- build a personal knowledge base in a new area of interest

- work with knowledge and personal perspectives in such as ways that new insights are gained

- use information wisely, for the benefit of others

The objectives should, of course, be interpreted in the light of the detailed descriptions of the categories describing experiences of information literacy. For example, learning to use information technology does not mean that the student should be able to use all information technology at his or her disposal; he or she should be able to learn to use whatever technology is required with the assistance of peers and available university services. The student should also experience the capacity of information technology for contributing to a personal program of information awareness. This interpretation of the objective is not only consistent with the category describing the information technology conception, it also ensures that students are empowered to take advantage of continual technological change instead of finding themselves armed with a suite of rapidly dating 'skills'.

When compared with other information literacy curricula, this list of outcomes is relatively short, and should remain relatively stable. This is because any changes would be made on the basis of research uncovering further variation in conceptions, rather than on the basis of the emergence of more resources or more new technology. If the outcomes of subsequent research follows the pattern established by ongoing investigations into conceptions of learning, we can expect changes to be minor.

Using conceptions of information literacy as a framework for curricula also allows educators to integrate conceptions of other phenomena, uncovered in previous studies that have a bearing on information use. Investigations into conceptions of learning, reading texts, literature reviews and computers, for example, would contribute to curricula designed along these lines.

Devising new teaching approaches Trigwell, Prosser and Taylor (1994, p.83) confirm that the strategies teachers adopt in their teaching are logically related to their intentions; essentially teachers adopt strategies to suit their intentions. It would not be unreasonable, then, for the outcomes of this study to be used in a lecture situation to transmit information about the varying conceptions, in a small group discussion to encourage students to consider alternative views, or in a socratic event to challenge students' thinking. Although these would all be legitimate ways of using the results, teaching approaches are required that are consistent with the relational information literacy model.

If learning information literacy is to be described as coming to experience effective use of information in new, and increasingly complex ways, then teaching information literacy can now be described as facilitating this change. Teaching, in the relational view, would aim to change the internal relations through which learners experience aspects of the world. Teachers who choose to work within the relational model would see their role as being to help students conceive of and experience information literacy in the full range of ways captured in the outcome space. Adopting this approach to teaching information literacy would be compatible with the shifting emphasis towards reflective and experiential modes of teaching and learning in information user instruction described in chapter three. It would also enhance learning to be information literate in the context of resource or problem based curricula.

To help individual teachers who want to adopt a relational approach to teaching information literacy, this study provides a major tool in the form of the categories of description. The categories provide clear pictures of the conceptions they could target in their teaching; they provide a framework which may help with diagnosing existing conceptions they provide pictures which may help students as well as teachers understand the differences between the various ways of interpreting the phenomenon. The categories enable teachers to pursue the task of ensuring that students can use the full set of conceptions and are able to determine which is most appropriate in a given context.

- Teaching strategies consistent with such an approach would revolve around: identifying how groups of students are conceiving of, or experiencing, information literacy

- helping students become aware of their own existing repertoire of conceptions

- helping students become aware of the range of possible conceptions

- helping students conceive of, and experience, information literacy in new ways

Each of the above directions is derived from the view that learning is about broadening one's existing repertoire of conceptions. They also follow established directions that have been explained in chapter three. In developing more specific strategies higher educators will need to grapple with questions such as the following:

- How may we ensure that students learn to conceive of information literacy in new ways?

- How may we encourage students to focus not on information technology but on information use?

- How should the categories be valued in different contexts?

- How can categories currently less well represented in teaching be better emphasised?

- How can students' ways of thinking about information be influenced?

Booth offers four principles which teachers can adopt to help students understand and change their ways of interpreting important phenomena. Teachers should:

- address the content of learning from the perspective of students' experience rather than from the perspective of the disciplinary framework
- identify educationally critical aspects of the phenomena to be taught and the teaching context
- ensure that learners reveal their experience of learning and subject it to reflection
- ensure that the tasks of learning are integrated into the world that the learners experience (adapted from Booth 1994, p 4.)

Evaluating existing curriculum Information literacy curriculum in higher education needs to embrace the complete range of conceptions if students are to become effective information users to the fullest possible extent. The categories, therefore, serve as a framework against which to test the content of any curriculum. This would help identify curricula taking an unbalanced approach to information literacy education. There is a danger, for example, that, with increasing emphasis on information technology, other elements of information literacy revealed by the categories will remain of peripheral interest.

The outcome space suggests that it would be possible to detail the various ways of thinking about information literacy, to which any curriculum attends, in a way which reveals the cluster of categories embedded in that curriculum. A curriculum which addressed students' familiarity with information sources and information technology without addressing the processes of recognising information needs, locating, evaluating and using information could be graphically portrayed as in Figure 7.2.

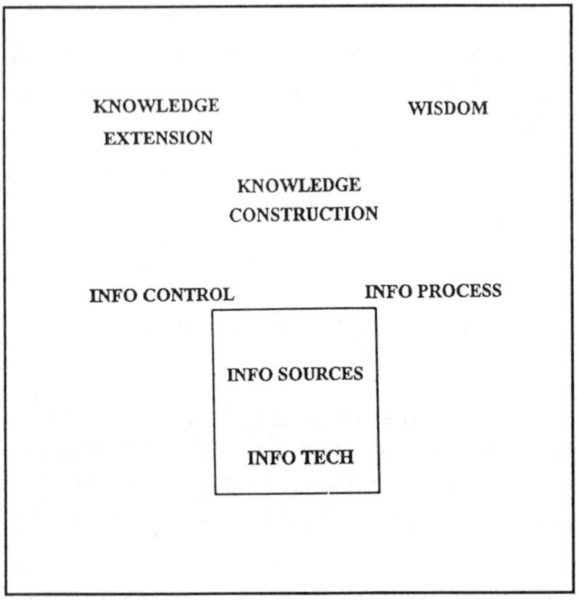

Figure 7.2   Curricula clustering around categories
one and two

Although further studies would need to be conducted to reveal how curriculum goals fit within this framework, it is relatively easy to group the categories into three clusters:

- the information technology and information sources conceptions

- the information process and information control conceptions

- the knowledge construction, knowledge extension and wisdom conceptions

It is not inconceivable that individuals or programs are likely to favour one subset of these groupings. Shown earlier in this chapter was that contemporary information literacy curriculum does not extend its interest beyond the information control and information process categories. For example, the Mann Library model (Olsen 1992) is largely designed around the information technology and information sources conceptions, with some leaning towards the information control conception. Bjorner's (1991) information literacy metacourse, however, is designed around the information process and, to a lesser extent, the information control conceptions. The resource based learning model has potential for focusing on the full range of conceptions, but at present appears to be designed around the information process conception, the emphasis being on 'Information Skills'. A *complete* information literacy program, however needs to operate across the artificial boundaries of these groupings.

The set of categories can also be used to analyse what students are learning in relation to each category. In learning information control, for example, category four suggests that learning to recognise potentially useful information is as important as being able to successfully store it for retrieval. Whether or not both aspects are equally treated would indicate whether or not changes needed to be made to the curriculum. Similarly, any curriculum targeting category six, the knowledge extension conception, should treat all three aspects of the category: the enhanced knowledge base, creative insight and the peripheral role of information technology.

Facilitating staff development for higher educators The results of this study can be used both to enhance higher educators' understandings of information literacy as well as to enhance information literacy education. Higher educators need to be made aware of:

- their own ways of conceiving of information literacy

- the many ways of conceiving of information literacy that comprise the phenomenon; the changing emphases on information technology and information use in the various categories

- the changing approaches to information (objective, subjective and transformational) in the various categories

- the socially distributed nature of information literacy

- the need for learners to operate within the complete framework, and not a limited subset

An enhanced awareness of the above could be accompanied by a challenge to evaluate curriculum and current approaches to information literacy education. Ideally, this would be accomplished within the broader framework of adopting a relational view of information literacy education. The arguments for doing so have already been outlined in chapter three.

For many higher educators adopting a relational approach to information literacy education would require changing their views of teaching and learning. Those educators who have already adopted learner-centred approaches, or those who are interested in reflective approaches to learning and competence, are more likely to develop an interest in the relational view.

In chapter three, four key principles (Ramsden 1988, p.26) were referred to, in adopting a relational view of information literacy education. These can now be revisited in the light of conceptions of information literacy uncovered. Higher educators would need to consider each of these and reflect on their implications for teaching and learning:

- *Learning is about changes in conception*—that is learning to be information literate is about developing new, more complex, ways of conceiving of, or experiencing, information literacy.

- *Learning always has a content as well as a process*—that is students should be learning about something (discipline content) as they engage in learning to be effective information users.

- *Learning is about relations between the learner and the subject matter*— that is learning to be an effective information user is about the relations between the learner and information.

- *Improving learning is about understanding the learner's perspective*— that is helping students to become better information users is about understanding their ways of conceiving of effective information use.

It is also important that educators be encouraged to reflect on the consequences of promulgating views of information literacy which emphasise individual autonomy. In both the information technology and information sources categories, there are subcategories which emphasise the need for support from information professionals and peers. Other subcategories convey how users become stressed when autonomy is emphasised. It is especially apparent from the participants in this study, that the view of information literacy as 'knowledge of sources' can place the individual concerned under severe pressure. It causes discomfort, stress and embarrassment, when knowledge is found to be lacking:

...the Reference librarians do not tell me all the time about new things coming in. So I'm quite embarrassed sometimes—when I don't know—so I'm conscious all the time of trying to keep up, just so that I'm not caught letting a student down. (Int. 10, p, 3, Librarian, Female)

Similarly, when independence is construed as an essential element of the information literate person, the need for other people can lead to poor self image and low self esteem. One interviewee has a negative view of herself as a researcher because she believes that independence is critical to information literacy. An important consequence of this view is that if information is not accessed independently it may not be accessed at all. Members of the academic community may be prepared to sacrifice information rather than subject themselves to the stresses of trying to locate it:

> I'm not really comfortable (trying to do things myself). I'm much happier when someone's holding my hand to help me....My daughter asked me if I could find a book for her. I still haven't done it. I probably won't do it. (Int.14, p.3, Staff Developer, Female)

Academic librarians who also perceive independence as critical to information literacy do nothing to alleviate this situation:

> If they are information literate, they won't need to bother—not bother ask—the librarian so many questions...so many people come in here and say 'Where's such and such?' , and you say 'Well go and look in the catalogue'. That person walks straight out of the door because they haven't been taken by the hand and shown where it is. (Int.7, p. 5-6, Librarian, Female)

Examining and understanding the service and educational implications of differing approaches to information literacy could form an important element of staff development for higher educators.

How does this study contribute to information literacy research?

In chapter four information literacy research was examined as a subset of information needs and uses research. Noted then, was that while a few information literacy researchers were adopting qualitative approaches, there was a strong tendency to focus on the views of information literacy expressed by information literacy scholars and opinion leaders rather than the experience of information users and the wider information professional community. In addition, researchers in the broader field of information needs and uses who were focusing on 'information users' in the research endeavour, were mainly adopting a cognitive approach. That is, they were interested in users' mental models of aspects of the world of information.

This study makes a number of contributions of relevance to researchers. It also opens a research agenda for information literacy, and may serve as a trigger for further studies of conceptions of phenomena in other information needs and uses research. These areas are discussed to highlight the possible influence of this study in future research.

Recent developments in information literacy and information needs and uses research

Current research literature reveals that little has changed in research on information literacy and information needs and uses. Important developments in such research are captured in recent papers about researching the phenomenon of relevance, and the role of information in society. These include:

- renewed interest in problems of meaning and the information user's experience as a vehicle for exploring meaning (Froehlich 1994; Park 1994)

- continued emphasis on the importance of adopting naturalistic approaches to explore users' experience (Park 1994)

- questioning of the need for 'definitions that are clear and distinct', and the suggestion that when meaning is sought on the basis of users' experience concepts are unlikely to be definable in a fixed and precise fashion (Froehlich 1994, p.128)

- focus on the value of hermeneutics for developing frameworks within which to model information systems and their users (Froehlich 1994, p. 130)

- analysis of the nature of the assumptions underlying different ways of thinking about the relationship between information and democracy (Dervin 1994)

Also of interest is the strengthening emphasis on research approaches which, like phenomenography, have hermeneutic and phenomenological underpinnings (Dervin 1994; Froehlich 1994; Park 1994). There is little evidence, however, of these consolidations of interest in the information needs and uses domain influencing ongoing information literacy research.

While my own research into conceptions of information literacy has been in progress a number of other studies have been completed and published, including:

- a follow up study of US information literacy scholars' consensus view of information literacy (Doyle 1996)

- a preliminary investigation of information literacy as a continuum in Australian education (SAFIL 1995)

- a study of the impact on academic achievement of integrated information skills instruction (Todd 1995)

- a survey of the place of information literacy education in US institutions of higher education (ACRL and the Middle States Commission on Higher Education 1995)

- an exploration of the role of the community college reference librarian in promoting and teaching information literacy (Herring 1994)

- an exploration of the role of information technology in facilitating information literacy for distance education students (Wilson 1994)

Most of these fail to fully adopt the approaches being argued for in the literature of information needs and uses research.

For example:

- they continue to assume that information literacy is a readily definable concept, generally adopting the information skills model as a benchmark (Herring 1994; Todd 1995; Wilson 1994)

- they demonstrate an interest in the views of opinion leaders and information literacy scholars rather than information users (Doyle 1996)

- only one of these studies has sought to research the experience of information users (Todd 1995)

- only one of the studies has adopted a naturalistic research design (Doyle 1996). Specific research strategies used include questionnaires (ACRL and the Middle States Commission on Higher Education; 1995; Herring 1994; SAFIL 1995 statistical analyses (Herring 1994), experimental design (Todd 1995), and the Delphi Technique (Doyle 1996)

Taken together, all of these studies continue to develop what Todd (1996) refers to as information literacy's fragmentary research base; he also comments that most of the existing research is 'methodologically unsophisticated' and contributes little to theory or practice. The few studies which do display methodological sophistication, for example Doyle's search for meaning using the Delphi technique and Todd's investigation of students' academic performance form a significant, though small, contribution to that research base.

Given the fragmentary research into information literacy, it is surprising that recent literature has contributed in only a limited way to the ongoing development of the information literacy research agenda. Gaps in the research endeavour that have been highlighted, include:

- the lack of academic scrutiny of information and its social role (Cronin 1995, p. 11)

- the need for evidence of benefits to learners of a focus on information literacy education (Todd 1996)

- the need for the strengthening of the information literacy research base (Todd 1996)

The most comprehensive listing of potential research questions were drawn together by Candy at the Second Australian Information Literacy Conference. A summary of these appears below:

- What is the connection between technology and futures for individuals?
- Does information from different sources have differential acceptance to learners?
- What support is there for the idea of information literacy in official statements by professional bodies and societies?
- To what extent is information literacy a generic accomplishment, and to what extent is it discipline- or domain- specific?

- How persuasive is modelling by teachers, lecturers, librarians, and other adults on influencing the behaviour of students and other learners in relation to information literacy?

- Within the new electronic dispensation...what will be the tests of trustworthiness or credibility of information?

- To what uses do people put information literacy?

- What sort of learning do people undertake which involves access to information, and what skills do they find that they need as they do it?

- How does information literacy intersect with the notion of socially distributed knowledge? (Candy 1996)

Contributions to the information literacy and wider research base

The Seven faces of information literacy has made both substantive and methodological contributions to information literacy research. The substantive contributions have been examined earlier in this chapter and chapters two, three and four. The main areas in which contributions have been made are summarised below. This study has:

- developed a relational model of information literacy

- proposed a focus on conceptions as a framework for information literacy research and scholarship

- developed a map of information literacy as it is conceived in higher education

- challenged conventional thinking about information literacy and information literacy education

In addition to these, a number of methodological contributions have been made. The study:

- provides an example of phenomenographic research as applied to information literacy

- demonstrates the value of adopting a phenomenographic approach to information literacy and information needs and uses research

- allows us to derive implications for information literacy researchers

- demonstrates that the research approach, phenomenography, has the potential to continue to advance theoretically as new studies are completed

The study provides an example of phenomenographic research as applied to information literacy

This study has shown how changes are required in how we think about studying information users in order to apply the phenomenographic approach to this area of research. The relational approach to research which was adopted in this investigation of higher educators' conceptions of information literacy, involved two significant shifts from what was the norm when the study commenced.

Firstly, there was a change from studying information users, to studying users' ways of conceiving the world. This meant that in this study conceptions, and not 'information users', were the object of research. That is not to say that information users were not of central importance to the research, but rather that users are seen as interacting with the world rather than being separate from it. Secondly, the study involved a change from seeing knowledge as being constructed by the user, to seeing knowledge as being a product of awareness, jointly constructed by information users and aspects of their world.

The study demonstrates the value of adopting a phenomenographic approach to information literacy and information needs and uses research

Already discussed in this chapter is how taking this approach has provided a deeper understanding of information literacy in higher education. Looking at information literacy as a phenomenon, that is the sum of people's conceptions or the subject-object relations through which it is constituted, has challenged the conventional view of information literacy as being a measurable attribute of people demonstrable through their ability to implement information skills processes. According to the outcomes of this study what constitutes information literacy is not fixed, it is fluid and contextually bound. Further, despite differing experiences of information literacy being appropriate in different circumstances, it is also clear that the nature of these experiences as described through the outcome space becomes progressively more sophisticated or complex. Consequently learning to be information literate, within the context of contemporary higher education, may be said to involve coming to conceive of effective information use in increasingly sophisticated ways. It is likely that equally important insights are likely to be gained through applying this approach to other objects of the information literacy and information needs and uses research. In general terms, we can conclude that the phenomenographic approach, that is investigating subject-object relations, is an effective strategy for illuminating information users' experience of the world.

The phenomenographic approach has proven to be a strategy which allows information literacy researchers to:

- accept the variation and fluidity of meaning associated with the concept of information literacy
- accept the variation and fluidity of meaning which is likely to be attributed to other
- elements of the world of information
- uncover variations in experience which are of use both theoretically and practically

These advantages will continue to make this approach attractive to information literacy and other researchers who are interested in information needs and uses.

The study allows us to derive implications for information literacy

Three important implications may by derived from this study which should be considered by future information literacy researchers. The implications each relate to one of the three areas of concern in this study—the meaning of information literacy, information literacy education and information literacy research. These are that:

- we cannot assume that the prescribed meanings associated with information literacy are shared by information users and information professionals

- we cannot assume that information literacy is best described as an attribute of persons, or that the information skills model best characterises information use processes

- our understanding of information literacy and related concepts will continue to deepen if the experience of information users is given priority in research

These implications further attest to the value of adopting naturalistic approaches, and specifically the phenomenographic approach in information literacy research. They also, however, stand as contributions to information literacy research in their own right.

The study demonstrates that the research approach, phenomenography, has the potential to continue to advance theoretically as new studies are completed

Because phenomenography is a comparatively new research approach it is not unusual for new studies to make some form of contribution to the approach. Three features of this study have the potential to advance the theory of phenomenography. The first is the nature of the outcome space. It is unusual to have a multiplane outcome space as an outcome of phenomenographic research. Yet the three elements involved in the outcome space, the meaning structure, the awareness structure and the way in which information was seen required this structuring in order to form a communicable map. Concurrent with the progress of this study, but quite separately, Marton, Watkins and Tang (1995) have also developed a different form of outcome space. In their case the outcome space of Hong Kong students' experience of learning was presented in two dimensions. This suggests that some phenomena at least are likely to reveal a complexity in the subject-object relations through which they are constituted which was not suggested by earlier studies.

The second is the separate analysis of the meaning structure and the structure of awareness in each category of description. It would seem, from this study, that for some phenomena the meaning structures and structures of awareness must both be revealed in order to capture a complete picture of the subject-object relation. Previous studies have examined either the one or the other of these elements treating them as equivalent. This study of conceptions of information literacy suggests, however, that the meaning structure and the awareness structure are not necessarily equivalent, and indeed may reveal different aspects of the form of the conception. Not surprisingly the two ways of viewing the subject-object relation are not incompatible, but rather complement each other. Together they reveal the logical relations between the categories allowing the outcome space to be constructed.

Thirdly, there is the clear identification of 'information' and not 'information literacy' as the object in the relation. Although the object in the relation, and the varying ways in which that object is experienced have been identified, it is the mediation of that object, that is the elements that form part of the relation, which constitute the experience of information literacy. Information literacy is experienced as a range of ways of experiencing effective information use. This suggests that, when we are researching conceptions of what appears to be an abstract rather than a concrete phenomenon, we can expect to find underlying the abstraction a more or less concrete subject-object relation. Thus, on the one hand, conceptions of a Geographical Information System (GIS), are about varying relations between the person and the GIS, and conceptions of essay writing are about varying ways of structuring the essay. Conceptions of love, on the other hand, may be found (hardly surprisingly) to be about the relation between a person and some other living being, whilst conceptions of beauty we could speculate to be about the relation between a person and the appearance of some thing.

Establishing a new research agenda for information literacy and information needs and uses

The successful completion of this study makes it possible to speculate about new directions for the research agenda for information literacy, and the wider field of information needs and uses based on a continuing adoption of the relational approach. As this study demonstrates that researching conceptions has both theoretical and practical value, researchers in these areas give serious consideration to making people's conceptions an object of study. The recommendations for future research which follow are based on developing the present study and adapting the approach to other aspects of information literacy research.

Building on the current study

Before conducting the empirical investigation being discussed it was speculated that the outcomes of this study would provide an initial benchmark of descriptions of information literacy which further research could confirm, refine or otherwise build upon. That benchmark is now available and the research agenda tentatively outlined in chapter four can be refined. Four main areas of research were proposed:

- people's experience of information literacy

- people's experience of learning information literacy

- teachers' experience of information literacy

- teachers' experience of students learning information literacy

In each of these areas *people* are information users including information professionals, and teachers are those responsible for information literacy education.

The areas were then subdivided to include a focus on one of each of the following pairs:

- conceptions of information literacy, or learning information literacy

- conceptions of information literacy, or learning information literacy, in specific contexts

- conceptions of specific phenomena, or learning about specific phenomena, which need to be understood in becoming information literate, for example the information life cycle, thesaurii and other elements of the information environment

- conceptions of vehicles, or learning about vehicles, through which information literacy is expressed, for example problem solving, decision making or research

The above agenda provides a broad framework within which the phenomenon of information literacy can continue to be investigated. More specific recommendations which fit within the framework are as follows:

Research Recommendation One: *That the present study be replicated in other higher education institutions.* This will help determine whether the conceptions uncovered in this study are present in other parts of the higher education sector. Replications of the study will also lead to the affirmation or modification of the outcome space developed here as a graphical representation of the phenomenon.

Research Recommendation Two: *That the present study be replicated amongst higher educators in other cultures.* This will help determine whether the conceptions uncovered in this study are also to be found in other cultural contexts. Such studies will reveal variation in conceptions of effective use of information across cultures, and will allow the construction of a supracultural outcome space for information literacy. This is of particular importance as more nations express an interest in information literacy, and as educational institutions increasingly deal with a multinational student population.

Research Recommendation Three: *That the present study be replicated amongst single groups of higher educators, for example librarians, staff developers, lecturers and learning counsellors.* Examining the conceptions of individual groups will make it possible to discover whether or not members of such groups are likely to operate within a subset of the broader outcome space. It is important for professional educators and staff developers in particular to know whether members of any group may be likely to adopt any of all the conceptions in the outcome space or whether they may be expected to choose from a limited number of these. Such studies will allow us to begin to address questions such as: Do librarians conceive of information literacy in the same way as lecturers?

Research Recommendation Four: *That similar studies be conducted drawing participants from a specific discipline base, for example science, engineering, education or the health professions.* This will help determine variation in conceptions amongst members of a particular discipline. Such studies will add depth to our understanding of information literacy and will reveal how conceptions in particular fields are related to the broader picture presented here.

Research Recommendation Five: *That similar studies be conducted amongst student groups.* This will help determine whether students' conceptions of information literacy coincide with or differ from the conceptions of those guiding their education. Such studies will be of particular importance to educators who are interested in helping their students conceive of effective information use in particular ways.

Research Recommendation Six: *That similar studies be conducted in a range of workplaces, the workplace being a key context within which information literacy is considered important.* Both horizontal studies, that is studies of employees at one level in the organisation, and vertical studies, that is studies of employees at a range of levels, could be implemented. Such studies are important because information literacy is being described as a 'generic skill' which employees may require of new graduates. Educators, as with students' conceptions, need insights into how ways of conceiving of information literacy in the workplace coincides with or differs from their own.

Investigating conceptions of other, related phenomena

The above recommendations are about furthering our understanding of the phenomenon of information literacy. The relational approach to research can also be adopted to investigate people's conceptions of other, related phenomena. These studies would be of interest to colleagues working in the broader field of information needs and uses as well as information literacy researchers. Some examples are suggested in the recommendations below:

Research Recommendation Seven: *That studies be implemented to discover people's conceptions of phenomena that are encountered in the process of becoming information literate.* We need, for example, to understand the variation in how people conceive of information problems, information technology, and information use contexts such as decision making, problem solving and research. Phenomena identified in chapter three as important include the world of information, online databases, indexing structures, telecommunications networks, scholarly communication, the information life cycle and information search processes. In the specific area of learning to search online electronic databases the need for studies to illuminate how users conceive of aspects of the online search experience has already been noted (Bruce 1994a, p.173). Such studies would inform educators as well as make it possible to devise new models of information users and their environments. When opening this area, however, researchers must be careful embrace the full range of interpretations of information literacy.

Research Recommendation Eight: *That the phenomenographic approach be tested as a device for the study of information and its role in society.* The study information and its role in society has already been described as 'a domain deserving of serious academic scrutiny' (Cronin 1995, p.11). Cronin also asserts that this scrutiny is not occurring. Researching conceptions of information is likely to be a useful technique for opening up this research domain. Such studies may also establish the importance of research on information literacy to this broader field.

Research Recommendation Nine: *That studies be implemented to discover how information is used in learning and everyday contexts.* Information literacy researchers must begin to examine closely variation in people's experience of information use in all kinds of environments, and to study the experience of learning to use information effectively. A recent study by Gerber, Boulton-Lewis and Bruce (1995) that examines how students interpret data contained in maps and charts provides an example of such a study in the educational arena. Park's (1993) study into how people interpret the value of bibliographic citations, although not phenomenographical, provides a further example of what may be possible. phenomenographic approach has a powerful contribution to make in this area with its emphasis on variation in experience, combined with the emphasis on a holistic approach to studying information use.

Information literacy is indeed a phrase with a meaning. It *is* a phenomenon that is worthy of being experienced, taught and researched. Its elusiveness, resulting from its association with other phenomenon such as information technology, literacy, computer literacy, learning to learn, library literacy, and information skills is overcome when it is treated relationally, as a way of experiencing the world. The paradigms that allowed the study to unfold can also be applied to learning situations and further research in this area

Interpretative research clearly has the power to transform the way in which we understand information literacy. Each of the recommendations provided reflects the importance given in *The Seven faces of information literacy* to understanding variation in how people relate to aspects of the world. If we continue to research information literacy in this way, it is likely that the 'information users', citizens, learners and scholars in our information age, will continue to challenge and help us reconstruct our understanding of this phenomenon. It is essential that we, as researchers, should abandon the attempt to artificially construct the phenomenon by creating our own descriptions or encouraging other information literacy scholars to do so. We must instead work at describing the experience faithfully or as has been done here, the variation in experience of those actively engaged in using information.

References

ACRL and Middle States Commission on Higher Education (1995). *Information Literacy in Higher Education: a report on the Middle States Region*, Commission on Higher Education, Philadelphia

Alexandersson, C. (1981). Amadeo Giorgi's Empirical Phenomenology, Department of Education, University of Goteborg, 1081:03

Aluri, R. (1981). 'Application of learning theories to library-use instruction', *Libri*, vol. 31, pp. 140-152

American Library Association (1983). *Evaluating Bibliographic Instruction: a Handbook*, Bibliographic Instruction Section, American College and Research Libraries, ALA, Chicago

American Library Association Presidential Committee on Information Literacy (1989). *Final Report*, ALA, Chicago

Andrews, Judith (1991). 'An exploration of students' library use problems', *Library Review*, vol. 40, pp. 5-14

Appleton, Margaret (1993). Teaching remote students to search information databases, Application for a national teaching development grant 1993/94, Committee for the Advancement of University Teaching

Arp, Lori (1990). 'Information literacy or bibliographic instruction: semantics or philosophy', *RQ*, vol. 30, no. 1, pp. 46-49

Aufderheide, Patricia and Firestone, Charles (1993). *Media Literacy: a report of the National Leadership Conference on Media Literacy*, The Aspen Institute, Washington D.C.

Baker, Betsy (1986). 'A conceptual framework for teaching online catalog use', *Journal of Academic Librarianship*, vol. 12, no. 2, pp. 90-96

Beck, C. (1989). 'Genevieve Walton and library instruction at the Michigan State Normal College', *College and Research Libraries*, vol. 50, no. 4, pp. 441-447

Beeler, Richard, J. (ed.) (1975). *Evaluating Library Use Instruction*, Pierian Press, Ann Arbor

Behrens, Shirley J. (1994). 'A conceptual analysis and historical overview of information literacy', *College and Research Libraries*, vol. 55, pp. 309-22

Behrens, Shirley J. (1992). 'Librarians and information literacy', *Mousaion*, vol. 3, no. 1, pp. 81-88

Behrens, Shirley J. (1990). 'Literacy and the evolution towards information literacy; an exploratory study', *South African Journal of Library and Information Science*, vol. 58, no. 4, pp. 353-358

Beyer, B. (1985). 'Critical thinking: what is it?', *Social Education*, vol. 49, no. 4, pp. 270-276

Biggs, John (1990). 'Teaching design for learning', in *Research and Development in Higher Education*, ed Bob Ross, vol. 13, Higher Education Research and Development Society of Australasia, Sydney, pp. 11-26

Birkett, William P. (1993). Information literacy in commerce and economics, Application for a 1993/94 National Teaching Development Grant, Committee for the Advancement of University Teaching

Bjorner, Susanne (1991). 'The information literacy curriculum - a working model', *IATUL Quarterly*, vol. 5, no. 2, pp. 150-160

Bodi, S. (1988). 'Critical thinking and bibliographic instruction: the relationship', *Journal of Academic Librarianship*, vol. 14, no. 3, pp. 150-153

Booker, Di (ed.) (1996). *Information Literacy and the Autonomous Learner,* Proceedings of the second national information literacy conference conducted by the University of South Australia Library, 30 November-1 December 1995, University of South Australia Library, Adelaide

Booker, Di (ed.) (1995). *The Learning Link: Information Literacy in Practice,* Auslib Press, Adelaide

Booker, Di (ed.) (1993). *Information Literacy: the Australian agenda,* Proceedings of the first national information literacy conference conducted by the University of South Australia Library, 2-4 December 1992, University of South Australia Library, Adelaide

Booth, Shirley (1994). 'On phenomenography, learning and teaching', in *Phenomenography, Philosophy and Practice,* eds Roy Ballantyne and Christine Bruce, Centre for Applied Environmental and Social Education Research, QUT, Brisbane, pp. 3-6

Booth, Shirley (1992). Learning to program: a phenomenographic perspective, Goteborg studies in educational sciences 89, Acta Universitatis Gothoburgensis, Goteborg

Booth, Shirley (1990). Students' conceptions of programming, programming languages and programming constructs, Occasional Paper 90.5, ERADU, RMIT

Borgman, C. (1986). 'The user's mental model of an information retrieval system: an experiment on a prototype online catalog', *International Journal of Man-Machine Studies,* vol. 24, pp. 47-64

Bowden, John (1995). 'Phenomenographic research: some methodological issues', *Nordisk Pedagogik,* vol. 15, no. 3, pp. 144–155

Bowden, John (1994). 'The nature of phenomenographic research' in *Phenomenographic Research: Variations in Method,* eds John A. Bowden and Eleanor Walsh, Office of the Director EQARD, RMIT, Melbourne, pp. 1-16

Breivik, Patricia S. (1993). 'Information literacy; what's it all about?', in *Information Literacy: the Australian Agenda,* ed. Di Booker, University of South Australia Library, Adelaide, pp. 6-18

Breivik, Patricia S. (1992). 'Education for the information age', in *Information Literacy: Developing Students as Independant Learners,* eds D.W. Farmer and T.F. Mech, Jossey-Bass, San Francisco, pp. 5-14

Breivik, Patricia S. (1991a). 'Literacy in an information society', *Community, Technical and Junior College Journal,* vol. 61, no. 6, pp. 28-9, 32-5

Breivik, Patricia S. (1991b). 'Information literacy', *Bulletin of the Medical Library Association,* vol. 79, no. 2, pp. 226-9

Breivik, Patricia S. (1991c). 'Literacy in an information society', *Information Reports and Bibliographies,* vol. 20, no. 3, pp. 10-14

Breivik, Patricia S. (1987). 'Making the most of libraries in the search for academic excellence', *Change,* vol. 19, no. 4, pp. 44-52

Breivik, Patricia S. (1985). 'Putting libraries back in the information society', *American Libraries,* vol. 16, no. 1, p. 723

Breivik, Patricia S. (1982). *Planning the Library Instruction Program,* American Library Association, Chicago

Breivik, Patricia S. and Gee, E.G. (1989). *Information Literacy: Revolution in the Library,* Macmillan, New York

Brock, Kathy T. (1993). Developing information literacy through the information intermediary process: a model for school library media specialists, Ph.D. Dissertation, Georgia State University.

Bruce, Christine S. (1995). 'Information literacy: a framework for higher education', *Australian Library Journal,* vol. 45, no. 3, pp. 13-26.–

Bruce, Christine S. (1994a). 'Educating end users of remote online systems', in *Encyclopedia of Library and Information Science*, ed. Allen Kent, pp. 155-182

Bruce, Christine S. (1994b). 'Research students' early experiences of the dissertation literature review', *Studies in Higher Education*, vol. 19, no. 2, pp. 217-229

Bruce, Christine S. (1994c). 'Reflections on the experience of the phenomenographic interview', in *Phenomenography, Philosophy and Practice*, eds Roy Ballantyne and Christine Bruce, Centre for Applied Environmental and Social Education Research, QUT, Brisbane, pp. 47-56

Bruce, Christine S. (1994D) 'Portrait of an information literate person', *HERDSA News*, vol.16, no.3, pp. 9-11

Bruce, Christine S. (1994e). 'Griffith University Information Literacy Blueprint', in *The Learning Link: Information Literacy in Practice*, ed. Di Booker, Auslib Press, Adelaide

Bruce, Christine S. (1992a). Research students' conceptions of a literature review, Masters Thesis, Faculty of Education, Queensland University of Technology, Brisbane

Bruce, Christine (1992b). 'Reflective practice in the library: an experiment with design students', in *Exploring Tertiary Teaching*, eds. Patricia Weeks and Denise Scott, Department of Administrative, Higher and Adult Education Studies, University of New England, pp. 64-73

Bruce, Christine (1991). 'Postgraduate response to an information retrieval course', *Australian Academic and Research Libraries*, vol. 23, no. 2, pp. 103-112

Bruce, Christine (1990). 'Information skills coursework for postgraduate students: investigation and response at the Queensland University of Technology', *Australian Academic and Research Libraries*, vol. 21, no. 4, pp. 224-232

Bruce, Christine S., and Candy, Philip C. (1995). 'Developing information literate graduates: prompts for good practice', in *The Learning Link: Information Literacy in Practice*, ed. Di Booker, Auslib Press, Adelaide, pp. 245-252

Bruce, Christine S., Weeks, Patricia and Crebert, Gay (1995). 'Teaching lecturers: modelling information literacy education', in *The Learning Link: Information Literacy in Practice*, ed. Di Booker, Auslib Press, Adelaide, pp. 239 244

Bunnell Jones, Linda (1992). 'Linking undergraduate education and libraries: Minnesota's approach', in *Information Literacy: Developing Students as Independent Learners*, eds D.W. Farmer and T.F. Mech, Jossey-Bass, San Francisco, pp. 27-36

Burchinal, Lee G. (1976). 'The communications revolution: America's third century challenge', In The Future of Organising Knowledge, papers presented at the Texas A & M University libraries centennial academic assembly, ED 168470

Burnheim, Robert (1992). 'Information literacy - a core competency', *Australian Academic and Research Libraries*, vol. 23, no. 4, pp. 188-196

Candy, Phil (1996). 'Major themes and implications: conference summary and future directions', in *Learning for Life, Proceedings of the Second Australian Information Literacy Conference*, ed. Di Booker, University of South Australia Library, Adelaide

Candy, Phil (1993). 'The problem of currency: information literacy in the context of Austalia as a learning society', in *Information Literacy: the Australian Agenda*, ed. Di Booker, University of South Australia Library, Adelaide, pp. 60-

Candy, Philip C. (1991). *Self-Direction for Lifelong Learning*, Jossey-Bass, San Francisco

Candy, Philip C., Crebert, Gay and O'Leary, Jane (1994). *Developing Lifelong Learners Through Undergraduate Education*, National Board of Employment Education and Training, AGPS, Canberra

CAUL (1995). CAUL Questionnaire—information literacy programs. Summary of Results. University of Newcastle

Cavalier, Rodney (1993). 'Why worry? I'm not', in *Information Literacy: the Australian Agenda*, ed. Di Booker, University of South Australia Library, Adelaide, pp. 19-27

Cheek, Julianne and others (1995). *Finding Out: Information Literacy for the 21st Century*, Macmillan Education Australia, Melbourne

Cody, S., Grassian, E. and Jacobson, T. (1993). Sample Bibliographic Instruction Course Syllabus, LOEX Clearinghouse

Colorado Department of Education (1994). Information literacy guidelines, State Library and Adult Education Office, Colorado Educational Media Association, Denver

Commission on Higher Education. Middle States Association of Colleges and Schools (1995). *Information Literacy. Lifelong Learning in the Middle States Region*, Commission of Higher Education,

Coombs, Merolyn and Houghton, Jan (1995). 'Information skills for new tertiary students; perspectives and practice', *Australian Academic and Research Libraries*, vol. 26, no.4, pp. 260-70

Coons, Bill, Schlabach, Marty and Barnes, Susan (1989). Evaluating the impact of an information literacy program, American Library Association, Caroll Preston Baber Research Proposal Application, Cornell

Cronin, Blaise (1995). Shibboleth and substance in North American Library and Information Science education. Keynote Presentation, ALISE (Association of Library and Information Science Education) Annual Conference, Philadelphia, February 1995

Curran, Charles (1993). 'Information literacy and the public librarian', in *Encyclopedia of Library and Information Science*, ed. Allen Kent, vol. 51, pp. 257-66

Curran, Charles (1990). 'Information literacy and the public librarian', *Public Libraries*, vol. 29, no. 6, pp. 349-53

Dahlgren, Lars Owe (1984a). 'Higher education—impact on students', in *The International Encyclopedia of Education*, eds T. Husen and N. Postlethwait, Pergamon Press, London, vol.4, pp. 2223-2226

Dahlgren, Lars Owe (1984b). 'Outcomes of learning', in *The Experience of Learning*, eds Ference Marton, Dai Hounsell and Noel Entwistle, Scottish Academic Press, Edinburgh, pp. 19-35

Dahlgren, Lars Owe and Fallsberg, M. (1991). 'Phenomenography as a qualitative approach in social pharmacy research', *Journal of Social and Administrative Pharmacy*, vol. 8, no. 4, pp. 150-156

Dall'Alba, Gloria (1994). 'Reflections on some faces of phenomenography', in *Phenomenographic Research: Variations in Method*, eds John Bowden and Eleanor Walsh , Office of the Director EQARD, RMIT, Melbourne, pp. 73-87

Dall'Alba (1991). 'Foreshadowing conceptions of teaching', in *Research and Development in Higher Education*, ed. Bob Ross, vol. 13, HERDSA, Sydney, pp. 293-297

Demo, William (1986). The idea of information literacy in the age of high technology, ED 282537

Dennis, Nancy (1990). 'New technologies for information retrieval: a three credit course for undergraduates at Salem State College', *Reference Services Review*, vol. 18, no. 1, pp. 39-46

Dervin, Brenda (1994). 'Information <----------> Democracy: an examination of underlying assumptions', *Journal of the American Society of Information Science*, vol. 45, no.6, pp. 369-385

Dervin, Brenda (1992). 'From the minds eye of the 'user': The sense-making qualitative-quantitative methodology', in *Qualitative Research in Information Management*, eds J.D. Glazier and R.R. Powell, Libraries Unlimited, Englewood, pp. 61-81

Dervin, Brenda (1977). 'Useful theory for librarianship: communication not information', *Drexel Library Quarterly*, vol. 13, pp. 16-32

McCrank, Lawrence J. (1991). 'Information literacy: a bogus bandwagon', *Library Journal,* vol. 116, no. 8, pp. 38-42

McHenry, K.E., Stewart, J.T. and Wu, J.L. (1992). 'Teaching resource-based learning and diversity', in *Information Literacy: Developing Students as Independent Learners,* eds D.W. Farmer and T.F. Mech, Jossey-Bass, San Francisco, pp. 55-62

McKinnon, David H., Macaulay, M. and McFadden, Mark (1993). An information literacy package for tertiary students, CAUT Application for a national teaching development grant 1993/94

Mc Nally, Mary Jane and Kuhlthau, Carol C. (1994). 'Information search process in science education', *Reference Librarian,* vol. 44, pp. 53-60

Marais, J.J. (1992). 'Evolution of information literacy as a product of information education', *South African Journal of Library and Information Science,* vol. 60, pp. 75-9

Marland, M. (ed.) (1981). Information Skills in the Secondary Curriculum: the Recommendations of a Working Group Sponsored by the British Library and the Schools Council, Methuen Educational, London

Marton, Ference (1995). 'Cognosco ergo sum', *Nordisk Pedagogik,* vol.15, no.3, pp. 165-180

Marton, Ference (1994). 'On the structure of awareness', in *Phenomenographic Research: Variations in Method,* eds John A. Bowden and Eleanor Walsh, Office of the Director EQARD, RMIT, Melbourne, pp. 89-100

Marton, Ference (1993). Towards a pedagogy of awareness, Paper presented at the EARLI Conference 1993, Aix-en-Provence

Marton, Ference (1992). Notes on ontology, Unpublished manuscript

Marton, Ference (1988a). 'Phenomenography: exploring different conceptions of reality', in *Qualitative Approaches to Evaluation in Education: the Silent Revolution,* ed. David Fetterman, Praeger, New York, pp. 176-205

Marton, Ference (1988b). 'Describing and improving learning', in *Learning Strategies and Learning Styles,* ed. R. Schmeck, Plenum Press, New York, pp. 53-82

Marton, Ference (1986a). 'Phenomenography—a research approach to investigating different understandings of reality', *Journal of Thought,* vol. 21, no. 3, pp. 28-49

Marton, Ference (1986b). 'Some reflections on the improvement of learning', in *Student Learning: Research into Practice—the Marysville Symposium,* ed. John Bowden, CSHE, University of Melbourne

Marton, Ference (1981a). 'Phenomenography—describing conceptions of the world around us', *Instructional Science,* vol. 10, pp. 177-200

Marton, Ference (1981b). 'Studying conceptions of reality—a metatheoretical note', *Scandinavian Journal of Educational Research,* vol. 25, no. 4, pp. 159-169

Marton, Ference and Neuman, Dagmar (1990). The perceptibility of numbers and the origin of arithmetic skill, Report 1990:05, Department of Education and Educational Research, University of Goteborg

Marton, Ference and Ramsden, Paul (1988). 'What does it take to improve learning?', in *Improving Learning: New Perspectives,* ed. P. Ramsden, Kogan Page, London, pp. 268-286

Marton, Ference and Saljo, Roger (1984). 'Approaches to learning', in *The Experience of Learning,* eds Ference Marton, Dai Hounsell and Noel Entwistle, Scottish Academic Press, Edinburgh

Marton, Ference, Carlsson, M.A. and Halasz, L. (1992). 'Differences in understanding and the use of reflective variation in reading', *British Journal of Educational Psychology,* vol. 62, pp. 1-16

Marton, Ference, Dall'Alba, Gloria and Beaty, Elizabeth (1993). 'Conceptions of learning', *International Journal of Educational Research,* vol. 19, no. 3, pp. 277-300

Marton, Ference, Watkins, David and Tang, Catherine (1995). Discontinuities and continuities in the experience of learning: an interview study of high school students in Hong Kong, paper presented at the 6th European Conference for Research on Learning and Instruction, August 26-31, 1995, Nijmegen

Megill, Janet (1993). Infotech/infoliteracy requirements to graduation, message to the Bibliographic Instruction list, 18th October 1993

Mellon, Constance (1990). *Naturalistic Inquiry for Library Science: Methods and Applications for Research, Evaluation and Teaching*, Greenwood, New York

Mellon, Constance (1986). 'Library anxiety: a grounded theory and its development', *College and Research Libraries,* vol. 47, no. 2, pp. 160-165

Mendrinos, Roxanne (1994). *Building Information Literacy Using High Technology: a Guide for Schools and Libraries*, Libraries Unlimited, Englewood

Merriam, Sharan B. (1988). *Case Study Research in Education,* Jossey-Bass, San Francisco

Moran, Louise (1995). National Policy Frameworks to Support the Integration of Information Technologies into University Teaching and Learning, Deakin University

Morris, Ruth (1994). 'Towards a user-centred information service', *Journal of the American Society for Information Science,* vol. 45, no.1, pp. 20-30

Mumford, A. (1986). 'Learning to learn for managers', *Journal of European Industrial Training,* vol. 10, no. 2, pp. 3-28

Murdock, Jeanne (1995). 'Re-engineering bibliographic instruction: the real task of information literacy', *Bulletin of the American Society for Information Science,* vol. 21, pp. 26-7

Murrey, Nancy (1993). Core competencies, message to the Bibliographic Instruction list, 20th October 1993

Nahl-Jakobovits, D. and Jakobovits, L.A. (1993). 'Bibliographic instructional design for information literacy: integrating affective and cognitive objectives', *Research Strategies,* vol. 11, no. 2, pp. 73-88

Naisbitt, J. and Aburdene, P. (1985). *Re-inventing the Corporation: transforming your job and company for the new information society,* Futura, New York

New South Wales Department of Education (1988). *Information Skills in the Schools*

Nordenbo, S.E. (1990). 'How do computer novices perceive information technology? A qualitative study based on a new methodology', *Scandinavian Journal of Educational Research,* vol. 34, no. 1, pp. 43-76

Oberman, Cerise (1991). 'Avoiding the cereal syndrome, or critical thinking in the electronic environment', *Library Trends,* vol. 39, no. 3, pp. 189-202

Ochs, Mary, Coons, Bill, Van Ostrand, Darla and Barnes, Susan (1991). Assessing the value of an information literacy program, ED 340385

Olsen, Jan Kennedy (1992). 'The electronic library and literacy', in *Information Literacy: Developing Students as Independent Learners,* eds D.W. Farmer and T.F. Mech, Jossey-Bass, San Francisco, pp. 91-103

Owen, Richard (1995). 'Chilling the community: information literacy and the Hindmarsh Island bridge', in *The Learning Link: Information Literacy in Practice,* ed. Di Booker, Auslib Press, Adelaide, pp. 37-46

Palmer, Judith (1991). 'Scientists and information: using cluster analysis to identify information style', *Journal of Documentation,* vol. 47, pp. 105-129

Palmquist, R.A (1992). 'The impacts of information technology on the individual', *Annual Review of Information Science and Technology,* vol. 27, pp. 3-42

Park, Taemin Kim (1994). 'Toward a theory of user-based relevance: a call for a new paradigm of enquiry', *Journal of the American Society for Information Science*, vol. 45, no. 3, pp. 124-134

Park, Taemin Kim (1993). 'The nature of relevance in information retrieval: an empirical study', *Library Quarterly*, vol. 63, no. 3, pp. 318-351

Penrod, J.I. and Douglas, J.V. (1986). 'Information technology literacy: a definition', in *Encyclopedia of Library and Information Science*, ed. Allen Kent vol. 40, pp. 76-107

Petterson, Rune (1994). 'Learning in the information age', *Educational Technology, Research and Development*, vol. 42, no. 1, pp. 91-97

Plomp, Tjeerd and Carleer, Gerrit (1987). 'Towards a strategy for the introduction of information and computer literacy courses', *Computer Education*, vol. 11, no. 1, pp. 53-62

Plum, S.H. (1984). 'Library use and the development of critical thought', in *Increasing the Teaching Role of Academic Libraries*, ed. T. Kirk, Jossey-Bass, San Francisco

Porter, J.R. (1992). 'Natural partners: resource-based and integrative learning', in *Information Literacy: Developing Students as Independent Learners*, eds D.W. Farmer and T.F. Mech, Jossey-Bass, San Francisco, pp. 45-54

Prosser, Michael (1994a). 'Some experiences of using phenomenographic research in the context of research in teaching and learning', in *Phenomenographic Research: Variations in Method*, eds John A. Bowden and Eleanor Walsh, Office of the Director EQARD, RMIT, Melbourne, pp. 31-55

Prosser,Michael (1994b). 'Using phenomenographic research in large scale studies of student learning in higher education', in *Phenomenography, Philosophy and Practice*, eds Roy Ballantyne and Christine Bruce, Centre for Applied Environmental and Social Education Research, QUT, Brisbane, pp. 321-332

Prosser, Michael (1993). 'Phenomenography and the principles and practices of learning', *Higher Education Research and Development*, vol. 12, no. 1, pp. 21-31

Prosser, Michael and Webb, Carolyn (1994). 'Relating the process of undergraduate essay writing to the finished product', *Studies in Higher Education*, vol. 19, no. 2, pp. 125-138

Prosser, Michael and Webb, Carolyn (1992). 'Qualitative differences in the process and product of undergraduate essay writing?', in *Research and Development*, vol. 15, ed. M. Parer, Higher Education Research and Development Society of Australasia, pp. 534 - 541

Rader, Hannelore (1995). 'Information literacy around the world', Paper presented at the 1995 IFLA Conference, Istanbul

Rader, Hannelore B. (1990a). 'Bibliographic instruction or information literacy', *College and Research Libraries News*, vol. 51, no. 1, pp. 18-21

Rader, Hannelore B. (1990b). 'Bringing information literacy into the academic curriculum', *College and Research Libraries News*, vol. 51, no. 9, pp. 879-80

Ramsden, Paul (1992). *Learning to Teach in Higher Education*, Routledge, London

Ramsden, Paul (1988). 'Studying learning: Improving teaching', in *Improving Learning: new perspectives*, ed. P. Ramsden, Kogan Page, London, pp. 13-31

Reichel, Mary (1990). 'Teaching students to evaluate information: a justification', *Reference Quarterly*, vol. 28, pp. 348-354

Roberts, A.F. & Blandy, S.G. (1989). *Library Instruction for Librarians*, 2nd edn, rev., Libraries Unlimited, Littleton

Roe, Ernest (1969a). '$27 million dollars worth of better education', *The Australian Library Journal*, vol. 18, no. 6, pp194-199

Roe, Ernest (1965b). 'The educational irrelevance of libraries II. Some possible solutions', *The Australian Journal of Education*, vol. 9, no. 3, pp. 191-201

Rowntree, Derek (1981). *Dictionary of Education*, Harper and Row, London

Rubens, Donna (1991). 'Formulation rules for posing good subject questions', *Library Trends*, vol. 39, no. 3, pp. 271-98

SAFIL (South Australian Information Literacy Forum) (1995). Questionnaire Results. To what extent is information literacy currently a continuum from compulsory schooling through to higher education? Unpublished Document

Saljo, Roger (1988). 'Learning in educational settings: methods of enquiry', in *Improving Learning: New Perspectives*, ed. Paul Ramsden, Kogan Page, London

Saljo, Roger (1979). 'Learning about learning', *Higher Education*, vol. 8, pp. 443-451

Samuelowicz, Katherine and Bain, John, (1992). 'Conceptions of teaching held by academic teachers', *Higher Education*, vol. 24, no. 1, pp. 93-112

Sandberg, Jorgen (1995a). How do we justify knowledge produced by interpretative approaches?, EFI Research Report, Stockholm School of Economics, The Economic Research Institute

Sandberg, Jorgen (1995b). 'Are phenomenographic results reliable?', *Nordisk Pedagogik*, vol. 15, no.3, pp. 156-164

Sandberg, Jorgen (1994). Human competence at work, PhD thesis, University of Gothenburg, Sweden

Sandberg, Jorgen (1991). Competence as Intentional Achievement, Occasional Paper 91.4 ERADU, RMIT

September, Peter E. (1993). 'Promoting information literacy in developing countries: the case of South Africa', *African Journal of Library, Archives and Information Science*, vol. 3, pp. 11-22

Sheridan, J. (1986). 'Andragogy: a new concept for academic librarians', *Research Strategies*, vol. 4, no. 4, pp. 156-167

Simmons, Howard L. (1992). 'Information literacy and accreditation: a Middle States Perspective', in *Information Literacy: Developing Students as Independent Learners*, eds D.W. Farmer and T.F. Mech, Jossey-Bass, San Francisco, pp. 15-26

Stanford, Lois (1992). 'An academician's journey into information literacy', in *Information Literacy: Developing Students as Independent Learners*, eds D.W. Farmer and T.F. Mech, Jossey-Bass, San Francisco, pp. 37-44

Stoan, Stephen K. (1991). 'Research and information retrieval among academic researchers: implications for library instruction', *Library Trends*, vol. 39, no. 3, pp. 238-57

Sullivan-Windle, Barbara (1993). 'Students' perceptions of factors influencing effective library use', *Australian Academic and Research Libraries*, vol. 24, no. 2, pp. 95-104

Sutherland, Stuart (1994). *The Macmillan Dictionary of Psychology*, Macmillan Press, London

Sutton, Stuart A (1994). Information literacy initiative, Part 1: Problem analyses and statement of response. The San Jose University Library, the School of Library and Information Science, and the Alquist Centre

Svensson, Lennart (1994). 'Theoretical foundations of phenomenography', in *Phenomenography, Philosophy and Practice*, eds Roy Ballantyne and Christine Bruce, Centre for Applied Environmental and Social Education Research, QUT, Brisbane, pp. 9-20

Svensson, Lennart (1989). 'The conceptualization of cases of physical motion', *European Journal of Psychology of Education*, vol. 4, no. 4, pp. 529-545

Svensson, Lennart (1984). 'Skill in learning', in *The Experience of Learning*, eds Ference Marton, Dai Hounsell and Noel Entwistle, Scottish Academic Press, Edinburgh, pp. 56-70

Svensson, Lennart and Hogfors, Christian. (1988). 'Conceptions as the content of teaching: improving education in mechanics' in *Improving Learning: New Perspectives*, ed. Paul Ramsden, Kogan Page, London, pp. 162-178

Svensson, Lennart and Theman, Jan (1983). The relation between categories of description and an interview protocol in the case of phenomenographic research, paper presented at the Second Annual Human Science Research Conference, Duquesne University, Pittsburgh

Svinicki, M.D. and Schwartz, B.A. (1988). *Designing Instruction for Library Users: a Practical Guide*, Marcel Dekker, New York

Takle Quinn, Karen (1991). 'Information literacy in the workplace: new education/training considerations', in *Information Literacy: Learning How to Learn*, ed. J. Varlejs, Mc Farland & Co, London, pp. 13-22

Tierney, Judith (1992). 'Information literacy and a college library: a continuing experiment', in *Information Literacy: Developing Students as Independent Learners*, eds D.W. Farmer and T.F. Mech, Jossey-Bass, San Francisco, pp. 63-72

Todd, Ross (1996). 'Information Literacy Research: charting the landscape and moving beyond the littoral zone', in *Learning for Life, Proceedings of the Second Australian Information Literacy Conference*, ed. Di Booker, University of South Australia Library, Adelaide

Todd, Ross (1995). 'Integrated information skills instruction—does it make a difference?', *School Library Media Quarterly*, vol. 23, no. 2, pp. 133-138

Trauth, E.M. (1986). 'A college curriculum for information literacy', *Education and Computing*, vol. 2, no. 4, pp. 251-58

Trigwell, Keith, Prosser, Michael and Taylor, Peter (1994). 'Qualitative differences in approaches to teaching first year university science', *Higher Education*, vol. 27, no. 1, pp. 75-84

Turner, Susan S. (1992). Emerging themes and patterns of information based teacher education curricula in response to NCATE Standards, Ed.D. Dissertation, University of North Carolina

Van Manen, Max (1990). *Researching Lived Experience*, State University of New York Press, New York

Vareljs, Jana (ed.) (1991). *Information Literacy: Learning How to Learn*, McFarland & Co, London

Verma, Surendra (1993). *Information Technology Dictionary*, Longman Cheshire, Melbourne

Walsh, Eleanor (1994). 'Phenomenographic analysis of interview transcripts', in *Phenomenographic Research: Variations in Method*, eds John A. Bowden and Eleanor Walsh, Office of the Director EQARD, RMIT, Melbourne, pp. 17-30

Walton, G. and Nettleton, S. (1992). 'Reflective and critical thinking in user education programmes: two case studies', *British Journal of Academic Librarianship*, vol. 7, no. 1, pp. 31-43

White, Herbert S. (1992). 'Bibliographic instruction, information literacy and information empowerment', *Library Journal*, vol. 117, no. 1, pp. 76,78

Wiggins, Marvin E. (1992). 'Information literacy at universities: challenges and solution', in *Information Literacy: Developing Students as Independent Learners*, eds D.W. Farmer and T.F. Mech, Jossey-Bass, San Francisco, pp. 73-82

Wilson, Vicki (1994). 'Information Literacy and Remote External Students: exploring the possibilities offered by new communications technologies', *Australian Academic and Research Libraries*, vol. 25, no. 4, pp. 247-252

Wright, Carol and Larson, Mary E. (1990). 'Basic information access skills: curriculum design using a matrix approach', *Research Strategies*, vol. 8, no. 3, pp. 104-115

Wurman, R.S. (1989). Information Anxiety, Doubleday, New York

Zaporozhetz, L.E (1987). The dissertation literature review: how faculty advisors prepare their doctoral candidates, Doctoral Thesis, University of Oregon

Zurkowski, Paul (1974). The Information Service Environment - Relationships and Priorities, National Commission on Libraries and Information Science, Washington DC, ED 100391

INDEX

Retrieve information, 135
  using the brain, 135
Roberts, A and Blandy, S, 44
Roe, E 4, 5
Ross Report, 6
Rowntree, D, 36
Rubens, D, 3, 54, 55, 56, 77

SAFIL (South Australian Forum for Information
  Literacy), 176, 177
Saljo, R, 81, 84, 88, 95, 103, 104, 106, 108
Samuelovicz, K and Bain, J, 84
Sandberg, J, 38, 40, 84, 85, 86, 89, 94, 104, 106,
  107, 108, 109
Scholarly knowledge, 3
School library, 5
Setting social direction, 72
Sheridan, J, 45, 56
Simmons, H, 8
South Africa, 2, 7, 165
South Australian Forum for Information Literacy, 176,
  177
Staff developers, 94
Staff development, 167
  for higher educators, 173
Stanford, L, 54
Stoan, S, 64, 65, 66
Structure of awareness, 122, 133, 138, 144, 148
Student based models, 49
Students
  postgraduate, 10
  undergraduate, 10
Study skills, 99
Sullivan Windle, B, 66
Sutherland, S, 36, 37
Sutton, S, 159, 162
Svensson, L, 84, 85, 86, 87, 96, 99, 105
Svensson, L and Hogfors, C, 168
Svensson, L and Theman, J, 84, 86, 99, 100, 101, 103
Svinicki, M and Schwartz, B, 44
Synthesis, 25

Takle Quinn, K, 3
Tasmania. Department of Education, 6
Taxonomic approach, 50
Teacher librarians, 4
Teacher training, 4
Teaching method, 4

Teaching practices, 12
Teaching strategies, 170
Technological literacy, 6, 147
The Middle States Commission on Higher Education,
  177
Theman, J, 108
Thinking skills, 55
Tierney, J, 46, 54, 55, 56
Todd, R, 12, 159, 162, 165, 176, 177
Traditional view of information, 65
Training of teachers, 5
Trauth, E, 23, 55, 56
Trigwell, K, Prosser, M and Taylor, P, 170
Turner, S, 67

Undergraduate curriculum, 8
Undergraduates, 66
  research processes, 66
United States, 5, 7, 165
Universities, 41
University libraries, 9, 43, 166
University of Gothenburg, 83
University of Queensland, 166
User education, 6, 11, 43, 45
User education programs, 46
User oriented research, 76
User's perspective, 83

van Manen, M, 83
Vareljs, J, 12, 34
Verma, S, 37

Walsh, E, 103
Walton, G, 44
Walton, G and Nettleton, S, 46, 55, 56
White, H, 12, 46
Wiggins, M, 46, 47, 54, 56
Wilson, V, 159, 162, 176, 177
Wisdom, 148, 149
Wisdom conception, 147, 161
Wise use of information, 149
Wright, C, and Larson, M, 47, 51
Wurman, R, 9

Zaporozhetz, L, 66
Zimbabwe, 5
Zurkowski, P, 4, 5, 31